# Mary Mag

## Christianity's Hidd

Other books by the same author

*The Encyclopaedia of the Paranormal (Ed.)*
*The Mammoth Book of UFOs*

With Clive Prince

*Turin Shroud: In Whose Image?*
*The Templar Revelation: Secret Guardians of the True Identity of Christ*
*The Stargate Conspiracy*

With Clive Prince and Stephen Prior

(additional historical research by Robert Brydon)
*Double Standards: The Rudolf Hess Cover-up*
*War of the Windsors*

# Mary Magdalene
## Christianity's Hidden Goddess

## LYNN PICKNETT

CARROLL & GRAF PUBLISHERS
New York

To all who have suffered at the hands of the Church

Carroll & Graf Publishers
An imprint of Avalon Publishing Group, Inc.
245 W. 17th Street
11th Floor
NY 10011
www.carrollandgraf.com

First published in the UK by Robinson,
An imprint of Constable & Robinson Ltd 2003

First Carroll & Graf cloth edition 2003
First Carroll & Graf trade paperback edition 2004

Reprinted 2004 (five times)

ISBN 0-7867-1311-9

Printed and bound in the EU

Library of Congress Cataloging-in-Publication Data is available on file

# Contents

# Illustrations

*Crucifixion with the Virgin, Mary Magdalene and St John the Evangelist* by
Niccolo dell' Abbate (1508–71), Galleria e Museo Estense, Modena, Italy/
Bridgeman Art Library.
*St John the Baptist,* 1513–16 (oil on canvas) by Leonardo da Vinci (1452–1519),
Louvre, Paris, France/Bridgeman Art Library.
*The Last Supper* 1495–97 (fresco) (post restoration) by Leonardo da Vinci
(1452–1519), Santa Maria della Grazie, Milan, Italy/Alinari/Bridgeman Art
Library.
*Madonna of the Rocks* (with the infant St John adoring the infant Christ accom-
panied by an Angel) c.1478 (oil on panel transferred to canvas) by Leonardo da
Vinci (1452–1519), Louvre, Paris, France/Giraudon/Bridgeman Art Library.
Blonde bewigged skull, said to be Mary Magdalene's, in the basilica of St
Maximin in Provence, France. Photograph: Clive Prince.
*The Black Virgin in the Chadaraita* given by Louis XI (1423–83) (oil on canvas)
by French School (17th century), Musee Crozatier, Le Puy-en-Velay,
France/Giraudon/ Bridgeman Art Library.
Bronze Egyptian statue of Isis suckling Horus, found at Saqqara, late period
(c.664–332 BC). Ashmolean Museum, Oxford.
Cott Nero E II pt2 f.20v *The expulsion of the Albigensians from Carcasonne:
Catharist heretics of the 12th and 13th centuries,* from 'The Chronicles of
France, from Priam King of Troy until the crowning of Charles VI', 15th century
by Boucicaut Master (fl.1390–1430) (and workshop), Chronicles of France,
1388, British Library, London, UK/Bridgeman Art Library.
The altar bas relief in the church of François Saunière in Rennes-le-Château,
France.
The statue of Mary Magdalene is all that remains after the Church dynamited the
de Coma's monastery.
The head of John the Baptist used as a sacramental drinking vessel. Drawing by
Yuri Leitch.

# *Introduction*

Inconceivable though it is now, for the average north country working-class family in late 1950s England, no Sunday would have been complete without attending at least one church service, possibly two, if the family budget stretched to a double donation for the collection box. People were generally more reverential and less sceptical then, and priestly authority largely went unquestioned. Whilst many found the church service boring, I was fascinated with everything that the vicar said. My mother called my interest in religion 'unnatural', but it was, in fact, the first step in what was to become a long and often traumatic journey, one that has eventually resulted in *Mary Magdalene: Christianity's Hidden Goddess*.

Despite my parents' doubts, I shall be forever grateful to them for introducing me to Evensong as a very small child, although this book – the final, honest result of that early religiosity – will clearly not meet with the approval of any Christian church. Yet I am intrigued to recognize that many years ago it would have so horrified *me* that I would have compromised my liberal sentiments to the extent of burning it, preferably publicly, and vigorously encouraging others to do the same. But in those days, I did not question my beliefs. Things are very different now.

I may have come a long way since my enthusiastic attendance at St Thomas' Anglican Church in the ancient city of York, but the memory of trying not to slide off the highly polished pew, while listening entranced to the powerful cadences of the King James Bible, is as vivid as yesterday. The recollection still works a curious magic.

My first tentative interest in Mary Magdalene came upon me like an encounter with an old friend as I sat transfixed, whilst the vicar, read in a monotone from the New Testament, in the lyrical language of the seventeenth century. Some of the most powerful passages had me trembling, such as the events leading up to Jesus' arrest and crucifixion – I could imagine all the drama and the agony of the terrible torture so vividly in my head that it left me shaken – a real traumatic experience for an imaginative child. Less brutal passages seemed to be directed at me personally.

According to the vicar's sonorous tones, Mary's sister Martha scolded her for not attending to the running of the house, preferring to be in deep discussion with Jesus.[1] I sat utterly rapt in the ancient story: he almost rebuked Martha for taking her sister Mary to task. This passage appeared to speak directly to me. One day after Sunday lunch I tried out the Magdalene's feisty response when asked to help with the washing up. 'You're a funny kid,' said my mother, eyeing me dubiously. But she let me off doing the dishes.

As I grew older I found myself in trouble with my teachers, but not because I was naughty. My parents would return from PTA meetings with what was to me an extraordinary message from my Religious Knowledge teacher – please tell Lynn *not to take it all so seriously*. However, very soon I was to take my innate longing for religious certainty to an extreme, and in doing so experienced at first-hand the extraordinary and unique phenomenon of conversion.

One rainy Saturday morning in York – unromantically outside a butcher's – I was approached by two young American Mormon missionaries, who asked me: 'Where do you come from? Where are you going? And why are you here?' Although I had just been confirmed as a member of the Church of England, no one had addressed those central questions: the confirmation classes had been lacklustre to say the least. There was nothing of the *spirit*, nothing to inspire, console or help transcend the everyday problems of life, and certainly no attempt to address life's central mysteries. I had been disgusted by the lack of personal belief among the clergy, and was becoming disillusioned with going to church. But now these two American boys from the Church of Jesus Christ of Latter Day Saints (as the Mormon religion is properly known) had brought about a miracle, as I stood in the muddy street with the smell of prime pork sausages assailing my nostrils. It was almost enough that they had asked those questions – I was already hooked.

And although my membership of the Mormon church was to last only a few years, I shall always cherish the extraordinary mystical experience of conversion, in which the whole world seemed reborn with me.

The nearest and most apt analogy is falling in love. I believed I had fallen in love with Jesus, or at least with what I then thought to be his 'true church', but perhaps it is truer to say I had fallen in love with the divine within me. I am enormously grateful to have had that experience, for it has helped me understand the passion of Christian converts and to sympathize with their emotional involvement in the religion, while at the same time increasingly denying the very basis of their faith.

I was intensely happy as a Mormon for just four heady years, often leaping keenly to my feet to speak before vast audiences at the church's many conferences.

Who would have believed that one so utterly persuaded and devoted could have lost it all virtually overnight? Ironically, my exit from Mormonism – and, as things turned out, from Christianity as a whole – was not caused by a sudden revelation about an error of doctrine, but about the way the officers of the church dealt with the emotional problems of a friend. I was so incensed by what I perceived to be their cold-heartedness and inflexibility that the anger acted like a cold douche. Overnight I lost my faith – and with it the world lost that alchemically transforming glow. How could that happen? How could a single bad experience rip away all the joy, all the certainty – even the apparently deep-seated belief that Jesus was Lord?

Although I was glad to put that church behind me – and indeed suddenly the many questions about its quaint and distinctly dubious doctrine that I had unconsciously buried came bubbling to the surface – I knew I had lost something of value that I would never have again. Abruptly, I found I was on my own in the big wide world, faced with the terrible trials of growing up without any comfort or spiritual joy to help me through. Beatlemania and boys were not enough. While no longer emotionally committed, inside I was as interested in religion as ever, although I was unprepared for the serial shocks to the system that some quite accidental discoveries produced in me, many of which form the basis of this book.

Although through my university years and later decades in London as a feature writer and journalist, I continued to be fascinated by such topics as Theosophy, Spiritualism, Witchcraft and unexplained phenomena – even becoming something of an expert on the paranormal – but inside I still burned to know the truth about Christianity. Perhaps I needed to know if the religion had failed me, or if I had failed the religion.

For many years I knew nothing about the myths and half truths from which the story of Jesus Christ was cynically constructed. Like most lay people – that is, non-theologians and non-clergy – I had no idea about the extent to which the New Testament has been subjected to an almost endless process of censorship of passages that presented the 'wrong' image of certain biblical figures. And even though I had been such an avid student of Religious Knowledge at school, I had no idea that the four Gospels only existed in the New Testament because they had been voted in by the bishops of the Council of Nicaea in the fourth century, a process deliberately designed to exclude a great many other books, some of which had at least as great a claim to authenticity.

As a Christian – with experience of both conventional and 'fringe' beliefs – I had never even heard of the other gospels. Even today, how many church-goers know of the existence of the *Gospel of Mary* (Magdalene), for example? Or the *Gospel of Thomas,* the *Gospel of Philip* or the *Gospel of the Egyptians*? And if they do, do they really believe that the only reason these books are not even being discussed as additions to the New Testament is that God inspired the original editorial board of the Council of Nicaea to reject them – and very similar works – and the editors' decision was final?

It was not until I was in my twenties that a chance reading of a book pointed out that Jesus was only one of many holy men – all claiming to be the Messiah – who were preaching and performing miracles in Judaea at that time. Today this seems innocuous enough, but to me, then, it was a lightning bolt. I suspect that there are a good many Christians who have no idea about the epidemic of Messiahs: one year alone saw over 400 messianic pretenders crucified in Jerusalem.

One of the most illuminating – and life-changing – revelations that came my way was the fact that Jesus' life had mirrored those of many mythical 'dying and rising gods' in that time and place who had been born on or around 25 December in humble circumstances (their births being announced by a star and attended by shepherds and magi), and who died on a Friday to rise triumphantly again within three days. These gods included Dionysus (adopted into the Church as St Denis), Adonis, Orpheus, Attis, Osiris and Tammuz. When I discovered the truth about the existence of these other gods I was almost beside myself with fury: how dare the clergy patronize their flock with a nonsense about Jesus being the only Messiah, and the only sacrificed god who died and rose again! And I thought Jesus had been *unique* . . .

A few years ago I appeared on a television programme on the subject of ancient religions, together with a vicar. He began by beaming genially at me, but once I brought up the subject of the plethora of other dying and rising gods, his bonhomie became strained. First he denied their existence, then when pressed, claimed that their story was a pale imitation of that of Jesus. I pointed out that it would have been hard to imitate a cult that was in the future – for all those other gods had been worshipped for centuries, some for millennia, before Jesus was born. The vicar was not happy. Finally, admitting that he had learnt about them at theological college, he mumbled that the cults of the likes of Adonis and Osiris were actually *rehearsals* for the coming of Jesus Christ. There is not a lot one can reasonably say to such a desperate response – but rest assured, I said it anyway.

As I developed a great curiosity about the ignorance in which believers are deliberately kept by churches whose theologians have long known the unpalatable facts, I tried to step back and see my reaction in perspective. I concluded that the new evidence I uncovered – which, amazingly, was largely already freely available in libraries – could stand or fall by itself.

Like many others, I was shaken and inspired by the British best-seller *The Holy Blood and the Holy Grail* by Michael Baigent, Richard Leigh and Henry Lincoln (1982), which provided another sort of epiphany for me. Set against a complex background of conspiracy and secret societies, the book contains what was then an amazing revelation, arguing that Jesus and Mary Magdalene were man and wife. Strange as it may seem now, when the idea was widely accepted or at least discussed openly, in the early 1980s this was revolutionary. Was Jesus really married – and to my long-time favourite?

I must stress that although I have since become considerably more sceptical about most aspects of that book, as later research revealed its serious flaws, but I admit I owe it a debt of gratitude. I will be forever grateful to Baigent, Leigh and Lincoln for providing a signpost to the new and distinctly dangerous country of thinking for oneself, without benefit of vicar or priest, and daring to look beyond the usual religious pap.

Then, in 1989, I met Clive Prince, with whom I was to write several books and confront life-changing new revelations about Christianity. Clive is one of nature's most gifted researchers, both dogged and intuitive, with a sharp memory and a gift for lateral thinking that is, in my experience, unsurpassed.

Our first joint work was *Turin Shroud: In Whose Image?* (1994) which entered the world of alternative history through the catalyst of the extraordinary heresy of Leonardo da Vinci, who also features in this book, with new and yet more outrageous revelations. (One in particular will be astounding.) By then addicted to research into the history of Christianity – in which the so-called 'heretics' played a major part, although this is usually ignored – Clive and I then moved on to a book that is closest to this present work, although both are complete in themselves and are not intended to be either mutually exclusive or in any way rivals. This was *The Templar Revelation: Secret Guardians of the True Identity of Christ* (1997), in which we delved into the secrets of esoteric groups such as the Knights Templar – and which Dan Brown acknowledges as one of the major authorities for his best-selling novel *The Da Vinci Code* (2003), about the mystical secrets surrounding Mary Magdalene. This sharpened our appetite to know more, and in daring to delve yet further, we discovered major elements that the Church has been so keen to cover up for so long.

*The Templar Revelation* opened a great many doors for us, and we were pleased to be invited to give talks to a wide variety of groups. Perhaps what was surprising was the fact that only one member of all our audiences was so outraged that he shouted at us from the floor! On our lecture tour of Europe we soon grew accustomed to one particular phenomenon: after each talk about Mary Magdalene (we gave a choice of two: the other being about John the Baptist), there was usually a queue of people waiting to ask if there was going to be a book solely about the Magdalene? So here it is. I hope you approve.

*Mary Magdalene: Christianity's Hidden Goddess* is clearly not aimed primarily at the rarefied inhabitants of Academe. But I must stress that nor does this book sit comfortably with the 'sacred bloodline' theory popularized by Baigent, Leigh and Lincoln and still so prevalent among certain other 'alternative' writers – the idea that the children of Jesus and the Magdalene created a semi-magical royal line in Europe, which may exist to this day. Although it is possible, even likely, that Mary did have children, any idea that argues that some people are inherently better than others because of a physical trait (in this case, their genes) is rather too close for comfort to the concepts used by the Nazis to justify some of the worst atrocities of the twentieth century. Being somehow 'holy' because of your blood group or genetic inheritance is but a short step away from declaring that people with different characteristics are inferior, less 'human'. The Magdalene story does not, and should not, depend on the bloodline theory, and it will not feature except in passing in this book. However, a quite different physical trait does account for a great many pages, not one that is in some way superior – for none are – but equally not a justification for the reverse assumption, and the appalling injustice that accompanies it.

This book does not present a single idea, declaring it to be the one inviolable answer, the only truth. From the very start I am admitting that my ideas may not provide the whole answer, indeed, in many ways this book is more about framing the right questions than offering new dogma. Writing 2,000 years after the events, who can in all honesty claim that they know all the secrets of so long ago?

Some of the evidence about the true nature of Mary Magdalene may be fragmentary and inconclusive. Yet even at its most tenuous, this evidence is considerably more than that for the Church's doctrine that Mary was a prostitute, for which there is none whatsoever.

Cautious attempts are now being made to revise the Magdalene's status by a few brave (usually American) Christian feminists, and even some academics and theologians: so far she has progressed to being tentatively acknowledged as the leader of Jesus' female disciples, or perhaps even the 'thirteenth apostle'. This is indeed progress – until recently it was not admitted that Jesus had any female disciples, let alone that he appointed a woman to join the holy circle of Peter, James, Andrew and the like – but to my understanding even these radical ideas go nowhere near far enough. For Mary Magdalene may have had a mere walk-on role in the New Testament, but in the Gnostic Gospels – largely, but by no means exclusively, those discovered in Egypt in 1945 – she was the *star*.

(Although it is tempting to welcome these books, caution is advised: while many do contain explosive information – and at least one, the *Gospel of Mary*,[2] contains some remarkable teaching in language that rolls deliciously off the tongue – some are marvellous examples of pseudo-mystical gobbledygook: impenetrable, giddy and silly.)

The Magdalene is consistently the woman, according to the more coherent of these forbidden books, whom Jesus simply called 'The All', or 'The Woman Who Knows All', and many groups of heretics – who secretly possessed similar texts – claimed that he bestowed on her the title of 'Apostle of the Apostles'. For all their occasional oddness, it appears that the heretics did have access to some secret knowledge about the real woman, for her personality cuts through the weirder accretions of mysticism so clearly and strongly as to seem incongruous. It appears that she was *not* merely the leader of the female followers, not just a disciple, nor even another Apostle, but the leader of the Apostles – in other words, the superior of the likes of Andrew or James, and even of Simon Peter. So . . . the question has to be asked: was this marginalized and maligned woman actually *Jesus' true successor*, and not Peter, whose alleged authority as the heir to the Kingdom has always formed the keystone of the Roman Catholic Church?

The same non-canonical books contain passages that immediately suggest the reason for their suppression. For Jesus, we discover, loved the Magdalene so much that he often kissed her on the mouth, which profoundly shocked his male disciples – at least one of whom was driven to threaten her life because of his jealousy . . . Clearly, there was more to the relationship between Jesus and the Magdalene than a spirited conversation about the relative values of religious discussion and housework. It may be something the Church has tried to prevent us from knowing, but I wanted to know about it – and the answers that presented themselves may prove surprising to others with similar backgrounds but open minds.

Many challenging questions are asked in this book. Was Mary Magdalene perhaps married to Jesus? Or was their relationship based on illicit passion? And although it is assumed that she was a Semitic Galilean, is it possible, as certain evidence strongly suggests, that she was *a black woman?*

Yet it is impossible to research the Magdalene in isolation: sooner or later profoundly disquieting questions have to be asked about the true nature of her lover Jesus. If you believe that he was the Son of God, then that is a matter for faith and no argument will shake your position, although you may well be shocked that such questions are raised in the first place. But if it is admitted that he was a historical character on a mission, then the way is clear for new evidence – and certain key clues – to be admitted.

Although at this point in time there can be few complete solutions to the historical problems about events of 2,000 years ago, fate – with a little help from long hours of research – continues to throw up some highly provocative connections. Fitting them together in a kaleido-scope of shifting images sometimes presents a fragmentary glimpse, the dim shape of a very human champion who challenges, head-on, nothing less than the established Christian Church itself. And in that awesome arena, Mary Magdalene finally holds the sword of justice.

LYNN PICKNETT
St John's Wood
London 2003

# PART ONE

# Mistaken Identity

# *Dirty Linen*

In a double grave on the edge of Glasnevin cemetery, in the Drumcondra area of Dublin, Ireland, lie the bodies of 175 girls and women, who in life suffered the shameful fate of being 'Magdalen laundresses'. Of the bleak list of names on the grey headstone, the first dates from 1858 and the last 1994. There is no religious symbolism on the stone.

These women were, in fact, for the most part re-interred, 133 of them having been previously buried in the grounds of High Park Convent, close to the stark place that was their life-long prison – and ultimately their lonely tomb. Yet it was not some sudden surge of compassion for these dead women that caused their names to be known, and the scandal of their stories to be hotly debated, when their bodies were reburied. It was simpler – and colder – than that: the Sisters of Our Lady of Charity, who ran the convent's Magdalen laundry, had sold the twelve-acre burial site for around £1 million and wanted it free of inconvenient corpses.

Their greed was their undoing. As the bodies were exhumed, questions were asked, for the 1990s was a decade of facing uncomfortable facts about the past, perhaps driven by a psychological imperative to enter the new millennium with a clean sheet, if not a clear conscience. Who were these women? Questions were asked about these – and suddenly, many, many more in other grey high-walled institutions all over Ireland: who were they, why were they so discounted and so discarded, and what did they represent? Pandora's box flew open: at first hesitantly – like all victims of abuse – former Magdalens, or members of their families, came forward to tell their stories, barely imaginable descriptions of lives of incarceration, degradation and the suppression of the human spirit. It was – and is – a massive scandal, but in a way not massive enough, for there are still many well-read and thinking people, particularly outside Ireland, who have never heard of it. Perhaps it is time to put that right.

Today in the centre of St Stephen's Green, Dublin, next to a magnificent magnolia tree, is a new wooden bench, bearing a metal plaque inscribed with little faceless heads and these words: 'To the women who worked in the Magdalen laundry institutions and to the children born to some members of those communities – reflect here upon their lives.'

## The shame of it

Who were the 'Maggies', and why were they shut away in those grim, grey institutions? Was it because they were hardened criminals, juvenile delinquents who attacked old ladies or beat up children? Hardly: in most cases it was because they were deemed 'fallen' (pregnant, or having had sex outside marriage) or even simply 'in moral danger' – which may mean nothing more than being on the brink of marrying a Protestant or going to the cinema too often with a boy – or for any reason that the local priest put forward, real or imagined. Sometimes it was only because they had tried to run away from home, or had stood up to abusive husbands, or had committed the terrible sin of being part of a loving but poor and fatherless family.

In all cases, the word of the priest – aided and abetted by local government officials – was law. No matter how hard you or even your family pleaded, if you were deemed 'fallen' or even perceived to be teetering on the brink of a tumble from grace, a Maggie you became. Inevitably, some girls were put away because they were just disliked, or failed to fit in. Being sent to the laundries was the ultimate form of bullying. Whatever the reason, official or unofficial, for the girls to be there, as the character of the sadistic Mother Bernadette (played by Tina Kelleger) said in the BBC programme

2

*Sinners,*[1] a graphic drama based on the lives of the Irish Magdalen laundresses in the 1960s, 'this is no holiday', adding later: 'you lost your rights when you succumbed'. (And when a young Magdalen went screaming into labour, the same nun told her briskly: 'If you die it's no more than you deserve.')

Many of the laundresses came straight from orphanages, also run by nuns, which were themselves little better than work camps, complete with beatings and semi-starvation. Mary Norris Cronin told Brian Macdonald of the *Irish Independent*[2] how her life was devastated when 'she and her seven brothers and sisters were sent to orphanages in 1940, simply because their widowed mother began to go out with a man'. While her brothers were sent to an orphanage in Tralee run by the Christian Brothers, she and her sisters found themselves in the hands of the ironically named Sisters of Mercy at St Joseph's Orphanage in Killarney, Co. Kerry. Mary was just twelve when her nightmare began.

'My mother was a much loved woman and this should never have happened. We were poor, but no poorer than our neighbours and we were all loved,' says Mary. The trauma of the separation was too much for her: soon after arriving at the orphanage, she began to wet the bed and was immediately singled out for particularly harsh treatment by a certain 'Sister of Mercy'. Mary tells of the reaction her plight drew from the sadistic woman put in charge of them:

> Sister Laurence used to beat me for wetting the bed. She also used to get me to carry the wet mattress on my head down a fire escape, across a yard and into a boiler house where it could be dried. As I was doing this the other children would all be chanting 'Mary Cronin wets the bed . . .'
>
> Sister Laurence would often wait until Friday to beat me. We used to have a bath on Fridays and she would come in when I was dripping wet and beat me, because it hurt more. But I would never cry and one lay nun [a nun who entered the Order without a dowry] who was nice used to tell me to cry, because she would then stop the beating.[3]

Even the slightest act of 'transgression' brought the wrath of the nuns on the children's heads: just dropping a spoon or holding a sock too long meant a beating. Two of the prettier girls had their heads shaved: a punishment for 'vanity' – although their genetic inheritance was hardly their fault – which clearly demonstrates the nuns' underlying fear and hatred of sexuality, as well, paradoxically, their personal jealousy of the girls' attractiveness. (Surely even their own faith should have prompted them to consider that if God had chosen to make the girls pretty, who were they to destroy his handiwork?) The nuns repressed their own femininity so ferociously that it was inevitable that they would also denigrate that of others. In fact, it is this tortured ambivalence about sexuality that underlies much of the problem of the historical Church, carrying clear reverberations into its increasingly troubled present.

## The disappearing toys

Mary, now in her sixties, harbours a deep anger that the authorities failed to stop this brutalization, which was being echoed in dozens of similar establishments around Ireland – and also in Scotland and the United States. She recalls what happened when the inspectors arrived to examine the living conditions at the orphanage:

> The nuns always got a phone call in advance from nuns in the other orphanages. We were all given new clothes, dolls were put on our beds and the ponnies [tin mugs] were taken away and the good delph put on the table. We also got special food. But when the inspector went away, everything was taken back and it was back to the dreadful food. The nuns used to make enough bread and dripping to last a week and it was awful.[4]

(Needless to say, the nuns themselves did not subsist on elderly bread and dripping.)

Few anecdotes illustrate more starkly the deliberate nature of the brutality the nuns so assiduously administered to the children under their care. It might be argued that times were different back in the 1940s and that children in those days expected to be beaten for infringements of the rules, but to give children dolls, clean clothes and good food – a little glimpse of heaven – *and then take them away* as soon as the inspectors had gone, leaves room for no other interpretation than one of deliberate cruelty. Great evil – not mere

4

error – was being perpetrated, and not just by one or two sadists (who, unfortunately, one might expect to find in any large group of people). It was institutional brutalization, and the only conclusion is that it was deliberately ignored or even tacitly encouraged by the Church.

Mary's nightmare was to continue even though she left the orphanage at the age of sixteen: she went to skivvy in the home of the sister of one of the nuns, but was reported for the heinous sin of going to the pictures a couple of times in the company of a young man. As a result, she was forced to undergo an internal examination by a (male) doctor, who duly pronounced her still a virgin. Nevertheless, she was sent to a Magdalen laundry for three years, after which she went to England, being inspired to speak out by meeting another young woman with a similar background, at another institution also run by the Sisters of Mercy – now also the subject of a police investigation.

## A reign of terror

The women slaved in the convent laundries for many hours a day – laundry work in more normal circumstances could be back breaking enough[5], but this was both hard physical labour and mental torture – even if a Maggie were close to giving birth, while nuns constantly circulated intoning prayers to which each Magdalen had to respond in the traditional manner. Failure to do so, or to obey any of the myriad rules of the establishment meant severe punishment: beatings with straps or canes, torture in various forms including the application of steam or heated irons, starvation and endless humiliation. One of the gravest kind of infractions was to behave in a way that was deemed discourteous to a nun, which may be nothing more than failing to bow to them when passing in the corridor. The system was geared to extract the last drop of slave labour, while inculcating in the girls a crippling sense of their unworthiness, of self hate – often reinforced by the endemic sexual abuse by the priests who were their spiritual confessors.

Meanwhile, they may have written letters to their families, but – as the 1990s' investigations demonstrated – few were actually posted. Often the nuns secretly simply tore them up, or tormented the families by telling them that their Maggie relative was dead or had moved to a distant institution. Sometimes, conversely – and this was much easier to maintain – they told the Maggies that their families had moved, perhaps to America, and had deliberately gone without a word. One can only imagine the effects of such actions on the young women, subsisting on dire food, regimented and abused, who were finally led to believe that even their own families had abandoned them. Hell was everywhere inside the walls, and suddenly there was nothing for them outside either: no human warmth anywhere in the world nor any hope of escape. The girls had been deliberately broken, as much as any inmate of a Hitlerian or Stalinist camp.

Recently, families searching the records for information about their missing female relatives have been hampered by the fact that the nuns routinely gave the incoming Magdalens new names – the first in a series of harsh tactics designed to soften them up, mentally and spiritually, to accept that they were sub-human chattels without rights, to whom no mercy would be shown and for whom there was no hope. In fact, for centuries, renaming had been a common practice in the wider world of slavery: as James Walvin writes in his *Black Ivory: Slavery in the British Empire* (1992) of the systematic breaking of the spirit of the cargoes of traumatized new arrivals from Africa at the sugar and cotton plantations of the Caribbean and North America:

> It was not enough that the planters had new slaves to augment their work-force; they also needed to change them, to render them disciplined in the ways of the New World. The first step was to give them new names. Re-naming involved an attempt to change a slave's identity, a denial of his or her former self, and offered both a convenience for white owners and a confirmation of their power.[6]

The children born to these fallen women were often sold as adoptees to rich Americans, but sometimes they were simply shifted to a neighbouring orphanage – although any contact between child and mother was forbidden and any infringements subject to the most severe punishments, including the child being removed to a remote institution where there was not even the slightest chance his mother would ever see him again.

The Maggies rarely went out, except perhaps in a crocodile, neat and tidy, to church on a holy day. Apart from that, they were locked away, night and day, behind high walls – and, incredibly, most often *under police guard*. Each Magdalen laundry usually had a couple of Gardai (policemen) regularly in attendance, to prevent escapes and bring back those who made it past the gates, although few dared to try, and even fewer had the energy. The policemen seemed to be there more as an outward and visible sign of oppression – a psychological deterrent – than for any truly practical reason. The women were locked away to stew in their 'shame', and everything was geared to not letting them forget it. (It is interesting that the current investigations into the Magdalen institutes should be carried out by the police, who had been present in most of the laundries and undoubtedly witnessed many horrors perpetrated against innocent girls and women. As there is more than an element of conflict of interest involved, perhaps there should be a truly *independent* investigation, with no possibility of religious or secular vested interest.)

## The scandal deepens
Significantly, while being taken out on a walk by the nuns, Mary and her fellow inmates were told to tear down posters on poles, saying that they had been put there 'by a bad communist man' – who, it transpired, was Dr Noel Browne, then promoting the caring and practical Mother and Child scheme. Any form of responsible family planning is, of course, still anathema to the Catholic Church: witness the fate of Mary Ann Sorrentino, the syndicated American columnist who was executive director of Planned Parenthood of Rhode Island from 1977 to 1987. As a direct result of her work for the organization, she was excommunicated in 1985, and now writes blistering attacks on the Church's recent history, especially its supreme disregard for the civil rights of women and children.

In 1998 she wrote of the Magdalens:

The Magdalen nuns saw their original mission as the salvation of prostitutes. In time, however, that definition was expanded to include young women guilty only of loving a man of their choice before they were married. This forced slavery, degradation and

7

punishment was being ordered by the same Irish bishops and Roman hierarchy content to overlook the sexual abuse of minors, sexual assault on communicants, and affairs sometimes resulting in the fathering of children by priests and others in church ranks, which the Irish courts continue to deal with to this day.[7]

Of course not all nuns are child-beating sadists, and not all priests prey sexually upon their flock. There are good people in the Catholic Church as elsewhere in the world, but the fact remains that the Vatican is so organized, and its officers so conditioned, that – as the evidence strongly suggests – it seems they have little grasp of what constitutes basic human compassion, let alone possessing, as they claim, nothing less than the monopoly of morality and religious truth.

On 24 April 2002, after a two-day meeting with the Pope, American cardinals agreed to streamline their rules on defrocking priests who sexually abused their flock – but after due consideration was given to the problem, it was announced that the only automatic dismissals are to be reserved for 'notorious' serial abusers of children. As Andrew Sullivan wrote in *The Sunday Times* (28 April 2002):

Notorious? How on earth, ordinary American Catholics were asking last week, does a child abuser's 'notoriety' have anything to do with how he should be disciplined? The church was still acting as if it were more concerned with its own reputation than with the lives of children. And notice the caveats: even a 'notorious' priest's abuse would have to have been 'serial' and 'predatory'. Under this rubric, a single instance could get him the easy treatment of the past. If the teenager made the advances, then the priest might also be handled with kid gloves. And if the priest kept it all quiet, who knows what might happen?

What, indeed? According to this new ruling, only 'notorious' abusing priests will even be considered for dismissal, which implies that those who manage to keep their abusing secret – or whose crimes are covered up by the Church – will automatically go scot free, as far as the Vatican is concerned. Clearly, it is not the crime that is the offence to the Catholic hierarchy, but the notoriety. There is to be no zero tolerance for what modern society – the moral majority of the world outside the Church – considers to be one of the few remaining truly unforgivable human-upon-human crimes.

Never has the Church looked so out of touch. Yet the problem goes far deeper than that: never has its very heart been exposed as being quite so rotten to the core, in its corruption and arrogance that seem suddenly to have their roots, not in some outdated practices, but rather perhaps in its whole belief system. When all decent people hate and condemn child abuse, there is surely something very wrong with a massive organization that claims moral and spiritual superiority yet fails even to begin to comprehend the problem.

The Magdalens seem now to be pitiful expressions of the way things used to be done, yet almost certainly the abuses would have continued almost unchanged if breaking scandals had not exposed them to the horrified outside world and in 2003 the award-winning movie *The Magdalene Sisters* (directed by Peter Mullan and starring Geraldine McEwan) brought the scandal to a much wider audience, girls who complained of the priests' abuse often disappeared into mental institutions.

The Magdalen laundries were not the exception that proves the rule, they *were* the rule. They did not represent a mere fractional blip on the progress chart of an otherwise loving, compassionate organization, but were instead its constant bottom line. Perhaps, though, one should feel a little compassion for the perpetrators of the cruelties, even for the ramrod straight nuns in their crisply starched wimples who took such delight in physically torturing and psychologically scarring young girls and unmarried mothers. After all, they, too, grew up in an institution that made human love a disgusting sin and degraded the joys of female sexuality. They, too, had no hope of a fulfilling career. In their place and time there was often a stark choice: either marriage or taking the veil. Women who for any reason were not the marrying kind or had never had an offer of marriage had little choice but become a nun, which all too often meant throwing themselves into a life of extreme repression and a pathologically violent repugnance for normal life. That there were any nuns who were *not* ignorant and bigoted sadists is perhaps more remarkable than the fact that there were so many who took out their many frustrations on the young in their care.

In fact, the religious women of Ireland have sunk a long way from the apex of their power when the Celtic Church was dominant. As Ean Begg notes in his classic *The Cult of the Black Virgin* (1996, revised edition), as a result of the rise of the Catholic Church: 'The rights of women were . . . repressed, though in the Celtic world they retained many of their considerable ancient freedoms. They even . . . took part in the celebration of the Mass in Ireland prior to the Norman Conquest.'[8]

It is surely a terrible irony that a country that was once so inspiring to religious women and offered them such opportunities, should have sunk so low as to produce generations of female sadists – in the name of the God of love, or more pertinently, *Saint* Mary Magdalene. However, there were also Magdalen laundries in Scotland (there was one in the area known as 'The Magdalenes' in Edinburgh[9]) and similar institutions in the United States – and of course there are Catholic orphanages everywhere, many of which have long been run on the same principles.

In the case of the laundries, there is no need to ask where their profits went: cynicism – and the evidence of history – supplies that answer. While the Maggies humped the endless filthy laundry and intoned their responses to prayers to Our Lady, or to Jesus in the name of Mary Magdalene, outside the world changed. Indeed, in the span of time encompassed by the dates on the stone in Glasnevin cemetery, things changed almost beyond belief – but only outside the gates. While the Magdalens continued to suffer in isolation, daily life outside moved from pen and ink to widespread computer literacy. In the same time-span indicated on the Glasnevin stone, the world was opened up by steam trains, ocean-going liners, aircraft and space shuttles. Men walked on the Moon. Wars came and went with their terrible legacies: from the Indian Mutinies and the Boer War, through the two global conflicts and the annihilation of Hiroshima and Nagasaki – even as recently as the first Gulf War – the Berlin Wall went up and came down again, symbol of the end of one manifestation suffering. And Ireland itself outside the laundry gates became unrecognizable:

finally an independent republic, a thriving modern state with a female president.

Something else happened in the big wide world that went unnoticed by the women and ignored by the Church: slavery was abolished in the British colonies in 1838 and in the United States in 1865 – yet the last Magdalen slaves emerged blinking into the outside world only a century and more later (and even then the advent of the washing machine and the increasingly inevitable scandal was more responsible for the closures than any sudden concern for human rights). From the time of the Gettysburg Address to the era of Beatlemania and beyond, generations of Catholic slave girls continued to suffer as if emancipation of slaves had never happened. Once a Maggie was signed into the laundry, she was just as much a chattel of the convent as any shackled African woman of the late eighteenth century was a possession of her slave-master.

Inside the high walls of the Magdalen laundries, nothing changed except the people, generation after generation of deliberately degraded womanhood. And all in the name of Mary Magdalene, the biblical woman said by the Church to have been a prostitute converted by Jesus. The ultimate 'fallen woman'.

It may be said that what went on in the Maggie laundries was not much worse than the crimes against humanity that were perpetrated in the old parochial workhouses throughout the length and breadth of Britain until the early twentieth century, where abuses of all sorts were the norm, and where families were split up on entry, never to be reunited. The workhouses – so blisteringly excoriated by the likes of Charles Dickens – were not Catholic organizations, but they did arise, similarly, from the contemporary interpretation of Christian mores. Male-dominated, harsh and unyielding, there is no doubt they had their roots in a patriarchy endorsed by the New Testament idea that the only people who counted in the Christian movement were men. And of course, the last British workhouse closed for ever with the advent of the Welfare State in the post-war years, whereas the reign of terror of the Maggie laundries only ended, or so the Church says, in the 1960s. But the last date on the Glasnevin tombstone is 1994.

And as a footnote to the reign of terror of the Magdalen institutes: Irish President Mary Robinson may have applauded the recognition of these women, calling the Glasnevin cemetery memorial 'historic', but it escaped few of those who had suffered that not a single nun or cleric attended the ceremony of remembrance, and no statement issued from the Church on that most poignant day in its history.

The full extent of the scandal may never be known. Religious institutions in Ireland were exempt from any legal compulsion to keep records or to make them accessible to outsiders.

## Successful marketing

It might be thought that using St Mary Magdalene's name in this way had little connection with the violence and horror that went on within the walls of the laundries. In a sense, that must be true. Having lived and died 2,000 or so years ago, the woman whose name 'graced' – or perhaps *dis*graced – those institutions, could not possibly have any direct connection with those abuses. Yet Mary Magdalene is one of the most potent brand names of the Church: an image that has not been merely adopted, but – as we shall see – has actually been so cleverly *created* by successive generations of spin doctors that just her name is synonymous with one powerful emotion: *shame* . . .

To mention Mary Magdalene to a traditional churchgoer is to evoke the image of a ripe young woman, dishevelled in the distress of her extreme – not to say excessive – penitence, as she looks back on her life of shame as a prostitute. Tears flow as she realizes she can do nothing to change the past, yet clearly she is obsessed with it, constantly wringing her hands as memories of her years of degradation, of selling her body to all comers, come flooding back.

Yet, in many respects, this is utterly wrong, both from a historical point of view (as we will see) and a moral stance. Never mind that she is supposed to have been forgiven her sins by Jesus – in which case her whining penitence smacks somewhat of ingratitude, or even disbelief in his power to do so – and never mind that after her conversion by him she has presumably begun a new life. The Church, certainly in the Ireland of the days when the Magdalen scandal was at its height, never stressed the idea that the forgiven, shriven Magdalene might jump joyfully from her chaste bed every new morning with a gleam in her

12

eye and a lust, no longer for wealthy male flesh, but for good works. She is not the patron saint of new beginnings as might reasonably be supposed: but instead the embodiment of looking back with utter horror, of self-loathing and the hatred of all womanly delights.

This radical shift of emphasis was no accident: the snivelling Magdalene was too useful to the Church to abandon for a more encouraging brand image, something that might be uplifting to girls with a sad past, filling them with a positive outlook on life. Forget it: she is the blunt instrument which the traditionally misogynist Church eagerly seized to beat up women.

The Irish Magdalen scandal naturally caused widespread outrage – UNICEF bleakly categorizes it as 'modern slavery' – and continues to do so, as the controversy grinds on. Certainly the wretched female inhabitants of the brutal Caribbean and American plantations would have had no difficulty in recognizing the familiarity of the regime of the Church-run chain of laundries. Yet the problem is not so much that it happened, but that the entire belief system upon which it was based is riddled with distortions, many quite deliberate on the part of the Church Fathers, which in a sick kind of logical process will *always* give rise to such abuse.

Individual members of the Church try to work a magical damage limitation as scandal after scandal rocks the organization, claiming that these are exceptions that prove the usual rule of decency and compassion. But although many voices now clamour for justice, a curious phenomenon has arisen that effectively plays into the Church's hands, enabling their protestations of innocence to have the ring of truth. Despite the many uncompromising attacks on such abuses in the broadsheet press, in their politically correct fervour to show tolerance towards all religions, liberal Westerners fall over themselves to ignore the wholesale abuse of human rights by the world's largest Christian organization.

No decent person wishes to see violence against devotees of any religion – bigots smashing synagogues or thugs beating up good Muslims – but surely there is a case for the prevailing attitude towards the corrupt and morally rotten to be challenged. History has demonstrated conclusively and repeatedly that some beliefs manifest as actions that are unequivocally and obviously evil, and that many of them are committed by supercilious hypocrites who take care to surround themselves with a 'holy' aura. How else can one possibly describe the underlying mores of a world-wide organization that refuses to dismiss its officers who are predatory paedophiles – unless, that is, they unfortunately get caught?

Somehow the Catholic Church is viewed through rose-coloured spectacles even by those who are not themselves members, because it is 'Christian' and therefore must be basically 'good'. But the problem can best be understood if reframed as the following question: how would most devout Christians respond if they uncovered a mere cult that refused even to condemn the vast numbers of paedophiles it harbours – unless they happen to be 'outed' in the press? *This is now official Vatican policy*. How would even Christian cult-busters deal with the problem of such a group that is happy to turn a blind eye to terrible abuse, and even tacitly encourage it? Any other religious organization with a similar record would be shut down and its leaders imprisoned or banned from entering the country.

Yet this is not only a massive, international organization, still much more widespread than any upstart cult, but also allegedly God's own organization, founded on the 'rock' of no less than Saint Peter. With the blessing of God himself, how can it possibly be evil, how can it even be *wrong*? Yet there is compelling evidence that it is, and even about the fundamental principles of the faith.

We know that the Church is God's chosen vehicle because it told us so. Having rid the world of its opponents through fire and sword, it continues to tell us so. (Even those who broke away from Rome with courage and inspiration as the Protestant movement are not totally free of many of the same misconceptions and the fundamental patriarchal domination of their flocks.)

Yet ironically much of this moral mess has its roots in the early Church's smear campaign against Mary Magdalene, a woman who hardly makes an appearance in the New Testament. Many people no doubt think it strange that she, of all religious figures, should be central to a major challenge to Catholics and other Christians, yet – as we shall see – she is the nightmare that has come back to haunt them. Over the centuries, thousands of the so-called 'heretics' have known elements of the truth about her, and been ruthlessly annihilated because of their secret knowledge. But some escaped the fire, and left extraordinary clues about a quite different interpretation of the Gospel story ...

## CHAPTER ONE

# *The Outsiders*

Whatever else she may have been, Mary Magdalene was an outsider – someone who failed to fit in totally with the people and culture in which she found herself – and it is above all this air of social unacceptability that has made her an icon to generation upon generation of those who, for whatever reason, find themselves outside the prevailing moral climate. And in the course of time others from that rackety and louche fraternity came to call her their own, cherishing what they believed to be her secrets, even in the face of terrible personal danger. A prime example of such a natural loose cannon became one of the most famous names in history, yet in certain respects one of the least known – a paradox both during his lifetime and since: indeed, never more so than now. One of his works became undoubtedly the most famous painting in the world, yet there is a central mystery about it, one that never fails to intrigue. As we shall see, however, it may well have been intended to represent Mary Magdalene – although with a very curious twist. It will come as no surprise to those who know the works of Picknett and Prince to discover that this audacious heretic was none other than Leonardo da Vinci, although there are now new insights – and certainly one rather incredible discovery – to reveal concerning his part in this astonishing story.

When the famous Florentine maestro died in France in 1519, there were only two paintings in his death chamber, both of which had particular significance for him personally. One was his last painting, *St John the Baptist*, a dark and curious work showing a knowing young man in animal skins pointing to the sky with his right index finger. Although familiar enough as the sign of the presence of the Holy Spirit in artworks of that time, because in Leonardo's paintings it is *always* a code for a heretical version of John the Baptist, Clive Prince and I have dubbed this 'the John gesture'.[1] Certainly, as we shall see, the Baptist held an unusual fascination for one so widely believed to be almost an atheist – a prototypical scientific rationalist – or at least someone who was rabidly cynical about religion.

But for now, it is the other painting he chose to keep in his last bedchamber that draws our eye: the weird and mesmeric *Mona Lisa*, whose eyes famously seem to follow one around, and whose mouth may or may not be intended to smirk knowingly or tauntingly (somewhat akin to the expression on the face of his John the Baptist). Perhaps disappointingly little lies beneath that impenetrable mask, or perhaps deep and dark emotions swirl in the forbidden depths: as the Victorian critic Walter Pater wrote, 'all the thoughts and experiences of the world have etched and moulded there, in that which they have power to define and make expressive . . . the lust of Rome, the reverie of the Middle Ages . . . [and] the sins of the Borgias'.[2] No doubt the artist would have been flattered – and amused – by this somewhat backhanded compliment about the world's most famous, if uncertain, smile.

Like the story of the arch-outsider Mary Magdalene, this most enduringly controversial of paintings prompts a series of questions, many thought to be unanswerable, but all of them asked – with fascination – nevertheless. Who was the Mona Lisa? Why is she smiling or smirking? Indeed, *is* she smiling or smirking, or is the impression simply due to the genius of Leonardo's unique brushwork, which creates a subtle effect, almost of shifting light? And if it was a portrait of some Italian or French lady, why was it never claimed by her family?

The answer to all of those questions may be simple, and characteristically – where that particular artist in concerned – little short of outrageous. Although famous for his art and designs for curiously advanced inventions such as the military tank and even the sewing machine, Leonardo da Vinci should perhaps be just as famed for his jokes and hoaxes. Author of the acclaimed biography *Leonardo: The Artist and the Man* (1992), Serge Bramley, said recently[3] that in most of the contemporary writings about the great Italian genius, among Leonardo's contemporaries three things usually prefaced any discussion of his works: his good looks, his stylish clothes and how funny he was. For Leonardo da Vinci was famous in his own day as a wit and practical joker – scaring the ladies of the court with mechanical lions and convincing a terrified Pope that he had a dragon in a box, for example.[4] But sometimes there was a dark, sharp and in some ways vicious edge to his jokes, some of which became major projects, perhaps even eclipsing his commissioned works in the amount of dedication, time and resources he devoted to them.

In *Turin Shroud: In Whose Image?* (1994) Clive Prince and I argued that it was Leonardo who perpetrated the astonishing and audacious – some would say disgusting and perverted – hoax of the Shroud of Turin, still believed by many to bear the actual image of Jesus himself. However, as the carbon dating of 1988 showed beyond doubt, it was a medieval or early Renaissance fake. Even so, the mystery in some respects only deepened, for the method of creating the image remained obscure. How could a primitive faker have created what is essentially a *photographic* image, over 600 years ago? Who had the intelligence and the nerve – and who was so completely oblivious to the threat to his immortal soul of faking Jesus' broken body and redemptive blood? Who else but Leonardo da Vinci?

The primitive photographic method he used to create the image of 'Jesus' on the Shroud is detailed comprehensively elsewhere,[5] but suffice it to say here that it seems Leonardo used the image of his own face in place of Jesus' – indeed, he was something of an obsessive in that way, using himself as model in most of his works (such as St Jude, significantly perhaps, the patron saint of lost causes, in *The Last Supper*). Through working his own dark magic on the Shroud, intentionally or inadvertently he created the template for most future images of Jesus: go into most churches and you will see Christ depicted as a tall, slim man with broad shoulders, a long thin face with reddish hair parted in the middle and a beard, sometimes forked. Although it has been argued that the face on the Shroud is very Semitic, it is not only curiously serene and mostly unblemished, but also the absolute spitting image of Leonardo da Vinci,[6] whose greatest fake and unknown work of genius largely set the trend for what Christ looked like among future religious painters and makers of stained glass and plaster statues. But if becoming the very image of the Son of God was an act of almost, some might say, satanic genius, it was at least on a par with his other great joke – although, of course, he could not have been sure how future generations would react to either of them, or whether they would simply be forgotten.

The *Mona Lisa*, it seems, was a self-portrait – just like St Jude in *The Last Supper* and other characters in his surviving works, such as the man down in the bottom right-hand corner of his unfinished *Adoration of the Magi* (which will be examined below), and assorted angels and saints, both male and female. This startling – and, on the face of it, sensational and unlikely – hypothesis was put forward in the 1980s by two researchers working independently of each other: Dr Digby Quested, of London's Maudsley Hospital, and Lillian Schwartz, of the prestigious Bell Laboratories in the United States. Both of them had noticed that the features of the 'female' face of the *Mona Lisa* were exactly the same as those of the 1514 self-portrait of the artist as an old man, drawn in red chalk, now in Turin.

The match of the faces was demonstrated beyond doubt using cutting-edge computer technology: QED, one might say – except of course that such a superficially outrageous theory by two non-art historians has been largely ridiculed or simply ignored by the academic establishment. Lavishly illustrated books on the subject of the 'mystery' of the painting continue to be published that barely mention this theory, if at all. Yet to the objective mind, there is no ignoring the fact of the *exact* match between the proportions of the face in the red chalk self-portrait and the *Mona Lisa,* and the fact that the artist was a known hoaxer, conjuror and illusionist (in great demand for court spectaculars), who was also obsessed with creating characters in his works in his own image. If, as seems to be the case, Leonardo *was* both the *Mona Lisa* and the face on the Shroud, then he had achieved a unique double coup: he not only became the universally recognized image of the Son of God, but also the 'Most Beautiful Woman in the World' – no wonder 'she' was smirking mysteriously!

Over the years, it has been suggested, sometimes even seriously, that the *Mona Lisa* was in fact a portrait of Leonardo's unknown female lover, which is considerably more unlikely than the self-portrait theory, on the grounds that he was almost certainly homosexual. When he was in his early twenties he was arrested, together with several other young men, on a charge of sodomy – although there was more than a hint of 'heresy' about their arraignment. Fortunately, due to friends in high places, these terrified young men were let off.

If the elusive image of the enigmatic woman was indeed a self-portrait, why did he do it, and why did he keep it with him until his dying day? Perhaps the answer is simply that he thought he had produced a masterpiece, and wanted to keep his best work close to him. Perhaps he liked the look of himself as a woman, beardless and in drag. Perhaps it never failed to bring a smile to his lips, just like the one in the painting. Yet there are reasons to consider that, like everything else he did, there was also a deeper reason, a more profound and fundamental layer bubbling away like a witch's cauldron under the slick urbanity, that made him the life and soul of the party, composed of shreds of experience and belief, of love and hate and passion and pain.

Like Mary Magdalene, the illegitimate and probably gay Leonardo was an outsider, a tormented genius without benefit of much formal education, humoured and flattered in the courts of the great, but always dependent on patronage, always wary, mostly alone – and never secure. Always the artistic prostitute, being paid to produce the trophy portrait or the famous religious fresco (and then, not always on time), forever on the outside looking in. As an outsider, he reached out across the dark centuries to another: perhaps the dragged-up Leonardo, in his lady's veil and strange, almost stuck-on bust, was supposed to represent the Magdalene herself. Certainly, it would have been very much in character, for – as we will see – he clearly felt strongly about the much maligned saint of long ago.

As described elsewhere,[7] Leonardo da Vinci's work – both celebrated and unrecognized – provided a portal for Clive and myself through which came an understanding of the subversive world of the heretical movements of Europe, and while it is not the intention to reproduce the arguments in detail here, one or two examples will be necessary as explanation before the latest discoveries are unveiled. (And if, as some critics suggest, our conclusions about Leonardo himself are awry, then curiously our discoveries about the wider heretical picture, which we came to through studying him, have proved to be correct.)

It is strange that of all Leonardo's works, so few have come down through the centuries to us today: of those that can with any certainty be ascribed to him, two are quite simply the most instantly recognizable and most prolifically reproduced of all works of art, ever. The first we have just examined, while the other is his now-restored fresco in the Church of Santa Maria delle Grazie near Milan, known the world over as *The Last Supper*. Its image graces buildings everywhere from Magdalen College, Oxford, to American chapels of rest, and is reproduced, almost like a holy talisman, on objects from pin cushions to stained glass and even brothel walls. (No doubt, too, some version of it hung on the otherwise bleak walls of the Magdalen laundries, like a badge of an uncaring male-dominated church, as the slave-girls eked out their days. If only they knew its secrets they might have taken heart.) Yet, once again, this most public of pictures not only hides one or two rather shocking secrets, but also actually displays clues about the real beliefs of the man who created it, still thought by many[8] to have been a devout Christian.

Some object to the very idea of Leonardo being a heretic, saying that as he painted such beautiful religious paintings of Jesus and the Virgin Mary, how can he have been anything but a pious Christian artist? Yet, as we shall see, he was indeed very different from a devout Christian, and some of the clues are there for all to see – after stripping away all accumulated layers of expectation and personal prejudice – in *The Last Supper*.

Leonardo himself, as St Jude, is second from the right (from the observer's viewpoint, see illustration), with trademark luxuriant beard and hair, both greying. As we shall see, it is no coincidence that he chose to depict himself facing away from the central figure of Jesus. Although almost in profile and not very large, one can still make out the unmissable nose dominating his face, and even the characteristic bump on the bridge (the so-called 'broken' nose on the Shroud image). Always a handsome man, Leonardo had been something of a fop in his younger years, curling his plentiful auburn hair and wearing almost outlandishly coloured clothes. Then something changed his outlook completely and he adopted what might be described as the Old Testament prophet look, with comparatively unkempt grey hair and long untrimmed beard, dressing in the dull flowing robes that were then affected by learned men, be they doctors of divinity, alchemists or magicians. Perhaps his days of being a camply pretty boy were over, or perhaps the complete change of image indicated that he had found something much more profound with which to occupy his mind as he matured.

While Leonardo gesticulates with his back to Jesus at one end of the table, strange things are going on elsewhere in this, the world's most familiar painting, which few people have remarked on. Just above table level, a disembodied hand points a dagger at the stomach of the third disciple on the observer's left: judging by the positions of the little group at that place, it belongs to no one there. Not only would any of the nearby disciples have had to have been a contortionist to twist his hand round in that position, but – if the culprit is the young St John 'the Beloved', on the left of Jesus – his arm must have been unnaturally long, almost as if extended like a telescope. Yet it can only be John's hand: all the others are facing the wrong way. Why should John, the young man whom Jesus called 'the Beloved', be acting in this aggressive fashion, particularly as he appears to be serenely oblivious to the activity around him? It is also odd that Leonardo should paint him dipping – almost swooning – so obviously sideways, away from Jesus, particularly because the Gospel of John describes him as leaning on Jesus' bosom during the historic meal of the Last Supper.

Closer inspection of the fresco leads the objective observer to ask the apparently ludicrous questions: are we really looking at St John? Indeed, are we really even looking at a *man*? Perhaps a clue lies in the shape that he makes with the figure of Jesus – a giant, outspread 'M' – and the fact that there is the glint of a gold necklace around 'his' neck, and a dark smudge where 'his' breasts should be. Surely this is no John, no male disciple, but a woman

21

whose name begins with M, who clearly should have been a central figure in the Last Supper, in Leonardo's eyes at least. This is Mary Magdalene, with a pale elfin face and tiny, feminine shoulders. Even the vague suggestion of a beard – a small frill of gingerish hair – does nothing to detract from her essential femininity.

There is also a clue about why Leonardo believed she should be in this scene in the fact that, in the artist's original coloration, her clothes are exactly the mirror image of Jesus' own robes: where he wears a blue robe and red cloak, her robe is red and cloak blue. The styles are identical. Is Leonardo's secret code hinting strongly that Mary Magdalene was Jesus' 'other half' – in any language, however metaphorical, his wife or intimate beloved? Yet even here there is, apparently, a twist: has Leonardo depicted the Magdalene's extreme sideways movement away from the central figure of Jesus simply for the purpose of composition, of providing one side of the spreadeagled 'M' shape? Or is there another, darker and more mysterious reason? Why should a lover or wife be trying to move so far away from her partner as to seem embarrassed, or perhaps wishing to distance herself from some aspect of his character, beliefs or actions?

Yet despite her facial expression of extreme serenity (which is always shared by members of the Holy Family in Leonardo's paintings), Mary does not seem to be secure. The disciple standing next to her appears to be slicing across her delicate neck with the back of his hand – hardly an accident, for all artists are particular about their composition, and Leonardo was fanatical about his, not to mention meticulous about the symbolism (after all, in his day there was a limited number of ways to express yourself for posterity: art was one, but it was dangerous if your beliefs were heterodox, so codes and symbols were necessary). But who is the disciple who seems so keen to cut across her neck? Which of the Twelve would want the Magdalene dead? This menacing white-haired figure is none other than St Peter, founder of the Church of Rome, and – as we will see – certainly no friend of Jesus' 'other half'. But note the composition: one arm of the 'M' is made up of the little knot consisting of the Magdalene/young John, St Peter – and Judas. We know that two of them expressed greater or lesser doubts about Jesus in their denial and betrayal, but what about the third . . .? Yet the Magdalene is not the only individual who appears to be threatened at the table: a disciple thrusts the 'John gesture' impertinently, almost insultingly or threateningly, into the oblivious Redeemer's face.

For the ritual whose essential purpose was to initiate the Christian ceremony of the bread and wine – representing Jesus' broken body and redemptive blood – there is no impressive chalice in front of Christ himself, only an insignificant, half-filled tumbler. There is plentiful bread, but little is broken. Is Leonardo, who chose to paint himself with his back to Jesus, trying to convey that in his opinion Jesus did not spill his blood or suffer to have his body broken for our sins? And although he draws our attention to Jesus' female 'other half', she appears to be threatened by her lover's – or husband's – own disciples. Perhaps, too, if the disembodied hand is meant somehow to be hers, then she posed some threat to them, too. Whatever it may mean, there is a lot of aggression at the table of the Last Supper, which Jesus himself, spreading his hands in empty space – with no significant amount of wine between them – seems not to notice. And let us not forget that the artist chose to depict himself with his back to Jesus. One way or another, Leonardo's famed religious work is hardly the epitome of pious Christianity, with its undertones of menace, hidden sexuality and dark secrets.

Perhaps it might be thought that Leonardo would also be a devotee of the Virgin Mary, drawn – like many homosexual men – to strong female figures. Yet of course an intrinsic demand of the classic gay female icon is that she must have suffered, preferably where relationships were concerned, and although Mary the Mother certainly suffered by losing her son in a horrific early death, by no stretch of the imagination could she have been said to have been unlucky in love. (With God the father of her firstborn, and the worthy Joseph her husband and father of her following children, surely she of all women had no room to complain.) Of course it is the Magdalene who perfectly fits the requirements of this role model, yet it is strange that a man who apparently distrusted the accepted version of Christianity so much should apparently risk public condemnation by insisting that she is smuggled into the Last Supper, albeit in light disguise as St John. Why should Leonardo be attracted to her in this way? Was it because the Church taught that she was the ultimate social freak – not just a woman in a man's world, but also a prostitute? Yet once again, surely Leonardo knew that she was supposed to have repented of her old unclean ways, so what was her attraction for him? Did he believe – or *know* – something about her that put her back in his more familiar emotional world, not as a penitent, but still an unrepentant feisty outsider? (And is it a coincidence that his St John/Magdalene is blessed with hair of a similar colour to his own?)

What was the source of his information about the underlying hostility among the disciples that he portrayed in the fresco of *The Last Supper*? For although the New Testament is clear that one disciple, infamously Judas, fell foul of the others, nowhere does it say either that Mary Magdalene attended the sacred meal on Jesus' last night alive, or that she was personally threatened by the Twelve on any similar occasion. Yet from our observation of his works with a new eye, clearly Leonardo believed that she was not only present at the Last Supper but was also threatened even as she sat close to Jesus himself – and he believed it enough to risk being 'outed' as a heretic and suffering atrocious torture and death. Where on earth could he have got such an apparently outrageous idea from?

Of course he need not have worried – if, indeed, he ever did – because his grasp of psychology was second to none. He knew that people only ever see what they want to see or expect to see, be it the 'miraculous' image of Jesus on a strip of chemically treated[9] cloth that masqueraded as his holy shroud, or the only too womanly attributes of a St 'John' in mirror-image clothes to Jesus – not to mention the existence of a disembodied hand complete with dagger that most people simply blank out. However, there is more – and some might think worse – in his other works of art, that leaves no doubt about his true inclinations and what amounts to his impressive, if shocking, credentials as a heretic.

Leonardo's challenge to the accepted view of Christianity is repeated in his other works. In his unfinished *Adoration of the Magi*, he painted himself in the bottom right-hand corner, once again turning vehemently away from the Holy Family, who sit in the lower centre of the picture, receiving the gifts of the Three Wise Men, an oasis of calm in what seems like a hive of activity, with crowds of people milling all around them and a battle with horses in the background. As usual with Leonardo, the secrets lurk in the detail and the carefully constructed symbolism. The Magi bow to a rather affected baby Jesus and a serene Virgin who is so pale as to be almost transparent, offering frankincense and myrrh – but no gold. As this was the classic symbol for alchemical perfection and kingship in Leonardo's day, was he perhaps implying that Jesus was not a rightful king, and not a perfect being – therefore by no means God incarnate?

On closer inspection of the picture two distinct groups of worshippers can be seen: those around Mary and the infant are nothing short of hideous. They stare out of sunken eyes, and their skinny bodies are ancient and cadaverous – almost like the walking dead clawing at the Holy Family in some surreal horror movie. But the other group beyond the zombies is very different, with their healthy, young bodies and uplifted faces as they appear to worship a tree, whose roots rise above the Virgin's head. This is a carob tree, symbol in Church iconography of John the Baptist, who of course either appears in person or is represented by the 'John gesture' in many of Leonardo's works, and for whom he obviously has the greatest regard. But again, this devotion appears to be very bizarre for one with such little time for Jesus and his mother, for was not the Baptist merely Christ's forerunner? (And, as we have seen, the artist died in the presence of two of his paintings: the *Mona Lisa* – probably himself as a woman, and possibly the Magdalene – and his painting of John the Baptist, in which some might also detect distinctly Leonardo-like features.) Why should this John be so important?

Before turning to the question of Leonardo's secret sources, we should take a new look at one of his other 'beautiful religious paintings': *The Virgin of the Rocks*, originally commissioned in April 1483, by the Confraternity of the Immaculate Conception (indeed, their very name perhaps inspired the artist's ultimate sacrilege) to be a single painting in a triptych for the altar of their chapel in the church of San Francesco Grand in Milan. In fact, Leonardo was to paint two versions: a more orthodox picture, which now hangs in the Sainsbury Wing of London's National Gallery – before which visitors speak in hushed tones, as if in the presence of something sacred – and the heretical one, which is in the Louvre in Paris.

The brothers of the Confraternity specified that the painting should depict a scene that, while not appearing in the Bible, was a traditional part of Church belief. This told how, during the flight into Egypt, Mary and Joseph and the baby Jesus met the young John the Baptist, together with his guardian, the archangel Uriel, in order that Jesus could confer on John the authority with which to baptize him in later life. Of course the story was fabricated specifically to provide an explanation for a puzzling anomaly: if baptism was such a sacred rite, then the baptizer must have greater authority than the individual who is being baptized – yet how could John the Baptist possibly have such authority over Jesus, the Son of God? The problem was embarrassing: hence the invented fable. No doubt this commission particularly appealed to Leonardo who, in his own ironic and savage way, appears to have had great fun with it.

Both versions are strange, brooding works, with the figures almost crammed into the bottom half, the upper half being composed solely of a mass of very dark rock, decorated here and there with a few weeds. Of course no one looks at the rocks: all eyes are on the figures, which is how Leonardo the psychological adept knew the vast majority of people would react. Indeed, considering what he has done in this painting, it was a good thing – certainly in his own lifetime – that they did concentrate on the figures, and saw nothing unusual, alarming or disgusting in the rest of the work.

But look at the Louvre version of the painting, which the artist had intended to be the only one. Members of the Confraternity that commissioned it were so horrified by what they perceived as its dire blasphemy – the saints had no haloes – that they threatened legal action. Leonardo then painted the more acceptable version that now hangs in London's National Gallery, the non-heretical version. But there is huge irony about the accusation of blasphemy. No haloes! *Is that all?* If the monks knew what heresies really lurked in the painting they would have had the artist burned, not sued . . .

We see Mary the Mother as the central figure, with her arm around a kneeling and submissive child, and the archangel Uriel – traditionally John the Baptist's protector – crouching on the other side of the group with an almost identical child who is clearly blessing the other infant. Obviously, says the conscious mind, the child giving the blessing must be Jesus, the one bestowing the authority on John (according to the traditional story invented by the Church), and the child kneeling in submission must be John, who is receiving the authority. *Yet the children are with the wrong figures.* Surely Jesus should be with his mother, and John with Uriel. If the picture is read in this alternative, more rational, way, then it is *Jesus who is kneeling in submission to John.* Such an interpretation might be suspect, had it not been for the evidence of the other paintings. Once again, as in the *Adoration of the Magi*, where the carob tree – a classic symbol for John the Baptist – is being worshipped by healthy young people and the Holy Family are the object of devotion by a group of ghouls, Leonardo is presenting an unequivocal *Johannite* (pro-John the Baptist) message. And his obvious love and regard for the Baptist, and contempt for Jesus and his mother, is only one aspect of a greater 'heresy' that includes the near-worship of Mary Magdalene. (Is it also significant that the Virgin's left hand hangs, claw-like, in the air as if clutching the top of a head, whose neck is indicated by the pointing finger of the angel? Mary's gesture is strikingly similar to that of Jesus' right hand in *The Last Supper*.) Yet before we leave *The Virgin of the Rocks* there is something else to note, although there are good reasons for any author who wishes to be taken seriously not to mention it at all.

A newcomer to these revelations might concede, even politely suspending disbelief, that perhaps there is a Johannite case to be answered in Leonardo's paintings, and even admire his subtlety and audacity in presenting such naughty imagery to the trusting gaze of the masses. But since the publication of *The Templar Revelation*, another example of Leonardo's extraordinary subliminal anti-Christian campaign has become only too apparent to Clive and myself.

This following revelation is so sensational, so apparently ludicrous, as to appear the product of a Freudian delusion, or an infantile fantasy. Yet it should be remembered that Leonardo was primarily a hoaxer, a joker, an illusionist – and that he *hated* the Holy Family (for reasons that will be discussed in later chapters). In the context of his jokes, it is wisest to forget everything that has ever been written or taught about Leonardo's 'serious' works; this is anything but redolent of rarefied art history or the nobler paintings that drew generations on the Grand Tour. Clive and I wrote in *The Templar Revelation* that Leonardo was subtle in presenting his secret heretical code 'for those with eyes to see' and did nothing that was 'the equivalent of sticking a red nose on Saint Peter'. But, as we discovered more recently, we were very wrong.

Do not think of the reverential hush of the great art galleries as the visitors tiptoe close to Leonardo's 500-year-old brushwork. Think more of giggling schoolboys passing naughty scribblings around behind the bike sheds – or the likes of the Britart stars such as Tracey Emin or Damien Hirst, whose own controversial genius lies in the savagery and delight of iconoclasm.

Although this feature can be discerned in both the National Gallery and Louvre versions of *The Virgin of the Rocks*, it is far clearer in the latter, the more truly heretical of the two works. A clue lies in the title of the painting: 'rocks' was Italian slang for testicles, as in the modern phrase 'getting your rocks off' – the equivalent of the crude modern British term 'balls'. And so it is that the reason for the mass of rocks above the Holy Family becomes shockingly obvious.

Almost growing out of the Virgin's head are two magnificent male 'rocks' – topped with a massive phallus that rises to the very skyline, comprising no less than half the painting. The offending article is created out of the mass of rock, yet it is clearly discernible, and is even impudently topped with a small spurt of weeds. Perhaps this is the equivalent of a 'Magic Eye' shape that takes time to filter through into the consciousness, depending on one's resistance to the idea – but it bears little resemblance to the common phenomenon of seeing animal shapes in clouds. This does not require an active imagination, simply the ability to see the painting anew, without any preconceptions or expectations. This is Leonardo the hoaxer and the heretic at his most audacious – and vicious. He created the grotesque male appurtenances deliberately, no doubt perversely and savagely inspired by the organization that commissioned him – the Confraternity of the *Immaculate Conception*. With a giant penis growing out of her head, he is clearly saying 'to those with eyes to see' that *this* is no Virgin.

Presenting our discovery of the secret of *The Virgin of the Rocks* to a conference hall of several hundred delegates in 1999[10] was not the intimidating – or even humiliating – experience we had feared. Clearly, there was some risk in being so openly and apparently outrageously iconoclastic about a great work of art, and we had discussed the pros and cons of making the revelation so public for some time beforehand. After all, we were proud of our reputation for sober research – even if some disagreed with our conclusions – and here we were putting it all on the line with what could so easily have been a huge embarrassment and a very damp squib. Would we be relegated to the ranks of those who see UFOs in the lights of planes and even in the glow of well-established stars? Would it be the end of our careers? After first giving a presentation to our agent and her friend, neither of whom are known as credulous fools, and being very heartened by their reaction, we went ahead, although the audience we chose has a particular reputation for cynicism and shrewdness.[11] As it happened, we need not have feared. Once the existence of the phallus had been explained – and its graphic lines only vaguely pointed out on the projected image – there was a sudden explosion of noise, a great roar as almost the entire hall rocked with the sort of laughter that comes with delight at the sheer daring of a joke, and which continued for some time. (Just one person complained he had failed to see the crucial object, but the rest of the audience soon put him right.)

As there is no doubt that the Louvre version of Leonardo's great religious work, *The Virgin of the Rocks*, is pure blasphemy, with some finality it might be concluded that Leonardo was not a member of the cult of the Virgin Mary. Nor did he have any time for her son, but on the other hand, he appeared to be utterly devoted to the Baptist and certainly convinced enough of Mary Magdalene's importance to paint her into *The Last Supper*. On the surface, this is very puzzling, for why revere two marginal New Testament characters and have nothing but contempt for those on whom the entire Christian story should focus? It seems like a most perverse case of missing the point.

Of course he could simply have developed his beliefs as a sort of private eccentricity, a personal iconoclasm that inspired those extraordinary – and otherwise inexplicable – features in what were publicly thought of as the ultimate pious works. Geniuses are notorious like that. Yet there is evidence that suggests that Leonardo was not alone in his beliefs, and that they were not simply the equivalent of Satanism, a puerile reaction against the teachings and strictures of conventional Christianity. Our own research, detailed in *The Templar Revelation* has shown that he was part of a massive underground movement of interlinked heretics, who may still hold secrets that could finally explode the already rocky foundations of the Church. For Leonardo da Vinci and his fellow believers may have had a secret source, perhaps even a lost Gospel, that led them to their passionate but dangerous convictions.

It is time to turn to the ancient texts – some well known biblical works, and some whose very existence is still not widely known by the average Christian – in an attempt to locate the fountain-head of Leonardo's heresy, and the truth about Mary Magdalene, the dark lady whose presence was such a threat to the men of the early Church.

## CHAPTER TWO

# *The Magdalene Alternative*

On the feast day of St Mary Magdalene – 22 July – in the year 1209 something utterly horrific and bewildering, yet at the same time somewhat magnificent, took place at Béziers, a small town now in the department of Hérault in Languedoc-Roussillon, south-western France. According to the Cistercian monk Pierre des Vaux-de-Cernat, writing in 1213,[1] every last inhabitant of the town went willingly to their deaths at the hands of the Pope's men rather than deny their passionately held belief that Jesus and the Magdalene were lovers – not even, they claimed, being legally married. This large-scale massacre is all the more remarkable because it was totally unnecessary: the Crusaders had only required that the towns-people give up a few heretics, but they reacted by siding with them so vehemently that they, too, became martyrs for this one hotly contentious issue.

Béziers had become something of a focus for local heretics. Although it is uncertain how far the Count of Béziers allied himself with their cause; he seemed to support it. This would not have been surprising; through their dedication and lifestyle the heretics had won a place in many hearts.

These were the Cathars or Albigensians, who roamed northern Italy (including Tuscany, where, two centuries later, Leonardo would jealously guard his own form of heresy) and the area of the Languedoc, Provence and the foothills of the Pyrenees. Through

31

their sincerity and the shining example of their lifestyle, they were popular with both the peasantry and the nobility. Indeed, so many members of the aristocracy were Cathar sympathizers that in everything except name the area was a Cathar state.

Yet the 'Cathars' were not one large homogenous sect as often presented, but a loose federation of several allied groups, many of which had their roots in the beliefs and practices of the Bogomils, named after the heretical priest Bogomil of Bulgaria. (The modern word 'bugger' derives from 'bogomil'.) Although to discuss 'the Cathars' as if they shared the same beliefs and practices is inaccurate, as their fate was largely the same, the term will be used without apology throughout.

One thing is certain, however: the Cathars were Gnostics like many other heretical groups before and since, believing that it is possible to have knowledge – or *gnosis* – of God without priestly intermediaries or the authority of the Church. Gnostics believed that God was accessible to the pure in heart – although the journey to the requisite mental and spiritual state was long and hard – envisaged as a sublime Light that was unimpeded by any material body. They believed that the 'Kingdom of God' *was* within them, not withheld or bestowed piecemeal by the rulers of a corrupt Rome.

As the Cathars never left any official written records of their doctrines and rites for posterity, it is difficult with any certainty to analyse them – and of course what accounts have remained tend to have been written by their enemies, largely the Inquisition, formed specifically to combat their heresy. While one should be cautious about accepting unquestioningly the views of the opposition, often there is a kernel of truth in some of their denouncements – as in the case of the Knights Templar. And, with due discernment, it is possible to reconstruct the Cathars' curious and dedicated lives from the plethora of records kept by the Inquisition – one Inquisitor alone gathered the testimonies of no fewer than 5,638 sworn witnesses[2] – besides the many terrified local functionaries in their pay, and even from the oral tradition of the area.

The Cathars believed they adhered to the beliefs and practices of the primitive, pre-Roman Church: rejecting the authority and rule of the Vatican and the role of the priesthood. Denying the monopoly of the Petrine legacy, the heretics eschewed everything that was associated with it, from its rites to the use of church buildings. It might be said that the Cathars were free-range believers, worshipping in private homes or in the open countryside, as the first Christians did in response to the preaching of the apostles.

Doctrinally, they were utterly opposed to the idea that Jesus had been a human being who suffered on the cross. To them – as Walter Birks and R. A. Gilbert write in their *The Treasure of Montségur* (1987): 'the life of Jesus was a model the good Christian must strive to copy, not a cosmic mystery which he must blindly accept on trust'.[3] Yet, somewhat confusedly, they saw Jesus as pure spirit, denying that he could ever have been incarnated in a body of tainted clay, and seeing his death as an allegory, not a harrowing reality of blood and agony. This theory of docetism (from the Greek meaning 'to seem') was common among Gnostics, whose hatred for the physical world prevented them from even considering that their Saviour might have been flesh like them. To most other Christians, of course, Jesus' physical life and particularly his terrible end was the whole point of the religion. To the Gnostic, in a sense, Man, too, was pure spirit – but one that had 'fallen' and was trapped inside a carnal envelope of the material body. Discussing the Cathars' beliefs about the real status of humanity's physical existence, Birks and Gilbert write:

Man . . . is composed of three parts: a spirit which is divine and remains always in heaven, a soul which has been separated from its holy spirit by its evil will in following Satan, and a body which is merely the work of Satan and to be rejected. They emphatically denied the resurrection of the flesh which is mere corruption.[4]

The Gnostics also categorically denied the possibility of Virgin birth, pouring ridicule on those who believed in it; the Mass was an error because Jesus had no body and bread was made of the hated matter, and the Old Testament was the work of Satan – its 'jealous God' being so obviously different from the Holy Father of whom Jesus spoke so lovingly.

The Cathars adhered to a rigid but in some respects quaint way of life, based on the all-consuming quest for personal purity, which they took to extremes – for example, favouring near-veganism rather than pollute their bodies and souls by ingesting anything that had reproduced through sexual contact (while avoiding meat, eggs and milk, they did eat fish, believing, like all medieval people, that fish reproduced asexually. Curiously, Leonardo also appears to have been a 'fishertarian'[5]). They aimed to achieve the status of *parfait(e)s* or *perfecti*, perfect beings, although many knew they would fail to live up to the extreme asceticism that was required, and reserved that particular initiation, the sublime transmutation from the physical and corruptible to the immortal and incorruptible, for their deathbeds. They travelled in twos (largely to provide a watchful chaperone), preaching and setting a good example to others through their own lives, which on the whole they did so successfully as to earn themselves the generic nickname of 'Les bonhommes' ('good men' or 'good people') among the local people, although technically the term only applied to those who had not reached *parfait* standards. The Cathars also returned to primitive Christianity in that they believed passionately in reincarnation[6] – which gave a poignant, but ultimately optimistic edge to their mass martyrdoms – although to them making 'a good end' as a martyr for the faith averted the need for further incarnations on the purgatorial Earth. They also rejected all forms of luxury and carnality. Benjamin Walker, in his *Gnosticism: Its History and Influence,* writes:

> The Cathars were uncompromising opponents of the whole ecclesiastical hierarchy, the liturgy and the sacraments. They rejected the worship of the Virgin Mary, and of icons and images, including the cross. In their eyes the established Church was the 'synagogue of Satan', and the altar the mouth of hell. The corrupt, luxury-loving, avaricious and immoral popes and clergy were the lackeys of the devil. In the same tradition of dissent, they opposed the pomps and vanities of magistrates and civil authorities because they upheld and supported the Church.

Despite the sanitized image of the Cathars as perpetrated by neo-Cathar New Agers (who claim them for their own, as a sort of prototypical enclave of vegetarian believers on the path of 'love and light'), undoubtedly their way of life was extreme and open to many possible abuses: for example, distaste for the pleasures of the flesh was reflected in a rite they called the *endura*, which was effectively suicide through the slow and terrible death of self-induced starvation or even taking poison – after being purified through the final baptism of the spirit known as the *consolamentum*.[7] To be free of the shackles of the flesh was their most ardent wish – for they saw this world as literal Purgatory, there being no hell to fear other than this – and to those Cathars faced with arrest, torture and death by fire at the hands of the despised Inquisition, the *endura* was no doubt preferable.

It seems that their loathing of procreation may have encouraged some members of the heresy to practise contraception in the form of sodomy (just as buggery provided the only certain contraception for Victorian prostitutes). Certainly, they were often accused of it: although of course such claims were routinely made by the heretics' enemies in the Church – and therefore one should exercise caution in evaluating the accusation – it seems that the Pope's men did have inside information. As Yuri Stoyanov writes in his *The Hidden Tradition in Europe* (1994):

Before becoming an Inquisitor, Rainerius Sacchoni had been a Cathar *perfectus* for seventeen years and in his *Summa on the Cathars and the Poor of Lyons*[8] furnished invaluable information on the beliefs, activities and locations of the dualist [Gnostic] churches.[9]

When the Cathars were at the peak of their spiritual success, their chosen heartland of the Languedoc was also prosperous and thriving, with science, the arts and learned discourse flourishing both in the courts and private houses. As Yuri Stoyanov writes:

In contrast to the prevalent climate in western Europe, Languedoc society was markedly more tolerant and cosmopolitan and had also attained a high degree of prosperity. With its distinctive and diverse culture Languedoc was a prominent centre of twelfth-century Renaissance . . .[10]

This era saw the rise of the Troubadour movement in the

Languedoc, the first awakenings of Romance literature and the subversive elements of 'courtly love' – a version of intense and erotic, but not sexual, love between the sexes that may have had its origins in the Gnostics' platonic 'love feasts' and the Cathar 'kiss of peace'.

It was also an area of unusual egalitarianism between the sexes – perhaps because the Cathars had both male and female preachers, as they believed Jesus had intended from the start. However, all that Golden Age was to be lost for ever through a terrible, if strangely little-known, series of massacres.

By 1244 over 100,000 Cathars were slaughtered by the specially called Albigensian Crusade (so named after the Cathar town of Albi), which began in 1208, in what was effectively the first act of European genocide – although this fact is rarely, if ever, taught in schools, even in France. Yet this crusade was remarkable for many reasons, not least because it involved Christians murdering other Christians in a Christian country on the pope's orders, and the dignity with which the thousands of Cathars met abominable torture and an agonizing, fiery death. Indeed, they actively trained for it, using what may well have been Buddhist-like states of trance, the secrets of which were passed to them during their first initiations. Like the earlier Gnostic Christians, they had both exoteric and esoteric levels of membership, their greatest secrets being passed on in secret only to those who had already proved themselves worthy of them. (Unfortunately, those who were so impressed by the Cathars' essential simplicity, faith and goodness that they sided with them against the Crusaders, often went to their deaths without the necessary training in pain control. This makes their conversion and conviction all the more impressive.)

One of the many long-term legacies of the Albigensian Crusade was the instigation of the Inquisition, originally set up specifically for the interrogation and execution of the Cathars. Significantly, the first so-called 'witches' to whom the Inquisition paid its terrible attentions were Cathars and their helpers from Toulouse and Carcassonne. In 1335 over sixty people were accused of attending the Witches' Sabbath, to which they all confessed – but only after the usual methods of persuasion were vigorously applied. One of the victims, a young woman, testified that she had attended the

Sabbath in order to 'serve the Cathari at supper'[11] (which, given their habitual asceticism, would hardly have been an onerous duty). Of course as a mere helper, she would not have known the mind control techniques for staving off the more exquisite of the pains of Inquisitorial torture.

The Church – and in particular Pope Innocent III – cast its avaricious eyes upon the land of milk and honey that was the Languedoc in those days and decided to take it for itself: the heresy of its inhabitants being a useful excuse for such dire depredations that the area never recovered. Today it is still the most economically depressed area of France, in stark contrast to the more famous 'south of France', the moneyed lushness of neighbouring Biarritz and Monte Carlo. The genocide that ended in the killing fields below the citadel of Montségur in 1244 created shock waves that reverberate to this day, including – although the area is outwardly Catholic – a distinctly wary attitude to the Church.

Like all Gnostics, the Cathars' belief in personal responsibility for the state of one's own soul was a direct threat to the Church, which has always been very careful – literally – to put the fear of God into its members to such an extent that they simply dare not stray from the straight and narrow path. To sin so alarmingly as to be excommunicated was the ultimate threat over life and property in an age where Hell was a grim and atrocious reality, so those who removed themselves from the threat of excommunication simply by refusing to accept the Church's authority were – by their utter rejection of the power of conventional clergy and their continued defiance – very dangerous. Who knows how many others they would infect with their evil heresies? Best to cut out the cancer before it could spread and undermine the very foundations of the Church.

Yet, as we will see, although lust for power and wealth was certainly a factor behind the creation of the Albigensian Crusade, there was indeed an underlying fear and hatred of the heresy involved, although perhaps not one that is commonly known or understood. There was clearly another major factor behind the Albigensian Crusade that began in 1208, one that involved dangerous secrets about Mary Magdalene, even hinting at the existence of an underground church that she herself founded . . .

## Courageous to the end

The Cathars built astonishing citadels on the very apex of dizzying, needle-like mountains all over the Languedoc, into the snowy foothills of the Pyrenees by the Spanish border, or occasionally simply took over more ancient fortresses, in which they waited, often besieged for many months, for the inevitable horror of capture, torture and an agonizing death. One by one, their strongholds fell, although not without some strange behaviour on the part of their enemies: overcome by the heretics' powers of resistance, and their dignity and sheer strength of character, many of the Crusaders themselves were converted to Catharism.

Although small bands of the heretics did manage to stagger on for a while in France, after a ten-month-long siege, the fall of Montségur finally took place on 2 March 1244, but not before the Crusaders had acceded to their request to remain in the citadel for a further fifteen days. After all, after so long another two weeks or so would hardly make any difference to the outcome – and in any case, the heretics would continue to starve, whereas the pope's men would not. What did they do in that time? Perhaps they spent their last fifteen days on earth in a measured rite whose purpose was to concentrate their will so that nothing – not even the towering flames their enemies were preparing in the fields below – could penetrate their self-energized force-field of perfected and sanctified strength. It is said that when the time came for them to give themselves up, despite their extreme physical weakness after their prolonged period of starvation, they ran shouting their love for each other and for God down the steep hillside – and, even joyfully, straight into the bonfires. As the flames consumed their hated flesh, it is said that some (presumably the ones who, despite making 'a good end', felt unworthy of eternal life) shouted from pyre to pyre that they would meet again in a future life. Among their number were Crusaders who had defected to their cause, for whom there had been no preparatory rites of protection against the agonies.

Of the many enduring mysteries about the Cathars there is one that has seized the imagination of many readers and researchers over the centuries: it is said that on the night before they gave themselves up, four Cathars got away with the 'Cathar Treasure' – but its nature has never been ascertained. What could it have been?

Their material wealth has mostly been accounted for, and in any case heavy bags of gold would have been virtually impossible to carry off down that almost perpendicular Pyrenean mountain. Some have suggested that they fled with a great secret, or a sacred book – indeed, the Cathars were known to possess a version of the Gospel of John, which they used in some of their holiest rites. Others argue that the Cathars took with them nothing less than the Holy Grail[12] – although what this was, or what form it took, is very much open to question. Some believe it was the cup that caught Jesus' blood as he hung on the cross, while others – most famously Baigent, Leigh and Lincoln in their *The Holy Blood and the Holy Grail* – argue that, as *sang réal* (literally 'royal blood'), it may be taken as 'holy blood', and refers to the bearers of the sacred bloodline of Jesus and Mary Magdalene. (The subject of the Holy Grail will be discussed in a later chapter.) Whatever the Cathars spirited away on that fateful night, they deemed it of the highest importance – and, as *perfecti,* they would hardly have shown much interest in the fate of a mere bauble or a strictly material object. Then again, why would it take four of them to carry whatever it was away to safety, away from the attentions of the Crusaders? Perhaps those who believe in the 'Holy Blood' theory are right, and these were the 'purest' descendants of the bloodline. Or perhaps they had four bundles of documents or books, or one book divided into four – wisely intending to send them in different directions to safe houses. Of course carrying sacred texts on their persons would not prevent these four Cathars from also taking their secret knowledge with them, to somewhere distant, beyond the persecution where the word might be kept unsullied – and perhaps even resurrected at some future time. Whatever they took with them was their most cherished object or secret, and the Cathars would go to any lengths to protect what they believed to be true and sacred.

### A perverse miracle

As we have seen, a perverse miracle of entrenched Cathar belief took place at Béziers, where between 15,000 and 20,000 ordinary townsfolk willingly went to their deaths on 22 July 1209. Just over 200 of them were Cathars, but the people of Béziers clearly shared at least one passionately held belief with the heretics.

The people had been given the opportunity to leave unscathed and hand over the Cathars in their midst, but refused to do so, siding with them against the pope's men, despite the awful fate they knew awaited them for doing so. 'Nothing could save them, not cross, nor altar, nor crucifix,' wrote Pierre des Vaux-de-Cernat. When the pope's legates were asked by the crusaders how they would know the heretics from the innocent townspeople, they received the now infamous reply: 'Kill them all. God will know his own,' which has become the cold-blooded rallying cry of all tyrannical bigots the world over. And it was no accident that the day of the massacre was 22 July, the feast day of St Mary Magdalene, for as Vaux-de-Cernat wrote:

Béziers was taken on St Mary Magdalene's Day. Oh, supreme justice of Providence! . . . The heretics claimed that St Mary Magdalene was the concubine of Jesus Christ . . . it was therefore with just cause that these disgusting dogs were taken and massacred during the feast of the one that they had insulted . . .

What made the townsfolk of Béziers so convinced of this heresy that they gave up their lives – and the lives of their children – rather than recant? While history is replete with stories of mass suicides and self-inflicted fiery holocausts among cults who have taken the most fantastic and ludicrously nonsensical doctrines to their hearts, there is every reason to believe that in this case at least the Cathars had some inside information on the subject, some evidence to prove their otherwise astonishingly heretical assertion about the relationship between Jesus and Mary Magdalene. Yet whatever this information was, its source was certainly not the New Testament Gospels of Matthew, Mark, Luke and John, but something that they recognized to be just as authentic – and perhaps just as holy. Their ferociously held doctrine about her relationship with Jesus was not even inherited from their precursors, the Bogomils, for as Yuri Stoyanov writes in his *The Hidden Tradition in Europe*: 'The teaching of Mary Magdalene as the 'wife' or 'concubine' of Christ appears, moreover, an original Cathar tradition which does not have any counterpart in the Bogomil doctrines.'[13] What was the source of the Cathars' secret knowledge about the Magdalene? And was their devotion to this belief about her behind their annihilation? It appears that the Cathars – who, as we have seen, were not so much one organization as a loose allegiance of many small groups of heretics – may have overlapped with a home-grown, Languedocian, cult of the Magdalene that owed nothing to the legacy of the Bulgarian Bogomils or any other heresy. Clearly, as far as the Church was concerned, Béziers was as good a place to start wiping it out as anywhere, which had the added bonus of killing two heresies with one blow. Except that it failed, certainly in the case of the Magdalene cult, as we will see.

## The marginalized Magdalene

There is something suspicious in the way Mary Magdalene is represented in the Gospels: on the one hand, she is clearly so well known that, unlike all the other women listed, she is described merely by name and not in terms of her relationship to a man, as his sister, wife or mother. This alone marks her out as significant. Yet, on the other hand, there is virtually nothing in the biblical texts to explain why so many at Béziers should be so devoted to her that they offered themselves up for a hideous death – and even then, not to defend her *virtue*, but by the usual standards of morality, in fact quite the opposite, as they believed she was Jesus' concubine.

It must be said that for one who inspires such fanatical devotion, Mary Magdalene is hardly a major character of the New Testament. Apart from a single appearance in Luke, she is not mentioned again by name until the crucifixion, when she appears to come out of nowhere, intending to perform the ultimate act of devotion to Jesus, the anointing of his dead body in preparation for his entombment. The three short verses in Luke (8:1–3) in which she is mentioned, read as follows:

> After this, Jesus travelled about from one town and village to another, proclaiming the good news of the kingdom of God. The Twelve were with him, and also some women who had been cured of evil spirits and diseases. Mary (called Magdalene) from whom seven demons had come out; Joanna the wife of Chuza, the manager of Herod's household; Susanna and many others. These women were helping to support them of their own means.[14]

This short passage is interesting for several reasons: clearly Jesus had female disciples – there can be no doubt about it – and they *kept* the menfolk out of their own financial resources. Indeed, if the Catholic Church's belief that the Magdalene was, or had ever been, a prostitute is correct, then we are faced with the unpalatable suggestion that Jesus and the likes of Simon Peter were happy to live off immoral earnings! Clearly, she and the other women had access to money, or were independently wealthy. (Also note that the wife of Herod's household manager was called Joanna, which was a new name in those days[15] and indicated that she was, or had been, initiated into the cult of John the Baptist – which, as we shall see, was not necessarily similar in all respects to that of Jesus himself.)

However, perhaps the most important aspect of those three short verses in Luke is, as Carla Ricci says in her book *Mary Magdalene and Many Others* (1994): 'Going through the indexes to whole stacks of exegetical and theological writings held in the Pontifical Biblical Institute showed me that these verses were almost left out.' She adds that 'little has been written, specifically and purposively, on Luke 8:1–3.'[16] Is this attitude of the gospel writers merely a reflection of their cultural disregard for Jesus' women followers, or does something deeper secretly taint the neglect of these verses? Is it the fact that they contain the name of the Magdalene, rather than it being simply, if offensively, a matter of male chauvinism getting the better of the gospel writers or their later editors? If the verses had been left out, she would have barely appeared – by name at least – in the whole of the New Testament, which is very odd, considering how important she clearly was to certain aspects of the Jesus story – not to mention to the heretics. In fact, this omission is downright suspicious, especially when one considers what has happened as a *result* of her marginalization.

The whole of the Apostolic Succession of the Catholic Church – the idea that its authority has come down unbroken from St Peter and therefore from Jesus himself – is based upon the 'fact' that Simon Peter was the first disciple to see Jesus after his resurrection. This was stressed by the German scholar Hans von Campenhausen, who says that because 'Peter was the first to whom Jesus appeared after his resurrection',[17] he became the first Christian leader (or 'pope'). Elaine Pagels, in her now-classic *The Gnostic Gospels* (1979), comments:

> One can dispute Campenhausen's claim on the basis of New Testament evidence: the gospels of Mark and John both name Mary Magdalene, not Peter, as the first witness of the resurrection.[18] But orthodox churches that trace their origin to Peter developed the tradition – sustained to this day among Catholic and some Protestant churches – that Peter had been 'the first witness of the resurrection', and hence the rightful leader of the church.[19]

She goes on: 'As early as the second century, Christians realized the potential political consequences of having "seen the risen Lord": in Jerusalem, where James, Jesus' brother, successfully rivalled Peter's authority, one tradition maintained that James, not Peter (and certainly not Mary Magdalene) was the "first witness of the resurrection".'[20]

No doubt the fiction that Peter should be leader because he was the first witness to the risen Christ was relatively easy to maintain in the days when the only Bible available was the Latin Vulgate and the Church's flock was largely illiterate, and therefore could not learn the truth for themselves. But these days there is no excuse for upholding this deliberate distortion of the truth, for in Mark (16:9) it states unequivocally: 'When Jesus rose early on the first day of the week [i.e. was resurrected on the Monday], he appeared first to Mary Magdalene, out of whom he had cast seven demons. She went and told those who had been with him and who were mourning and weeping. When they heard that Jesus was alive and that she had seen him, they did not believe it.' Nothing could be clearer: it was the Magdalene, not Simon Peter, who saw the risen Jesus first, yet the Church does not accept that this undermines the concept of the Apostolic Succession because they still largely refuse to countenance the idea that *women could be disciples*. But if they were good enough to finance Jesus' mission, and follow him devotedly, surely doesn't that make them his disciples? And when all the men except John the Beloved deserted their master – out of fear for their own skins – only the women attended his lonely and horrific ordeal on the cross. Surely that alone qualified them as disciples – even, if necessary, honorary men.

Judging by the three contentious verses from Luke given above, the women, while not being considered part of the Twelve, were clearly an important part of his retinue. In Mark their devotion is underlined, at the critical time of Jesus' death on the cross:

> Some women were watching from a distance. Among them were Mary Magdalene, Mary the mother of James the younger and of Joses, and Salome. In Galilee these women had followed him and cared for his needs. Many other women who had come up with him to Jerusalem were also there.[21]

Yet according to the Gospels, it was the Magdalene who encountered the risen Jesus first, believing him to be a gardener. It was when he simply spoke her name: *'Mary'*, that she recognized him through her tears. If it could be demonstrated that not only did Jesus have female disciples but that the Magdalene was the most important of them, then this is a major issue and should cause some serious heart-searching among Roman Catholics today. If Jesus chose to show himself to Mary, *not Peter,* then this threatens a somewhat fundamental change. Although there is much theological pontificating on this subject, the essence is very simple: if there is a shred of doubt about the first person to see the risen Christ then the whole of the authority of the Catholic Church is dangerously in question.

Like the later men of the Church, the gospels of the New Testament behave strangely whenever the Magdalene is in the frame. For example, the last eleven verses of the Gospel of Mark, in which she is specifically mentioned as having been the first to see the resurrected Jesus, and his rebuking of the male disciples for their lack of faith, were not originally included in the earliest manuscripts[22] – showing the same ambivalence towards the women, and specifically the Magdalene, that nearly caused the list of the female disciples to be omitted from the text of the Gospel according to Luke. Then there is the apparently gleefully snide – almost spiteful – and definitely unnecessary description in Mark of 'he appeared first to Mary Magdalene, *out of whom he had cast seven demons*',[23] and again in Luke, where it says: 'Mary (called Magdalene) *from whom seven demons had come out*'[24]. Obviously the writers of the Gospels were very keen not to let us forget that this was a woman with a tainted past. They may even protest too much: is there perhaps an element of a smear campaign here against a woman who was so well known for some reason that it was sufficient to call her simply 'the Magdalene'? There is a lurking suspicion that the men who wrote the biblical gospels would have preferred to leave this intriguing character out of their text altogether, if they could have got away with it. Obviously, questions would have been asked in some quarters if *the* Magdalene had not appeared, although there is a sense that this would not apply to the editing out of Joanna or Susanna. Why was she too important to leave out but somehow too disturbing – or even downright dangerous – to describe in any detail? Who was Mary Magdalene, and why should the writers of the Gospels, like the enemies of the Cathars, have been wary, perhaps even afraid, of her power?

## CHAPTER THREE

# *Sacred Sex and Divine Love*

> The divine lover is spirit without body
> The physical lover is body without spirit
> The spiritual lover possesses spirit and body
> Ibn Arabi[1]

Who was the mysterious Mary Magdalene, so carefully squeezed to the very outside edge of the New Testament by the Gospel writers? Where did she come from, and what made her so threatening to the men of the emergent Roman Church?

In *The Templar Revelation,* Clive and I wrote about the enduring controversy surrounding this pivotal biblical character:

The identification of Mary Magdalene, Mary of Bethany (Lazarus' sister) and the 'unnamed sinner' who anoints Jesus in Luke's Gospel has always been hotly debated. The Catholic Church decided at an early date that these three characters were one and the same, although it reversed this position as recently as 1969. Mary's identification as a prostitute stems from Pope Gregory I's *Homily 33,* delivered in 591 CE, in which he declared:

'She whom Luke calls the sinful woman, whom John calls Mary, we believe to be Mary from whom seven devils were ejected according to Mark. And what did these seven devils

47

signify, if not all the vices? . . . It is clear, brothers, that the woman previously used the unguent to perfume her flesh in forbidden acts.'[2]

The Eastern Orthodox Church has always treated Mary Magdalene and Mary of Bethany as separate characters.[3]

The Catholic Church has always been canny in its presentation of the Magdalene, recognizing her value as role model for the hopeless women under their control, such as the Magdalen laundresses. As David Tresemer and Laura-Lea Cannon write in their Preface to Jean-Yves Leloup's 1997 translation of the Gnostic *Gospel of Mary Magdalene* (which is discussed in the next chapter):

Only in 1969 did the Catholic Church officially repeal Gregory's labeling of Mary as a whore, thereby admitting their error – though the image of Mary Magdalene as the penitent whore has remained in the public teachings of all Christian denominations. Like a small erratum buried in the back pages of a newspaper, the Church's correction goes unnoticed, while the initial and incorrect article continues to influence readers.[4]

Yet perhaps it would be unduly hasty to dissociate her from all suspicion of 'prostitution' in an excess of modern zeal to rehabilitate her. Several researchers have pointed out that the 'seven devils' that were allegedly cast out of her may be a garbled reference to the seven underworld gatekeepers of the pagan mysteries,[5] and may provide a valuable clue about her real background. Indeed, in the pagan world there were the so-called 'temple prostitutes', women who literally embodied and passed on the sacred 'whore wisdom' through transcendental sex: clearly, outside their own culture they would be viewed as little more than streetwalkers, especially among the male disciples, imbued with the moral and sexual strictures of the Judaic Law, in the Holy Land.

Traditionally, the Magdalene was understood to be the woman who comes out of nowhere to insist on anointing Jesus with costly spikenard from an alabaster jar – indeed, in Church iconography she is usually portrayed carrying the jar. In Luke (7:36–50) we read how when Jesus dined at the home of a hospitable Pharisee, a woman 'who had lived a sinful life in that town' discovered that Jesus was there, she went up to him, bathing his feet with her tears and pouring 'perfume' on them. Unmoved by this scene of apparent devotion, the Pharisee 'said to himself' (although how the author knew about it is hard to imagine), 'If this man were a prophet he would know who is touching him and what kind of woman she is – that she is a sinner'.[6] To offset the criticisms, Jesus then tells the parable of the two debtors, one who owes a little and the other who is massively in debt, both of whom have their debts cancelled by the money lender. He asks which of them would be more grateful, and the Pharisee, whom we discover to be called Simon, replies the one who owed the most.

Jesus then praises the woman's actions, saying to Simon:

'Do you see this woman? I came into your house. You did not give me any water for my feet, but she wet my feet with her tears and wiped them with her hair.

'You did not give me a kiss, but this woman from the time I entered has not stopped kissing my feet. You did not put oil on my head, but she has poured perfume on my feet.

Therefore, I tell you, her many sins have been forgiven – for she loved much. But he who has been forgiven little loves little.'[7]

(Heart-warming though this may be, it has given rise to some curious hedonistic sects over time, founded on the idea that in order to gain the greatest benefit from God's forgiveness, one should sin as much as possible first.) While the other guests mutter about the nature of a man who takes it upon himself to forgive sins, Jesus tells the woman that her faith has saved her.

Although a similar episode appears in all four Gospels, only in Luke is it set in the town of Capernaum at the start of Jesus' ministry. The woman is an obscure member of his following – apparently unknown and unnoticed until that moment – and remains unnamed. In this version, the purpose of including the incident is clearly to delineate Jesus' power to forgive sins. The woman herself is not important.

On the other hand, John's Gospel (12:1–8) explicitly explains that the incident – clearly a species of anointing – takes place at the home of siblings Martha, Lazarus and Mary at Bethany, and it is Mary who performs the anointing on Jesus. Earlier (11:2), John's description of the raising of Lazarus from the dead stresses that it was his sister Mary who later anoints Jesus. Neither the Gospel of Mark (14:3–9) nor Matthew (26:6–13) name the anointing sinner, but both state that it happened at Bethany two days (as opposed to the six days of John's Gospel) before the Last Supper and the subsequent dreadful events of the arrest and crucifixion of Jesus. But they set the event at the house of another Simon – not a Pharisee this time, but a leper.

Clearly, Mary of Bethany is the same as the unnamed sinner who anoints Jesus' feet. So why did Luke so conspicuously fail to mention the woman's name, and set the scene in Capernaum, at the beginning – not the end – of Jesus' mission? Did he simply have the wrong data with which to fashion his version of the story? The answer may lie in how he deals with the episode of Martha and Mary (which provides such a useful excuse for not helping with household chores – see the Introduction): he tells of how Jesus and the disciples arrive at an unnamed village (in the King James version it is deliberately vague – 'a *certain* village') where he visited the sisters Martha and Mary. Why not mention the name of the place? The other gospel writers clearly knew it. And why not include Lazarus? Obviously there is something about Bethany and that particular family that makes Luke – and to some degree the other chroniclers – uncomfortable. To a greater or lesser extent they all fudge the issue while ensuring that they include the incident, as if it were too well known and too important to leave out altogether.

In fact, the family at Bethany are key figures in the highly charged events at the end of Jesus' ministry. He sets out from Bethany on his last journey to Jerusalem, and although the Twelve appear to know nothing about the tragic outcome – which is, after all, the entire purpose of his mission and the whole of his life – the family at Bethany may even have made some of the most important arrangements, including providing the donkey on which Jesus rode into Jerusalem.[8] They knew that the Old Testament prophecies about the Messiah must be fulfilled, and ensured that they were, down to the last detail, but instead of being given centre stage by the Gospel writers as major players in the Jesus story, they are embarrassedly sidelined. But why?

Was it because there was more than an element of self-fulfilling prophecy about the way they created the role of Messiah for Jesus from the descriptions given in the Old Testament – or was there another reason for this suspicious off-handedness?

A clue may lie in the discovery in 1958 by Dr Morton Smith (subsequently Professor of Ancient History at Columbia University, New York) in the library of an Eastern Orthodox church at Mar Saba, near Jerusalem. Although the discovery has been dealt with in detail elsewhere,[9] suffice it to say here that he found a copy of a letter from Clement of Alexandria, a second-century Church Father, which – sensationally – includes quotations from a 'secret gospel', said to have been written by Mark. Essentially, his letter is a reply to one Theodore, who had written for advice about how to deal with a heretical sect called the Carpocratians (after their founder, Carpocrates), whose religious practices included sexual rituals – sex as a sacrament, the whole concept of which horrified the leaders of the Church. What is particularly interesting is that this group claim to have received this doctrine as secret teaching from Mary Magdalene, Martha and Salome . . .[10]

Significantly, Clement admits that the 'secret' gospel *is genuine and contained the esoteric teachings of Jesus that were intended to be kept from the ordinary Christian*. This is astounding. The Church Fathers are admitting that Jesus actually practised *Sexual Mysteries* . . . Even the idea of Christianity as a mystery school, with secrets to be kept hidden from the average member, is disturbing: Christianity, unlike myriad other cults and the dark world of occult secret societies (such as Freemasonry), has always been seen to be completely open. Yet here is not only clear evidence to the contrary, but an indication that the *secret* teaching of Jesus was essentially sexual in nature.

Not only does this show that the early church leaders were only too willing to censor material that had at least an equal claim as the rest to be taken seriously by the rank and file of the members, but also that eminent figures such as Clement were happy to lie about it to prevent it becoming common knowledge. Essentially the Church leaders were deliberately misrepresenting Jesus' teaching for their own ends. So what are the passages that offended the likes of Clement so much that they had to go? In fact, as he unwittingly made clear for future generations by quoting them in his letter, only two short passages had to be excised from the secret version to make it into the biblical gospel.

The first is another version of the raising of Lazarus, although he is merely described as a 'youth of Bethany'. Six days after he is raised from the dead (as in the version in John's Gospel), it tells how the youth came to Jesus 'wearing a linen cloth over his naked body', staying with him throughout one night, during which he was 'taught . . . the mystery of the kingdom of God.'[11] As we wrote in *The Templar Revelation:*

Rather than a miraculous resurrection, therefore, the raising of Lazarus seems to have been part of some kind of initiatory rite in which the initiate undergoes a symbolic death and rebirth before being given the secret teachings. Such a rite was a common part of many of the mystery religions that were widely practised in the Greek and Roman worlds – but did it, as some readers may deduce, also include a homosexual initiation?[12]

Morton Smith believed it did, as obviously did the heretical sect of the Carpocratians (and possibly other groups, such as the inner circle of the later Knights Templar) – not to mention Clement himself, who was clearly worried about the effect this little passage would have on others if they knew of it. Of course wearing a sheet and spending the night with a teacher or guru does not necessarily imply some kind of sexual rite passed between them, but it must be considered as a possibility.

However, the whole episode of the raising of Lazarus is important in any case, for it is one of the incidents that is featured in John's Gospel alone of all the four, and is even cited by theologians to prove that this gospel is less authentic that the others. But according to Clement, it appeared in at least one of the others but was then removed, as if it contained something too controversial, too challenging to the carefully screened version of the Christian message that was being established as the 'Gospel truth' by the likes of Clement. And this example of the editing out of the story of the raising of Lazarus from at least one of the other Gospels actually supports the authenticity of John, rather than denies it.

The other verse that Clement refers to as causing such displeasure among churchmen in the lost Gospel of Mark – but clearly one that excited great interest among the apparently wild and sacrilegious Carpocratians – appears, on the surface, to be completely innocuous. It does, however, provide the missing link that scholars have long puzzled over between two otherwise unconnected, but sequential, sentences in the canonical Gospel of Saint Mark (10:46): 'Then they came to Jericho. As Jesus and his disciples, together with a large crowd, were leaving the city, a blind man, Bartimaeus . . . was sitting by the road side begging . . .' Why tell the readers that Jesus went to Jericho and then apparently left it immediately? Obviously something had been deleted, and it was this, as supplied by the lost – and secret – Gospel of Mark: 'And the sister of the youth whom Jesus loved and his mother and Salome were there, and Jesus did not receive them.'

Implicit in this short passage is a particularly far-reaching implication: there is another young man who is described as 'the Beloved', and that is young John, who, in John's Gospel, famously leans against Jesus' chest at the Last Supper (and who appears to morph into the Magdalene in Leonardo's fresco). 'The . . . youth whom Jesus loved' is Lazarus – he is described in these terms in John's Gospel (chapter 11). In fact, 'Lazarus' is Greek for 'Eliezer',[13] 'Elijah' or 'Elias' – and as John the Baptist was commonly thought of as the reincarnation of Elias/Elijah, so the young man of Bethany is effectively called 'John' *twice* by the gospel writers, although 'Lazarus' is a clever device to obscure the fact. Why should they be so coy about a putative connection with the man who was so honoured to baptize Jesus in the Jordan? The conundrum becomes more problematic when the fact that the Baptist baptized at *another* place called Bethany – 'Bethany across the Jordan'[14] – or so the Gospel writers would have us believe, yet there is evidence that it was the same place after all.

The sister of John the Beloved is Mary of Bethany: just as the Gospel writers have obscured the identity of the brother, so they have attempted to divide Mary of Bethany into the unnamed sinner and Mary Magdalene – and Mary and John/Lazarus were intimately connected with the strangely dubious place called Bethany. Yet once again there is consternation in the ranks of the Church about that mysterious and clearly controversial family; enough, at least, for them to seek ways of removing them from the canon altogether, and if that is not possible, by fudging the story whenever they are mentioned. And Clement thought that Mark had written this secret Gospel while residing in the Egyptian city of Alexandria, which was, as we will see, intimately connected with John the Baptist . . .

If nothing else, this episode illustrates very clearly that from the outset the canonical Gospels have been subjected to a process of very subjective editing and censorship and that they are absolutely not the dispassionate, straightforward accounts of Jesus' life and teachings that most Christians still believe them to be. Unfortunately, the canonical Gospels – and, indeed, many non-canonical ones – are first and foremost works of propaganda and should be approached with exactly the same spirit in which we evaluate the party political pamphlets put through our doors before an election.

So for reasons that remain somewhat obscure – but which appear to have some connection with a *belief* that the Bethany family were involved in something distasteful, perhaps even a form of sexual rite – Martha, Lazarus (or John the Beloved) and Mary were deliberately and systematically marginalized by the editors of the New Testament Gospels, and also by the subsequent leaders of the Church; and Mary of Bethany appears to have been one and the same as the unnamed sinner who anoints Jesus with the costly unguent. But was she the same as Mary Magdalene?

Significantly, immediately after describing the anonymous woman's anointing of Jesus, Luke tells how Jesus and the Twelve travelled around with women (8:1–2) who included 'Mary (called Magdalene)', perhaps as if he had her on the brain after his hard work in carefully portraying her as the unnamed sinner with the perfume. However, in John's Gospel the anointer is explicitly named as Mary of Bethany, and her being a 'sinner' is omitted. Luke's choice of words in describing her moral status is very interesting: it is *harmartolos*, meaning one who has committed a crime against the Jewish law, although this does not necessarily imply prostitution. It is a term taken from the sport of archery, meaning missing the target and may refer to someone who for whatever reason does not keep the religious observances – or does not pay the taxes, possibly because she was not actually Jewish.[15]

Mary of Bethany is also described as having unbound or uncovered hair, which no self-respecting Judaean Jewish woman would do, for it represented sexual licence, as it does to Orthodox Jews and Muslims in today's Middle East. Indeed, Mary wipes Jesus' feet with her hair – a curiously intimate, not to say iconoclastic, action for an apparently unknown woman to perform in public. This would have been regarded as utterly scandalous by the disciples. As Timothy Frcke and Peter Gandy write in their book *Jesus and the Goddess* (2001): 'According to Jewish law, only a husband was allowed to see a woman's hair unbound and if a woman let down her hair in front of another man, this was a sign of impropriety and grounds for mandatory divorce.'[16] They conclude that: 'This incident, then, can be seen as portraying Jesus and Mary as either man and wife or as libertine lovers with scant regard for niceties.' This conclusion, however, makes certain assumptions, and although the subject of Jesus as a married man will be dealt with later, suffice it to say here that he appears to have such little concern for even the most entrenched Jewish customs as to appear either hugely insensitive – or a foreigner . . . Indeed, early Christian texts referred to him as *ho allogenes* (the foreigner).[17]

Nowhere in the canonical gospels does it describe that Jesus drove seven demons out of Mary of *Bethany*, although they never waste an opportunity to tell us that about Mary Magdalene – indeed, although Mary of Bethany outrageously wore unbound hair and was 'harmartolos', apparently Jesus proceeds to stay with her and her family as if nothing were amiss. Perhaps it is his familiarity with an ex-sinner that disturbed the disciples and Gospel writers – if, indeed, *she were ever a sinner*. (And there would be that knotty problem of the men of the mission living off her immoral earnings.) There is another interpretation of the anointing, however, which, while providing answers to many of the questions about that strange little episode and the real character of Mary of Bethany (and possibly, therefore, also of Mary Magdalene), is profoundly unsettling to those brought up in the Christian tradition. This is the idea that the anointing was not a haphazard, spur-of-the-moment action by a sobbing sinner, which took Jesus as much by surprise as anyone else, but that it was a pre-arranged sacred ritual, the purpose of which was unknown to the twelve men.

Indeed, a hint of this creeps into the Gospel of Mark, in which the disciples 'rebuked her harshly' for wasting money on such expensive perfume, which 'could have been sold for more than a year's wages and the money given to the poor'.[18] Jesus' response is quick and vehement:

Leave her alone . . . Why are you bothering her? She has done a beautiful thing to me. The poor you will always have with you, and you can help them any time you want. But you will not always have me.

She did what she could. She poured perfume on my body beforehand to prepare for my burial. I tell you the truth, wherever the gospel is preached throughout the world, what she has done will also be told, in memory of her.

Yet in this, Jesus only partly got his wish, for although the story is well known and regularly read out in church services, she mostly remains anonymous – and the solemnity and purpose of the rite is absolutely unknown. As Tresemer and Cannon write of Jesus' prophecy that wherever the Gospel is preached, the woman's actions will be known:

How is it, then, that all Christians do not remember and revere this memorial, so clearly marked by their teacher? Why do most people know her as the reformed prostitute, rather than as what seems more likely – a ministering priestess with a deep understanding of the thresholds of the spirit world?[19]

There is also a hint of Mary Magdalene here, for this woman prepares his body for burial, and she, too, was involved in the burial rites of Jesus. Were they, in fact, the same woman, her identity having been carefully trifurcated, just as John the Beloved also became Lazarus?

The sense of distaste that surrounds Mary of Bethany appears to rest largely on the anointing of Jesus – but surely this is an excessive reaction to the apparent squandering of even a vastly expensive ointment. In fact, a clue about the importance of this little ritual can be found in Jesus' title of 'Christ' – or, in Greek, *Christos*, which means 'the anointed one'. There is only one anointing mentioned in the New Testament – *and it is performed by a woman*. That, presumably, is the major reason why the male Jewish writers were so keen to play it down, to portray it as the work of a sinner, or a crazily feckless action of some anonymous (and possibly hysterical) woman. Whereas the idea of Jesus as God came largely from the later Christians, a Jewish Messiah was expected to be anointed – or 'christened', although certain chosen ones in the pagan world were also marked out as special in this way.

Only two people in the New Testament performed rites on Jesus: the first was the baptism by John the Baptist in the River Jordan, and the second was the anointing by Mary of Bethany at the end of his mission. Both of them are connected with Bethany, and both are deliberately marginalized by Matthew, Mark, Luke and John – and so is Mary Magdalene, who comes out of nowhere virtually to take charge of the events after the crucifixion.

Mary of Bethany made Jesus into the Christ by anointing him with spikenard that had, almost certainly, been specifically bought and kept for that purpose. This was no frivolous or impulsive gesture, but an integral part of what he was about – and the male writers were determined to make it as meaningless and as obscure as possible to undermine not only its value to Jesus himself, but also the value of the woman who performed it. Yet women did not perform sacred religious rites in Jewish practices at that time – indeed, it was ruled that 'women, slaves and children' were exempt even from saying the ritual prayers in the home[20], let alone officiating in the more important rituals of the synagogue or Temple – so why did Jesus allow Mary of Bethany to take such a significant role?

## The foreigners

As we have seen, a woman could even be divorced on the grounds of appearing in public with unbound hair – so heinous was the sin – and here Mary of Bethany, a 'harmartolos' woman, one who somehow misses the Jewish mark or is outside the religious law, seems utterly oblivious to the outcry her actions would cause. More significantly, not only does Jesus not rebuke her for flouting the Judaic law, but he tacitly encourages her by turning on those who criticize her behaviour.

Both of them are behaving like foreigners in a strange land: no wonder they are not understood, particularly by the Twelve who, time after time, we are told, fail to understand Jesus' teaching or the whole point of his mission. Mary of Bethany may be an outsider, but she appears to share some kind of private secret with Jesus – and they are both outsiders.

If the anointing were not a Jewish custom, then to what tradition did it belong? In their time there was a sublimely sacred *pagan* rite that involved a woman anointing a chosen man both on the head and feet – and also on the genitals – for a very special destiny. This was the anointing of the sacred king, in which the priestess singled out the chosen man and anointed him, before bestowing his destiny upon him in a sexual rite known as the *hieros gamos* (sacred marriage). The anointing was part of the ritual preparation for penetration during the rite – which did not have the same emotional or legal ramifications as the more usual form of marriage – in which the priest-king was flooded with the power of the god, while the priestess-queen became possessed by the great goddess. Without the power of the woman, the chosen king could never reign and would be powerless. Barbara G. Walker explains:

> Marriage with the earthly representative of the Goddess, in the form of the queen, was essential to the position of kingship: this was the original meaning of 'holy matrimony' (hieros gamos). Akkadian kings apparently went on military expeditions chiefly to prove themselves worthy of the sacred marriage.[21]

The concept of the sacred marriage is essential to the understanding of Jesus and his mission, and his relationship with the most important woman in his life – not to mention two highly significant men . . . The persistent image of Mary of Bethany/Mary Magdalene as a whore begins to make sense when it is realized that this ritual is the ultimate expression of what the Victorian historians called 'temple prostitution' – of course with their arrogant and hypocritical puritanism and sexual repression, this should not surprise us – although the original term for the priestess involved was *hierodule*, or 'sacred servant'. It was only through her that a man could achieve knowledge of himself and of the gods. In the epitome of the sacred servant's work, the *hieros gamos*, the king is sanctified and set apart – and of course immediately after the biblical anointing, Judas betrays Jesus and the machinery for his ultimate destiny through the crucifixion is set in motion.

(Distant echoes of this are to be found in a curious ceremony performed on 16 June 1633 when Edinburgh welcomed the newly crowned Charles I. At West Port he was greeted by what appeared to be a sea-nymph, dressed in blue-green and wearing a peculiar headdress representing a castle with turrets. She was known as 'Princess Magdalene'.[22] Here we have a species of royal priestess hailing the new monarch, just as Mary of Bethany/the Magdalene singled out and anointed Jesus as the sacred king. And the representation of the Princess as a sea nymph is a clear echo of the ancient associations of the name 'Mary' or 'Mari' – as Barbara G. Walker writes: '[Mari was the] basic name of the Goddess known to the Chaldeans as Marratu, to the Jews as Marah, to the Persians as Mariham, to the Christians as Mary: as well as Marian, Miriam, Marianne, Myrrhine, Myrtea, Myrrha, Maria, and Marina. Her blue robe and pearl necklace were classic symbols of the sea, edged with pearly foam.'[23])

The sacred marriage was a familiar concept to pagans of Jesus' day: versions of it were commonly performed by the devotees of various other dying-and-rising god cults, such as that of Tammuz (to whom there was a temple in Jerusalem at that time), and the Egyptian god Osiris, whose consort Isis breathed life into his dead body long enough for her to conceive the magical child, the hawk-headed god of courage, Horus. Indeed, Tresemer and Cannon state unequivocally that: 'Her appearances with special oils to use in anointing Jesus Christ place her in the tradition of priests and priestesses of Isis, whose unguents were used to achieve the transition over the threshold of death while retaining consciousness.'[24] Indeed, this places her in the specific context of the shamanic tradition of Egypt, which is only now being acknowledged.[25] As a shaman – or, at the very least, a gifted shamanic helper[26] – she would have officiated during Jesus' agonizing crucifixion and spiritual visits to the invisible realm, protecting and guiding him during the most dangerous moments of his union with the gods. If indeed, he did not die on the cross – as many of the heretics believed – the crucifixion may be seen as the major shamanic initiation of his life. What happened to him afterwards is uncertain and controversial, and lies outside the scope of this book, but clearly he would never have been the same again, and may have been virtually unrecognizable even to those who had known him well.

In all versions of the sacred marriage, the representative of the goddess, in the form of her priestess, united sexually with the chosen king before his sacrificial death. Three days afterwards the god rose again, and the land was fertile once more.

Mary of Bethany used spikenard to anoint Jesus' feet – it may be significant that in the eastern Tantric (sacred sex) tradition, this particular unguent was specified for use on the hair and feet.

## The female eunuch

Clearly, this woman who anointed Jesus was very special, a great priestess of some ancient pagan tradition – but was she also Mary Magdalene, as the Church claimed until 1969? Recently, there have been moves to rehabilitate the Magdalene by stressing that she was *not* one and the same as the unnamed sinner, or previously sinful Mary of Bethany. As the Magdalene has become a role model for all liberal-minded modern Christian women, celebrated for the steadfastness of her devotion to Jesus and her obvious importance among his disciples, increasingly it is thought an insult to ascribe sinfulness to her – however much she was forgiven by Jesus. The politically correct Magdalene is emphatically *not* a sinner. Yet it does seem that the two women *were* the same, and that the Gospel writers had their own reasons for splitting her into two separate women – and successfully marginalizing both of them. The last thing these men wanted was for their readers to connect the two, for then there would be a chance that Mary's true importance and distinctive role would be uncovered: when that happens, much of the carefully constructed edifice of the patriarchal church immediately begins to crumble. It is interesting that both the Church's contradictory pronouncements about the Magdalene have proved advantageous to them: as a hysterical penitent she was a useful role model for women who threatened to become uppity – such as the slave girls of the Maggie laundries – but now she is not a sinner, not the same as Mary of Bethany, she has lost any suggestion that she was a priestess of enormous power. In both cases the men of the Vatican successfully made this potent woman into the archetypal female eunuch, and the irony is that many of the more liberated female Catholics have been persuaded that it is a *good* thing that she is no longer associated with Mary of Bethany! They see this as progress, when in fact it is nothing of the sort.

Of course most Christians do not expect hidden agendas or secret subtexts from the Gospels – just the unvarnished truth, no matter how unsophisticated the phraseology might be. Yet, the New Testament is riddled with what we today would call 'spin', and much of it is basically propaganda for certain groups and viewpoints. Accounts of incidents are garbled or run together to give a spurious impression, certain places and characters are unnamed, while words are put in the mouths of some characters that are nothing short of outright fabrications. Where those books are concerned, there is no such thing as the 'Gospel truth', and one of their most significant victims is Mary of Bethany. We have examined the role and identity of the Mary who was sister to Martha and Lazarus (John the Beloved), now let us consider the clues concerning the true nature of the mysterious woman known as the Magdalene.

### Where was Magdala?

This enigmatic woman, who was so obviously a central part of the mission of Jesus, is referred to in the Bible as 'Mary Magdalene' or simply 'the Magdalene', which conveys a pervasive sense that the Gospel writers expected their readers to know who she was, recognizing her name immediately. (Even so, she is hardly a central figure in the Gospels of Matthew, Mark, Luke and John, almost as if she were included only because she was too famous to be left out completely. Perhaps the authors were afraid that if Mary Magdalene were omitted altogether, their reading public would want to know why.) Her name is usually taken to mean 'Mary of Magdala', referring to her place of origin. This early twentieth-century analysis gives a largely conventional interpretation, which is still generally accepted today:

Mary Magdalene is probably named from the town of Magdala or Magadan . . . now Medjdel, which is said to mean 'a tower'. It

61

was situated at a short distance from Tiberias, and is mentioned ... in connection with the miracle of the seven loaves. An ancient watchtower still marks the site. According to Jewish authorities it was famous for its wealth, and for the moral corruption of its inhabitants.[27/28]

(Note how the writer reinforces the traditional association between the Magdalene and 'moral corruption' by linking her with her alleged place of origin, the sink of sin, 'Magdala'. As far as conventional commentators were – and to some extent still are – concerned, no opportunity must be wasted to drag her name through the mud.)

What of the commonly held belief that her home was on the shores of Lake Galilee? We know from the first-century Jewish chronicler Flavius Josephus that the town now called el Medjdel or Magdel today was known as Tarichea in the days of Jesus' mission – *not* Magdala. And it does seem strange that if she came from Galilee she alone of all local female disciples should be called by the name of her town: surely this would have caused confusion among the other women – who in a large group – would almost certainly have come from the same place? As just one of a crowd of women from the environs of Magdala, why was she alone called *the* Magdalene? Surely it would be analogous in a modern London-wide mission to single out just one woman as 'the Eastender'. She is also described as 'Mary *(called Magdalene)*', which is a very different form of words from the likes of, for example, 'Simon of/from Cyrene'. Once again, there is a suggestion of deliberate obfuscation, perhaps one implication being that *some* people may call her Mary of Bethany, while others know her as Mary Magdalene.

In fact, nowhere in the New Testament does it spell out where Mary comes from, which has led scholars and churchgoers merely to assume that she hailed from the shores of Lake Galilee – even though it must be said that there are more compelling reasons to believe she may have come from elsewhere: perhaps as a truly exotic foreigner. Indeed, as we will see, there is persuasive evidence that Jesus himself was not from those parts, although the assumption that he was a Jew from Galilee is so entrenched as to be deemed an unassailable fact.

62

The Bible rarely ascribes places of origin to its named characters – including Jesus. (Simon of Cyrene and Saul of Tarsus are among the few notable exceptions.) One of the many mistranslations of the New Testament that still has the power to amaze when corrected is the title 'Jesus of Nazareth', which should read 'Jesus the Nasorean'. Although it is known that Nasoreans were members of a group of sects who collectively used that name, they remain largely mysterious. However, the word itself derives from the Hebrew *Nostrim*, meaning 'Keepers or Preservers . . . those who maintained the true teaching and tradition, or who cherished certain secrets which they did not divulge to others . . .'[29] Of course this is particularly thought-provoking – even perhaps a little shocking – in the context of Jesus, who is usually thought of as being the founder of a unique, God-given religion, and not as a disciple or follower of someone else's.[30]

In any case, the town of Nazareth does not appear in any of the contemporary Roman records, on any maps, in the chronicles of the Jewish historian Flavius Josephus, or in the Talmud. So revered by Christians today, it seems that Nazareth did not exist until after the fall of Masada in the eighth decade CE, and did not properly flourish until 300 years after Jesus' death. (It is interesting in this context to ponder on the possible home town of Mary the Mother, which is usually taken to be Nazareth. But as it was non-existent in her day, where did she come from? Even if, like many other women, she followed Jesus around to some extent, she must have had a base in Palestine – but if so, where was it?)

There is a curious tunnel vision, shared by many scholars even today – and certainly by most Christians – about the land where Jesus taught. It is as if tiny Galilee were completely cut off from all other countries and all other influences. In the collective mind, it was an area of Yahweh-worshipping Jews, metaphorically cordoned off from the wider world. However, as Burton L. Mack writes in his *The Lost Gospel: The Book of Q and Christian Origins* (1994): 'In the world of the Christian imagination Galilee belonged to Palestine, the religion of Palestine was Judaism, so everyone in Galilee must have been Jewish. Since this picture is wrong . . . the reader must have a truer picture in mind.'[31] Not for nothing was Galilee known as 'the land of the Gentiles', having extensive trade links with the other nearby cultures, standing at the heart of a network of trade routes leading to Babylonia, Syria – and neighbouring Egypt.

Galilee in the first century was renowned for its heady mix of sects, religions and races, and had something of a reputation as a centre for heresies. It was such a hotbed of religious subversion and radical free-thinking that the authorities of the Jerusalem Temple were no more popular there than the Roman army of occupation. It attracted not only traders but also travellers from distant lands bringing with them dangerous and exciting new ideas, and Mary Magdalene – *the* Magdalene, the stranger, singled out for her uniqueness in some way – was almost certainly one of them.

In fact, there is no necessity to endeavour to crowbar her into a Galilean setting, for there are at least two other intriguing alternatives for her place of origin: although there was no 'Magdala' in Judaea in her day, there was a Magdolum in Egypt – just across the border – which was probably the Migdol mentioned in Ezekiel.[32] There was a large and flourishing Jewish community in Egypt at that time, which was particularly centred on the great sea port of Alexandria, a seething cosmopolitan melting pot of many races, nationalities and religions, where John the Baptist had his headquarters[33], and perhaps where the Holy Family had fled to escape the depredations of Herod's men. There were other groups of Jews, both orthodox and heretical, scattered throughout Egypt in the first century, and their influence on the growth and development of Christianity – although largely ignored or dismissed by academics – was considerable. Unlike the ubiquitous, much-lauded Greece, Egypt is still seen by academics as the poor relation of historical influences, which may – as we will see in a later chapter – prove to be a grave mistake.

If the Magdalene were really from the Egyptian town of Magdolum, this could provide a clue as to why she was so sidelined – after all, despite the exciting mix of nations and religions in Galilee at that time, human nature has always been suspicious of foreigners, and the gospels make it clear that few were more insular in their attitudes than the likes of Simon Peter, at least at the beginning of the mission. Indeed, the Acts of the Apostles reveals that it was only as a result of a vivid dream after Jesus' death that Peter realized that the Gentiles were worthy of the Gospel.[34]

However, if the Magdalene was a *priestess* from Egypt, that would increase the Jewish men's hostility to her a thousandfold. Not only was she an outspoken and independent woman of means, but also invested with pagan authority! The men would be very wary of her, but the reassuring presence of Jesus would no doubt keep the full force of their animosity at bay, his dominant personality holding them fast. It may be that he was such an astoundingly charismatic leader that he held his disciples under a kind of spell: but there would still be mutterings in corners and seething resentments: while he could do no wrong, she was a different matter. They would have had great reservations about the foreign priestess who constantly tagged along. Or Jesus could have had some other kind of hold over his followers – if they believed him to be rightfully the Messiah there would be little problem in indulging his personal whims (although they might well still grumble among themselves), or if he had political or military power, potential or real, with which he had impressed this group. After all, his immediate band of disciples included Judas Iscariot, or 'Judas *Sicarii*', and Simon the Zealot – both members of what we would call terrorist groups (although they would call themselves freedom fighters, agitating against the Roman occupation).

Perhaps there was another reason why the Magdalene was treated so badly by the men of Jesus' following. While she may have lived in Egypt – after all, we know that both the Baptist and Jesus himself lived there for several years – perhaps that is not where she came from originally. Indeed, it may be significant that for many years there was a Magdala in Ethiopia, a remote hilltop fortress in the south of the country, which was the site of a major battle between the local people and the British Army in 1868, the consequences of which rumble on controversially to this day.[35] This rocky outcrop is now called Amra *Mariam* (Mary): although the Ethiopians today generally revere the Virgin Mary over Mary Magdalene, these place names indicate that there is a long association with the latter in that area, perhaps – unthinkably to many – it may even have been her birthplace or home.

An Ethiopian background would certainly have made her extremely exotic and perhaps disturbing to the insular men of Jesus' mission such as Simon Peter. Despite what politically correct revisionists may claim now, the British Empire did not invent racism: if the Magdalene were *black*, outspoken, rich, a pagan priestess – and Jesus' closest ally (to say the least) – the Twelve might well have floundered in a sea of uneducated emotions at the sight of her, born of fear of the alien, the unknown.

Perhaps on the surface the idea of a black Magdalene may provoke howls of ridicule – after all, it may be fine when casting a new production of *Jesus Christ Superstar,* but surely it has no basis in historical fact. Yet there are several thought-provoking traditional connections between the Magdalene and blackness, which are examined – together with their implications for the Christian story – in a later chapter.

The use of Mary's name in the Bible is interesting: she is pointed out as '*the* Magdalene', which sounds almost flippant – as critics might say 'la Thatcher' with more than a touch of irony, of the erstwhile British prime minister. Seen in that light, 'Mary *called* Magdalene' may be some kind of nickname, just as the gospels call the founder of the Church 'Simon called Peter', which appears to show that 'Peter' (or 'Petros' in Greek, meaning 'Rock') was a joke, perhaps referring to his height or bulk. Some[36] have even suggested it should be rendered as 'Rocky' (as in Sylvester Stallone's famous boxing character), as homage to Simon's reputation as something of a bruiser.

Perhaps, though, 'Mary called Magdalene' refers to a title, rather than a place name or facetious nickname. Indeed, as Margaret Starbird points out in her 1993 examination of the Magdalene cult, *The Woman With the Alabaster Jar*: 'In Hebrew, the epithet *Magdala* literally means "tower" or "elevated, great, magnificent".'[37] One interpretation of 'Magdala' is indeed 'tower' – the 'Princess Magdalene' who greeted Charles I in Edinburgh wore a headdress in the shape of a turreted castle – although it may more properly be understood in its metaphorical sense as 'elevated' or 'great'. And in many other languages the adjective or name 'Magda', while strictly carrying the definition of 'maiden' implicitly means 'magnificent [female] one', while 'Magna' simply means 'great', as in the Latin 'Magna Mater', the title of the Great Mother goddess. In her book *The Woman's Encyclopedia of Myths and Secrets*, Barbara G. Walker writes of the definition of 'Magna

Dea': '"Great Goddess" of Syria, worshippcd especially at Hicrapolis, "Holy City". The same title was applied to all Goddesses throughout the Roman empire, which was verging on a concept of female monotheism when Jewish, Persian and Christian patriarchy intervened.'[38]

But if 'the Magdalene' is a rank, perhaps indicating that she was the Chief Priestess of some ancient pagan cult, or in any case suggestive of great magnificence, who gave her the honour? Certainly not the Gospel writers, who obviously found the whole subject of the Magdalene uncomfortable – and, as we will see, neither was this kind of praise likely to originate with the famous Twelve, especially Simon Peter, who clearly found her particularly difficult even to be in the same room with[39], let alone happily bestowing a title of greatness upon her. However, although one searches in vain through the biblical texts for any information that would account for Mary's 'greatness', there is plentiful evidence from other sources that not only was she 'magnificent' in her own right, but that Jesus himself recognized that she was a woman of extraordinary power . . .

**Bride of Christ?**

But was the obviously close relationship between the Magdalene and Jesus due to their being legally man and wife, as some – most seminally Baigent, Leigh and Lincoln in their 1982 book *The Holy Blood and the Holy Grail* – have claimed? If they were, there is a very strange silence about it in the New Testament, for despite what Christians (especially Catholics) may think today, priests and rabbis in the Holy Land were *supposed* to be married, for to abstain from procreation was (and still is, among Orthodox Jews) seen as an insult to God. Indeed, celibacy won censure from the elders of the synagogue, and perhaps also mutterings about unnatural lusts among the congregation. For a Jewish rabbi, it would have been very odd if Jesus were *not* married, but if he had a wife, surely she would have been mentioned – as 'Miriam the wife of the Saviour', or 'Mary the wife of Jesus'. There is never any phrase that might remotely be interpreted as alluding to his legal spouse, but was this because there was no such person, or because his wife was known but disliked so intensely and on such a scale that the canonical

Gospel writers decided to ignore her? Or because they had married in a ceremony that the Jews did not recognize? But if, as the Gnostic Gospels overwhelmingly suggest, Jesus and the Magdalene were committed and passionate lovers, why did they stop short of putting their relationship on an official footing? As we have seen, the astonishingly brave citizens of Béziers believed passionately that they were unmarried lovers. (Many commentators have argued that the Wedding at Cana, where Jesus turned the water into wine, was in fact his own – largely because he and his mother appeared to be the hosts. But perhaps it was merely the wedding feast of a close relative, over which they presided: in any case, some writers suggest that the miracle at Cana never happened, being based on a myth from the story of the pagan dying-and-rising god Dionysus.[40])

Apart from there being some kind of legal proscription on their love – such as being close blood relatives or being legally married to someone else at the time – there seems little reason for them not to have made a public commitment to each other. Could this reluctance to tie the knot have been because they were not, in fact, Jewish at all in the generally accepted sense and therefore could not be married in a synagogue? And it is significant that pagan priestesses, even those involved in sacred sex, were often required to be otherwise celibate and remain unmarried.

In any case, we know from the Gospels that there were mutterings in the ranks of Jesus' disciples because although the Baptist's followers were allowed to marry, they were not. And those, such as Simon Peter, who were already married, were encouraged to leave their families behind and follow Jesus, which sits uncomfortably with the modern Christian idea of Jesus being somehow the god of happy families. (Curiously, though, Jesus' mission was not otherwise famous for its puritanism: according to the gospel of Matthew[41] – and, indeed, non-canonical sources – Jesus himself had a reputation for drunkenness and gluttony, certainly compared to the more notably abstemious Baptist's disciples, who often fasted and prayed.) Although there was this proscription on marriage, there were still undertones of sacred sexuality, of sexual or at least erotic rites associated with the movement, which suggest that while permanent and legal alliances were frowned upon, ecstatic – and perhaps even unique – sacramental rites, such as the *hieros gamos*, did take place. Of course if sexual relationships were out of bounds for all the members of the movement *except* for Jesus and the Magdalene (and possibly, although even more controversially, her brother), that might go a long way towards explaining the hostility with which she was treated by the men.

We can only speculate, but it may be significant that the citizens of Béziers had no such doubts, being so certain that Jesus and the Magdalene were *lovers* that they went to their deaths to defend what they saw as the facts, pure and simple. And Leonardo depicted them in mirror-image clothes in *The Last Supper,* as if they were their mutual other half. How did these people who lived in the much later medieval and Renaissance times know with such utter certainty about Jesus' and Mary's relationship when there was not so much as a breath of it within the Church? Did they have access to a secret gospel, which was then hidden again, rather than let the Pope's men find and destroy it?

While maintaining a caution against being over-persuaded by writings outside the accepted Christian canon simply because they are heretical, it is nevertheless very instructive to examine the versions of 'forbidden' books that have occasionally resurfaced over time. What light can the recovered Gnostic Gospels shed on the passion of Jesus Christ and Mary Magdalene, who lived their curiously significant lives over 2,000 years ago and in a distant land?

# Apostle of the Apostles

In December 1945, Muhammad Ali, an Arab peasant, together with his brothers, accidentally made a major historic discovery in the labyrinth of mountain caves near the town of Nag Hammadi, in Upper Egypt. Digging for the soft mountain soil known as *sabakh* – used locally as as fertilizer – they unearthed a massive (3 foot/ 1 metre-high) red earthenware jar, which at first they left intact, for fear of its harbouring a *djinn*, or evil spirit. This consideration was rapidly overtaken by a more pressing one – perhaps it contained treasure, a long-lost hoard of gold with which to alleviate the crippling poverty in which their family lived. Such thoughts banishing fear of any lurking djinn, stoutly they smashed the container open – only to be initially disappointed to discover a stash of ancient books: thirteen leather-bound volumes of closely-written papyrus.

For many years no details were known of this find – although there were plenty of rumours about what happened to it – and the exact circumstances that followed immediately after the volumes were found are still unknown. Ali later claimed that his mother, Umm-Ahmad, being ignorant of their potential value, burnt some of the papyri in her oven, which has provoked a mixture of outrage and condescending amusement among the international academic community at her ignorance of their worth. Just think what treasures, perhaps even astounding theological and historical revelations, the peasant woman no doubt happily committed to the flames! How ironic that the world's most sensational theological discovery for decades should meet with such a fate!

Yet there is something about this little tale, so well worn by now, that fails to ring true. Perhaps Ali's mother really was so desperate for kindling that the story is no more than the unvarnished truth, but it does seem odd that, even if ignorant of the historic worth of the find, she would treat anything that had a potential value on the flourishing antiquities market in such a cavalier manner, given the straitened circumstances in which she and her family were forced to live. Egyptians, particularly the most impoverished, have always shown great regard for anything that might be sold – the sight of the poorest of the poor sitting by the roadside in Cairo trying to sell not only dead but decomposing and stinking camels is common enough. Surely the first thing Ali would have said when he returned home with his bundle would have been (words to the effect of): 'Mother, take care of these, they could be valuable'? Life can be strange and people do act foolishly, but there is the distinct feeling of a convenient myth about this incident. Perhaps Ali sold the missing papyri separately, to another buyer who has chosen not to have them published, and concocted a story blaming his mother for lost volumes to cover for any potential embarrassment. (For all he knew, what are now known as the Gnostic Gospels mention papyri that should have accompanied them. Questions would be asked: far better to invent an accidental burning.)

There is the possibility that he sold the 'burnt' volumes directly to an agent of the Vatican, which has since chosen to keep them secret, for reasons of its own. Indeed, if these putative missing books were anything like the ones that did eventually find their way into the public domain, it is little wonder that it was deemed advisable not to make them widely available.

The Nag Hammadi papyri we know of underwent a complicated series of adventures,[1] many of which were connected with the Vatican's ardent desire to prevent their very existence from being widely known. Although this conspiracy to remove certain Christian texts from the public gaze had begun as early as the third century, the relentless process continues to this day. As David Tresemer and Laura-Lea Cannon say – almost teasingly – in their Preface to Jean-Yves Leloup's translation of the Gnostic *Gospel of*

*Mary Magdalene* (not itself one of the Nag Hammadi finds: it came to light in Cairo in 1856): 'The story of the suppression of early Christian gospels reads like an adventure novel – book burnings, secret meetings of small sects found out by the authorities, exiles, executions, and so forth.'[2]

For the first 200 years of the new religion of Christianity, all manner of writings on the life and teachings of its founder and his disciples circulated around the Roman Empire. Scholars estimate that the biblical Gospels were not the first Christian writings: Matthew and Luke are usually dated from around 80 CE, Mark about a decade earlier and John as late as 100 CE. Although the very first major books of the New Testament were the letters of Paul, dating from around 50 CE, unfortunately he was not remotely interested in the details of Jesus' earthly life or personal relationships, concentrating instead on his religious significance – and, more incidentally, the problems of organizing the early Church in the Roman world.

## Women's rites and Gnostic wisdom

However, the famous four Gospels were by no means the only sacred writings in circulation: indeed, because of the hundreds of scrolls being passed from group to group there was a huge variation in doctrine and practice, although there were certain major differences between what is now understood to be the Christian way of life and what was common enough then. It may be surprising to discover that in those exciting but confused early days, there was a strong female presence among the leaders of the Church. Women prophets were especially popular in the late second century, much to the disgust and chagrin of the likes of the church father Hippolytus, who wrote:

And being in possession of an infinite number of their books, they are overrun with delusion, and they allege that they have learned something more through these than from law, and prophets and the Gospels. [Although some of these 'infinite number of . . . books' *were* Gospels, Hippolytus and his colleagues only recognized those that upheld their particular viewpoint.] But they magnify these wretched women above the apostles and every gift of Grace, so that some of them presume to assert that there is in them something superior to Christ . . . They introduce, however, the novelties of fasts, and feast . . . alleging that they have been instructed by women.[3]

But did this feminine empowerment represent a form of subversion, or was the very early Church an equal opportunities organization? And if so, did this extraordinarily liberal attitude begin with Jesus himself? It is strange to consider that the furore about the suitability of women priests, and the immense condescension that accompanies their ordination even now, may represent not a new and enlightened era for the churches, but a very timid attempt to return to the old glory days.

Clearly, the proliferation of books in the first and second centuries somehow encouraged women to believe that they could take a major part in Christian worship, yet one searches the New Testament in vain for any direct evidence that this was so, just as the canonical Gospels are so evasive about the real role of Mary of Bethany/the Magdalene – whose name may mean 'magnificent'.

Tresemer and Cannon explain how today's New Testament came about:

In 325, [the Roman Emperor] Constantine convened the Council of Nicaea where it was decided which texts would become the standards of the Church – those that we now know as the canonical Gospels – and which would be suppressed. Those not chosen as standard were attacked – sometimes violently – for many years. Indeed, the bishops at the Council of Nicaea who disagreed with Constantine's choices were exiled on the spot.[4]

After the alleged burning of some of the Nag Hammadi discoveries by Muhammad Ali's mother, the remaining books (or 'codices') came into the hands of Professor Gilles Quispel, the distinguished historian of religion at Utrecht University in Holland. On translating the first line of the first document, he was astounded to read the momentous opening line: 'These are the secret words which the living Jesus spoke, and which the twin, Thomas, wrote down.'

Elaine Pagels, in her major work *The Gnostic Gospels* (1979) – indeed, although many have attempted to write on the subject, hers is still the major reference work that is almost reverently cited by virtually all other commentators – writes:

> Quispel knew that his colleague H.-C. Peuch, using notes from another French scholar, Jean Doresse, had identified the opening lines with fragments of a Greek *Gospel of Thomas* discovered in the 1890s. But the discovery of the whole text raised new questions: Did Jesus have a twin brother, as this text implies? Could the text be an authentic record of Jesus' sayings?[5]

(Although the question of Jesus as a twin lies outside the scope of this book, of course if true it seriously challenges the whole notion of Jesus as the unique Son of God, and Mary his mother as virgin at one stroke.)

The papyri of Nag Hammadi proved to consist, in Elaine Pagels' words, of: 'fifty-two texts from the early centuries of the Christian era – including a collection of Christian gospels, previously unknown. Besides the *Gospel of Thomas* and the *Gospel of Philip*, the find included the *Gospel of Truth* and the *Gospel of the Egyptians*, which identifies itself as "the [sacred book] of the Great Invisible [Spirit]"[6]. Another group of texts consists of writings attributed to Jesus' followers, such as the *Secret Book of James*, the *Apocalypse of Paul*, the *Letter of Peter to Philip*, and the *Apocalypse of Peter*.'[7]

On delving further into his exciting find, Quispel discovered that these discoveries were 1,500-year-old Coptic (first-millennial Egyptian) translations of much older works that had been written in Greek, like the books of the New Testament. He noted that they belonged to the type of early Christianity known as 'Gnostic' – which, as we have seen, derives from the Greek word *gnosis*, or 'knowledge', for Gnostics laid great stress on knowing God for oneself in one's own heart and soul, rather than only comprehending him through the intermediary of priests. Indeed, they believed that knowing one's own heart and soul is an essential part of the process of becoming one with God. As Elaine Pagels writes: 'Orthodox Jews and Christians insist that a chasm separates humanity from its creator: God is wholly other. But some of the gnostics who wrote these gospels contradict this: self-knowledge is knowledge of God; the self and the divine are identical.'[8]

Professor Quispel discovered that although the text of the *Gospel of Thomas* reinforced many of the teachings and mores of the New Testament books, there was a somewhat disturbing – and clearly exciting – added dimension: information that would certainly cause more than a few raised eyebrows among Christians everywhere. In the event, of course, while ordinary believers are free to buy Ms Pagels' book and the few others on the subject, they are by no means encouraged to do so by their spiritual leaders. It is true to say that the vast majority of Christians have only the vaguest awareness of their existence. Of course this ignorance of the lost gospels is tacitly encouraged by those at the top, for much of the content of the books of Nag Hammadi effectively challenges the New Testament certainty in several fundamental ways and contains some truly explosive material, not least regarding the nature of Jesus' relationship with Mary Magdalene. The powers that be are no doubt right – from their own perspective – not to breathe a word about these books to their flock, for surely centuries of careful conditioning could be undone in as little time as it takes to read the following passage, for example, taken from the *Gospel of Thomas*:

. . . the companion of the Saviour is Mary Magdalene. But Christ loved her more than all the disciples, and used to kiss her often on her mouth. The rest of the disciples were offended . . . They said to him, 'Why do you love her more than all of us?' The Saviour answered and said to them, 'Why do I not love you as I love her?'[9]

It may not be too facetious to suggest that Jesus' response should be read with a rising note of incredulity at the men's naïveté, with the following emphasis: 'Why do I not love *you* as I love *her*?' Although some commentators have tried to explain away this, and other similar passages, as merely a reflection of a typically tactile Gnostic friendship – their meetings were characterized by passionate hugs and kisses – it must be said that this clearly does not apply in the case of the Magdalene and Jesus. There is distinct evidence that this was not a platonic relationship – as the Cathars and the doomed citizens of Béziers believed so passionately. The word used for 'companion' in this particular passage says it all. This is the Greek *koinonos*, which specifically means 'consort' or 'companion *of a sexual nature*', an intimate partner and – by implication – sharer in her lover's most private thoughts, not simply a close friend in God. If the disciples, both male and female, were merely fond of the first-century equivalent of New Age hugs, the acrid jealousy of the men would be hard to understand, but if the likes of Simon Peter believed that although he *should* have been part of Jesus' inner circle – as indeed, do all Christians, everywhere – gallingly, his Master was more inclined to spend his time with this woman, all is explained. Here the disciples express their offence at the fact that Jesus and Mary were, in the fashionable language of today, an 'item' – which they clearly felt was to their own detriment on the mission. One can almost hear them asking, 'Who is this *woman* who knows all our Lord's secrets, and is always with him, night and day?'

From just that one passage in the long-hidden Gnostic gospels, inklings of the root of the strange aversion to Mary Magdalene in the conventional scriptures can be discerned. Already there is the uncomfortable suspicion that if the *Gospel of Thomas* was founded on fact, and Mary really was Jesus' constant, and intimate, companion, the Church fathers would still have metamorphosed her into a penitent whore, no matter how insulting this would be to both her memory and that of Jesus himself. The image of a strong Christ might be very useful to them, but the strong woman at his side had to be dropped from the equation: it seems that a feisty, intelligent – and above all *sexual* – companion of Jesus was just one role model too many, as far as they were concerned. (It is also instructive to consider the generations of 'Maggies' who were shut away as slaves, often because they had done no more than visited the cinema with a young man unchaperoned – and compare their 'sins' to the apparent reality of a Jesus who seemed so besotted with the woman and who caused such outrage to St Peter by fondling and kissing her publicly.)

### Denouncing the heretics

Although the Nag Hammadi texts were only discovered in 1945, there were many similar books in circulation at the very beginning of the Christian era, all of which were declared to be heretical by the Church Fathers in the middle of the second century. Around the year 180, Bishop Irenaeus of Lyons, France, wrote a blistering five-volume attack on the product of such books, promising to: '. . . set forth the views of those who are now teaching heresy . . . to show how absurd and inconsistent with the truth are their statements . . . I do this so that . . . you may urge all those with whom you are connected to avoid such an abyss of madness and of blasphemy against Christ.'[10]

Elaine Pagels points out that, 'He denounces as especially "full of blasphemy" a famous gospel called *The Gospel of Truth*,'[11] and asks: 'Is Irenaeus referring to the same *Gospel of Truth* discovered at Nag Hammadi?'[12] Was the 1945 discovery a copy of a book that circulated through the Christian world in the early centuries of the first millennium, or perhaps even the original text, having been buried when the heretics feared that all their sacred books would be destroyed in the same fires that burnt their own flesh? It hardly matters, for certainly some version of such a book had been known in the second century onwards, even then provoking the sort of reaction that it still elicits from many of the more orthodox Christian quarters.

The problem for the Church and its age-old conspiracy to create its own useful version of Christ is that there is no knowing how many Gnostic Gospels there are somewhere out there in the world, and when a particularly explosive one will jump forth like Banquo's ghost at the feast in a singularly threatening manner. And although many of these are mere fragments, or are so fancifully or impenetrably written as to appear ludicrous, a fair number seem to have an equal claim to 'authenticity' – whatever that may be, although one may take it to mean that they are close enough to the time and place of Jesus' mission and have a suitably serious tone – as the New Testament Gospels.

There are differences, however: the biblical Gospels tend to be more or less chronological narratives of Jesus' mission: where he went and whom he met, interspersed with a good deal of teaching by parable and wonder-working. The Gnostic Gospels, on the other hand, are much more concerned with the spiritual message, the inner – and often secret – knowledge, and the question of how to set about perfecting the human soul. The New Testament tries very hard to present an open Christianity with no secrets and no mysteries (although there are hints of private rites at Bethany, and in any case various saints and mystics have introduced them over the years) whereas the Gnostics' version of the fledgling religion is essentially based on a series of initiations, an occult hierarchy based on the concept that the greatest secrets are only given to those who prove themselves worthy – like the later Cathar religion. The New Testament Christianity is largely exoteric, for the masses – while the Gnostics cherished their esoteric nature and relative exclusivity. Both groups, of course, believed that they alone represented Jesus' true teaching, and – paradoxically – they may both be right to some degree, for taken together, the New Testament and the Gnostic books may well represent Jesus' public and private teachings respectively. There is a great emphasis among the 'forbidden' books on secret initiation into a kind of mystery school, which probably involved some kind of sexual rite. In any case, whatever it was, as it featured the Magdalene so prominently, it had to be repressed.

There is another major difference between the two systems: the Bible's religion, coming from a Jewish perspective, is male dominated, and is therefore the one that 'won', but the more cosmopolitan Gnostics – many were Egyptian or African – were egalitarian, with women preachers, prophets and even baptizers[13]. (Many were remarkable for their powers of prophecy, speaking wildly and colourfully when possessed by the spirit, in much the same way as both New Age channellers and evangelical Christians do today. Conventional Christianity was irritated and embarrassed by this, and in this at least one may sympathize.) The Church Father and theologian Tertullian, who set himself the task of returning Africa's Gnostics to the straight and narrow path of biblical Christianity, wrote: 'The very women of these heretics, how wanton they are! For they are bold enough to teach, to dispute, to enact exorcism, to undertake cures – it may be even to baptize.'[14] The two systems may have bickered back and forth about many differences on the matter of dogma, but the question of women priests was absolutely central, and a real threat to the emergent Roman Church – as, indeed, it still is.

The reason for the Gnostic openness to women was that, on the whole, the heretics tended to believe in both a feminine and a masculine divinity (although caution should be exercised here, for some Gnostics were at least as virulently anti-female as the mainstream Church). Elaine Pagels writes:

> . . . several gnostic groups describe the divine Mother as part of an original couple. Valentinius, the teacher and poet, begins with the premise that God is essentially indescribable. But he suggests that the divine can be imagined as a dyad: consisting, in one part, of the Ineffable, the Depth, the Primal Father; and, in the other, of Grace, Silence, the Womb, and 'Mother of the All'.[15]

She goes on: 'Valentinius reasons that Silence is the appropriate complement of the Father, designating the former as feminine and the latter as masculine because of the grammatical gender of the Greek words.' But clearly there is something other than mere grammar at the root of this: 'He goes on to describe how Silence receives, as in a womb, the seed of the ineffable Source; from this she brings forth all the emanations of divine beings, ranged in harmonious pairs of masculine and feminine energies.'[16]

Although the Gnostics were given to fantastically complex and fanciful cosmologies and angelic hierarchies that spiral out of control – which regularly brought down the ridicule of several church fathers upon their heads, for when the Gnostics were silly they were extremely silly – there was an essential simplicity about them. Believing that they mirrored the mandate of Jesus himself, they tended to uphold the spiritual equality of women, often openly and in defiance of the early Roman Church.

Indeed, the Gnostics – whether or not they consciously supported the feminine – seem to have naturally honoured those qualities that are associated more with women than men. The great psychoanalyst Carl Gustav Jung believed the Gnostics were important because they expressed 'the other side of the mind', celebrating and encouraging the more spontaneous and emotional reactions to life that conventional Christianity sought to suppress.

In the recently discovered Nag Hammadi text *Trimorphic Protennoia* (*The Triple-formed Primal Thought*), a divine female figure speaks:

I am the Voice. It is I who speak within every creature . . . Now I have come a second time in the likeness of a female, and have spoken with them . . . I have revealed myself in the Thought of the likeness of my masculinity.

[. . .]

I am androgynous. I am both Mother and Father, since I copulate with myself . . . and with those who love me . . . I am the Womb that gives shape to the All . . . I am Meirothea, the glory of the Mother.[17]

(It is interesting that the recent adoption of some Anglican congregations of 'inclusive language' such as a prayer that 'the Holy Spirit will move amongst us and that we may recognize Her presence and co-operate with Her work' should cause such a furore[18] for two reasons: it is hardly a new approach, as the Gnostics were so notably 'inclusive' nearly 2,000 years ago, and the Holy Spirit should be feminine, as Jesus himself recognized – as we shall see.)

Many of the Gnostic texts are not strictly gospels, but poems and hymns – even magical formulae: all in their unique way being heartfelt expressions of profound emotion and spirituality. One poem, *Perfect Consciousness*[19] includes a strangely stirring declaration by a female power:

I am the first and the last. I am the honoured one and the scorned one. I am the whore, and the holy one. I am the wife and the virgin. I am (the mother) and the daughter. I am called Sophia by the Greeks and Gnosis by the foreigners. I am the one whose image is great in Egypt and the one who has no image among the foreigners. I am she whose wedding is great, and I have not taken a husband . . . I am knowledge, and ignorance . . . I am shameless; I am ashamed. I am strength, and I am fear . . . I am foolish, and I am wise . . . I am godless, and I am one whose God is great.[20]

Here there is all the paradoxical nature of the archetypal goddess, and of the essence of emotion itself – rejoicing in the irrational and the contradictory, and welcoming the intellectually impossible as a gateway to God. Here, too, is a statement of the importance of the feminine in Egypt – 'I am one whose image is great in Egypt, and the one who has no image among the foreigners'. In Egypt, the concept of the powerful woman could flourish as nowhere else in the known world at that time – but as ever, particularly among the moneyed classes. Whether she was from Tarichea, Magdolum or further afield, a wealthy and independent Magdalene who was familiar with Egyptian openness would have had enormous difficulties with the hidebound and reactionary Galilean men.

The Gnostics used the metaphor of paradox in one of their most maligned symbols – the physical form of the hermaphrodite, who carries both sets of sexual characteristics in the same body, representing the divine union of God with initiate, and also the coming together within each person of the disparate selves, the equal but opposite genders. The hermaphrodite, to the Gnostics and to other heretical groups such as the more serious and mystical of the alchemists, represented nothing less than human perfection. Is it a coincidence that Leonardo da Vinci was obsessed with hermaphrodites and covered his notebooks with them? As we have seen from the barely hidden images and symbols in his works, he had nothing but contempt for the Holy Family – certainly Mary the Mother was singled out for that particularly vicious attack – but, so it seems, enormous respect for both Mary Magdalene and John the Baptist. Perhaps Leonardo had access to some ancient Gnostic documents, or at least a secret tradition (although no doubt he would have put very much his own gloss on them). And, intriguingly, there is a French Rosicrucian poster dating from the nineteenth century that shows Leonardo as the 'Keeper of the Grail', the guardian of the sacred and secret mysteries of the heretics. What did Leonardo know that came from the Gnostics? How did he know that Mary Magdalene was not just Jesus' *koinonos* – interestingly a masculine word – but also his right-hand 'man'? The issue is very much one of Mary Magdalene's own power, and underlines the probability that great – and *authentic* – secrets survived in Europe in the heretical underground.

## Baptizing women

Yet who or what gave the heretics the idea that women could be preachers and baptizers? Once again, one looks in vain in the very

Jewish New Testament books, which merely reinforce their cultural and religious stance on the place of women in the life of the community. As Karen Armstrong points out about the Jewish purity laws in her book *The End of Silence: Women and Priesthood* (1993):

> Taken to its logical conclusion, these purity laws almost disqualified women from the Jewish nation. This was graphically clear in the Temple which had just been completed by King Herod in the time of Christ. This Temple depicted the various grades of holiness in a series of concentric circles. On the inside was the Holy of Holies which could only be entered by the High Priest once a year on the Day of Atonement. In front of the Temple was the court of the priests, inaccessible to laymen. Surrounding this was a courtyard for the laymen of Israel; next came the court of women and after that the court of the goyim, the gentiles. When a woman was menstruating or ritually impure after childbirth, she was not even allowed to enter the court of women and was officially in the same category as the gentiles.[21]

Jewish prejudice against women in religious activities is reflected quite clearly in the New Testament letters ascribed to Saul of Tarsus (later Paul), which – characteristically devoid of biographical detail about Jesus – never mention Mary Magdalene or Jesus' appearance to her in his resurrected state in the garden. Indeed, he goes out of his way to reinforce the male prerogative, saying:

> . . . Christ died for our sins, according to the Scriptures . . . was buried . . . was raised on the third day according to the Scriptures, and . . . appeared to Peter, and then to the Twelve. After that he appeared to more than five hundred of the brothers at the same time . . . Then he appeared to James, then to all the apostles . . .[22]

Note the careful use of the word 'brothers' – as far as Paul was concerned, *no* women saw the risen Christ. And it has always been assumed that 'all the Apostles' simply meant the men – what else could it mean, for surely everyone knows that Jesus only had male Apostles? While there are objections among Christians even now about allowing – often extremely reluctantly – Mary Magdalene and the other women like Joanna and Salome into the general mass of 'disciples', there is strong evidence from the Gnostic texts that she was not merely a disciple, but actually *the leader of the Apostles*. The Gnostic 'heretics' commonly referred to her as 'The Apostle of the Apostles' (*Apostola Apostolorum*), or even more explicitly 'The First Apostle', believing that Jesus had given her the title: indeed, according to the Nag Hammadi and other Gnostic accounts, he went even further, referring to her as 'The All' and 'The Woman Who Knows All', reinforcing the idea that she alone of all his followers, male or female, knew his inner secrets. And it may not be a coincidence that the great Egyptian goddess of love, Isis, was known as 'The All'.

These books were hidden at Nag Hammadi in the fourth century, after relations between the victorious Roman Church and the 'heretical' Gnostics had become dangerously hostile. Soon the Gnostics would be marginalized to such an extent that their beliefs and scriptures would be ridiculed as nonsense, while they themselves were either martyred (a fate for which the Gnostics, on the whole, the Cathars apart, did not share the enthusiasm of the mainstream Christian saints, believing that as life is a gift from God, actively welcoming death for any reason is a grave sin) or managed to keep their beliefs secret, and their practices safely underground, away from prying eyes.

But what was it that made the Gnostics such a threat to the Roman church – and why are their long-lost scriptures routinely ignored in sermons, seminaries and Bible discussion groups today?

## A bitter feud

One Gnostic Coptic text that had surfaced well before the 1945 Nag Hammadi books was known as the *Pistis Sophia*, or *Faith-Wisdom*, which was bought by the British Museum in 1785, and appears to be the work of two different writers: one a careful, fine hand and the other the shaky writing of an old man.[23] In this book, Jesus returns twelve years after his ascension into heaven and gathers his closest disciples around him to exchange views on his teaching. Spiritual wisdom is personified as 'Sophia', and her convoluted spiritual adventures – always striving to be in and of the 'Light' of perfection – comprise the major theme of the protracted catechizing by Jesus of the disciples, and indeed vice versa. Although essentially concerned with the Gnostics' favourite subject of the 'Mysteries', and the complicated realms of heaven and hell, which frankly makes most of it unreadable, *Pistis Sophia* is nevertheless significant because it presents a very different picture of Jesus' relation with Mary Magdalene from the conventional story. It also makes abundantly clear the antipathy with which the male disciples viewed her: it seems that Simon Peter absolutely loathed her . . .

*Pistis Sophia* shows how the Magdalene – together with other women, such as the disciple Salome – constantly step forward to answer Jesus' questions with enormous enthusiasm, intelligence and not a little one-upmanship. This does not go down too well with the men. One can almost see the Magdalene and her sisters in the Light elbowing the likes of Simon Peter out of the way, as schoolchildren might vie for the attention of the teacher. In the Sixth Book of *Pistis Sophia*, Peter says: 'My Lord, let the women cease to question, in order that we may also question', to which Jesus replies by telling the women to allow the men to speak: but, apparently it never occurred to him to shut them up himself.

Perhaps unsurprisingly, this constant triumph of the women irritates the men: Philip, who is acting as scribe for the question-and-answer session complains that his duties prevent him from taking an active part, while the Magdalene is always the centre of attention. (Jesus duly allows him to speak.) The entire book is peppered with the phrase 'And Mary continueth again . . .' Peter, in particular, becomes extremely irritated and agitated by her success in holding the floor, saying: 'My Lord, we will not endure this woman, for she taketh the opportunity from us and hath let none of us speak, but *she* [my emphasis] discourseth many times.'[24]

In the Fifth Book of the *Pistis Sophia*, there is this little interchange between Jesus and Mary, in which she hints heavily that she understands his teachings better than the others:

Mary said: 'I shall behave badly to question thee. Be not wroth with me if I question on all things.'
Jesus said: 'Question what thou wilt.'

85

Mary said: 'My Lord reveal unto us . . . that also my brethren may understand it.'

The slight air of condescension seems to imply that she and Jesus share the secrets, and that her catechizing of him along with the others is merely an artifice, so she can pretend to be just another disciple, as ignorant as the others.

That there is more to this scenario than a passing knock to the men's egos, can be understood from another passage from the *Pistis Sophia*, which describes how the Magdalene came forward after Jesus' teaching, saying:

My Lord, my mind is ever understanding, at every time to come forward and set forth the solution of the words which [thou] hath uttered; *but I am afraid of Peter, because he threatened me and hateth our sex.*[25] [My emphasis]

This astonishingly vivid little scene seems to have the ring of truth, as if the extreme hostility with which Peter viewed the Magdalene was so well known that it came down clear through the years, even though much of the rest of the content of the books may be fantasy, fabricated long after the time of Jesus' mission. One would therefore expect that any personal interchanges they described would similarly be works of the imagination – presumably presenting Jesus' disciples as all sweetness and light. But this is not the case: it is as if the writers felt free to play with Jesus' words (almost certainly to suit their own interpretation), but the animosity between the Magdalene and Simon Peter was simply too well known to ignore or present in any other way for posterity. There are no platitudes here, but an extraordinary scene of real personal tension, only diffused – and then merely temporarily – by Jesus smoothing matters over. (For example, by making it clear that everyone who is 'filled with the spirit of light' may have an equal chance of speaking.)

It may well be that the important point in the Magdalene's complaint to Jesus about Peter – as far as she was concerned – is not so much he hates all women (although the consequences of that would be truly devastating when his Roman Church began to flex its misogynist muscles), but that he has actually physically threatened her. Quite apart from being notably lacking in Christian love and goodwill, it reveals how tenuous her personal safety was: she was only protected as long as Jesus was around. And it does seem an extreme reaction to her extraordinary success in attracting the teacher's attention. Clearly, there was some other factor that made her an object of hate by Simon Peter – who, judging by all the writings about him in both the Bible and the Gnostic Gospels was dim, hot-tempered and something of a bully. Indeed, the word 'yob' may not be misplaced, at least in the initial stages of his following Jesus. The Gnostic Gospels describe how his constant lack of understanding drives his exasperated master to utter at least one sharp rebuke. He is simply at the end of his tether with Peter's inability to grasp the meaning of his words.

The imbalance of the Magdalene/Simon Peter relationship is also underlined in the Gnostic *Gospel of Mary Magdalene*, in which she reacts sharply to his apparent suggestion that she fabricated a vision of Jesus. It reads:

> Then Mary wept, and answered him: 'My brother Peter, what can you be thinking? Do you believe that this is just my own imagination, that I invented this vision? Or do you believe that I would lie about our Teacher?' At this, Levi spoke up: 'Peter, you have always been hot-tempered, and now we see you repudiating a woman, just as our adversaries do. Yet if the Teacher held her worthy, who are you to reject her? Surely the Teacher knew her very well, for he loved her more than us . . . Let us grow as he demanded of us, and walk forth to spread the gospel, without trying to lay down any rules and laws other than those he witnessed.'[26]

The *Gospel of Mary Magdalene* also has her memorably rousing the depressed and fearful disciples after Jesus has ascended. It describes how:

> The disciples were in sorrow, shedding many tears, and saying: 'How are we to go among the unbelievers and announce the gospel of the Kingdom of the Son of Man? They did not spare his life, so why should they spare ours?' Then Mary arose, embraced them all, and began to speak to her brothers: 'Do not

remain in sorrow and doubt, for his Grace will guide and comfort you. Instead, let us praise his greatness, for he has prepared us for this. He is calling upon us to become fully human.' Thus Mary turned their hearts toward the Good, and they began to discuss the meaning of the Teacher's words.[27]

The *Gospel of Mary Magdalene*, unlike many other Gnostic texts, is lucid and beautiful, and contains many sophisticated yet easily comprehended teachings, such as the Teacher's response to a disciple's question about whether that which is made of physical matter will live for ever: 'All that is born, all that is created, all the elements of nature are interwoven and united with each other. All that is composed shall be decomposed; everything returns to its roots; matter returns to the origins of matter. Those who have ears, let them hear.'

And to a question from Peter about the nature of the 'sin of the world' the Teacher responds: 'There is no sin. It is you who make sin exist, when you act according to the habits of your corrupted nature; this is where sin lies . . . This is why you become sick, and why you die: it is the result of your actions; what you do takes you further away [from the Kingdom of the Son of Man].'[28]

This is an extraordinarily modern way of thinking, prefiguring the insistence of today's holistic therapists (and, increasingly, many mainstream physicians) that negative thoughts and habits (which equate to 'sin' and 'corrupted nature') may actually create illness of mind and body. (It would also be music to the ears of the Christian Scientists, who believe that all illness, and even death itself, is caused by 'error'.)

Of course not all the Gnostic scrolls have this remarkable clarity of vision: it must be said that much of the text of the *Pistis Sophia* is impenetrable gobbledegook that may have lost a good deal in the translation or may only have been intelligible to other Gnostics of that time and place. (Some verses may be in code, as where Jesus gives the 'words of power' to use in order to banish the pain of torture – disappointingly, this magical formula is only a meaningless string of letters. Perhaps, though, something similar was used by the Cathars during their fatal ordeal – in their case, fortunately to great effect.) But the *Pistis Sophia*, despite its tendency to ramble quaintly – and sometimes, to modern eyes, hilariously – does contain some gems, such as this very plain statement by Jesus: 'Mary, thou blessed one, whom I will perfect in all mysteries of those of the height, discourse in openness, thou, whose heart is raised to the kingdom of heaven more than all thy brethren.'[29]

Later, in the same text, he declares: 'Where I shall be, there will also be my twelve ministers. But Mary Magdalene and John, the virgin [John the Beloved or Lazarus], will tower over all my disciples and over all men who shall receive the mysteries . . . And they will be on my right and on my left. And I am they, and they are I.'[30]

If Jesus ever really proclaimed the superiority of Mary and young John in the group – and taken together, the evidence suggests he did – one can imagine the feelings of the rough Galilean men, not easily persuaded to give way to women. This would have applied especially to the Magdalene, who seems gloriously oblivious to the sensitivities of the others, although there may be other reasons for their dislike of her. The text of the teaching may often prove impossibly hard work for modern readers – even seeming downright ludicrous in many places – but once the individuals speak and reveal their characters, the words lights up.

## The code of the hermaphrodite

This inside knowledge of the clash of personalities within the coterie of Jesus' closest disciples seems to have been shared by the wider Gnostic community, for similar sentiments appear in other previously lost gospels. Simon Peter's hostility to the Magdalene – and to women in general – is also reflected in passages such as this brief declaration of Simon Peter to Jesus, taken from the *Gospel of Thomas*: 'Let Mary leave us, for women are not worthy of life'. If to the modern eye this appears to be a flat statement of shockingly extreme and unashamed misogynism, perhaps even more disturbing is Jesus' response, which on the surface appears to endorse Peter's hatred of women: declaring that Mary must 'become male' in order to become a 'living spirit, resembling you males. For every woman who will make herself male will enter the Kingdom of Heaven'.[31] Elaine Pagels interprets this not as an attack on the Magdalene personally by Jesus (one has the feeling that even he would never dare openly criticize Mary the Magnificent), but on the whole subject of sexuality.[32] She may be right – certainly the Gnostics, such as the Cathars, often had a rigorously puritan attitude to sex (at least in theory), but there is evidence, as we will see in a later chapter, that both Jesus and John the Baptist saw things differently: to them, sacramental sexual ecstasy was in quite a separate category from common-or-garden licentiousness.

In any case, a more modern interpretation of Jesus' words may be that he is *empowering* the women, just like men, through the sacred mediation of the Light. And it may be significant that several Egyptian goddesses, such as Isis, were sometimes portrayed with beards, the idea being that as men were powerful and women were weak, to take on male characteristics would automatically bestow greater potency on the woman.

This concept of the blending of the male/female found its way into other Mystery enclaves. Several groups of heretics, notably the Knights Templar and the more serious alchemists, were fascinated with the symbolism of the hermaphrodite, human beings with both sets of fully developed primary and secondary sexual characteristics. And as we have seen, Leonardo was also obsessed with hermaphrodites – he sketched a good many in various states of rather obvious arousal[33] and indeed his hybrid St John/Mary Magdalene in *The Last Supper* may be seen as such a representation – and although it is very likely that they also carried a profound spiritual meaning for him, the general flavour of these works is one of lovingly crafted, and over-the-top, personal pornography. Leonardo always wrung the last drop of personal satisfaction from all his works of art.

He also produced a little sketch entitled *Witch With Mirror*, which depicts a young and beautiful witch admiring herself in a hand-mirror, but the back of her head takes the form of an old man (very probably Leonardo himself, once again). Not only does this combine genders, but also unites widely separated age groups, producing the perfect paradoxical being: at the same time, both genders and therefore neither exclusively, and both young and old.

As a witch she is using magic in some way, perhaps to create the illusion of the double-image. Similar characters are to be found in the symbolism of alchemy, where – in some respects like the Cathar *perfecti* – the master alchemist finally achieves the 'Great Work', and transcends both gender and mortality, transmuted into something divine and other, yet remaining this side of the gates of death.

Magic, heresy and alchemy all thrived in the areas of France in which the doomed Cathars lived out their short but intense lives – and this is also where the Magdalene was said to travel after the crucifixion and live out her days. What secrets are there still to be found in the less well travelled areas of the south of France where the historical Magdalene is believed to have lived and died?

## CHAPTER FIVE

# *The French Connection*

There are several legends about Mary Magdalene travelling to France (or Gaul as it was then) after the crucifixion, together with a varied assortment of people, including a black servant girl called Sarah, and Mary Salome and Mary Jacobi – allegedly Jesus' aunts – besides Joseph of Arimathea, the rich man who owned the tomb in which Christ was laid prior to the resurrection, and St Maximin (Maximus), one of the seventy-two closest disciples of Jesus and the first bishop of Provence. Although the details of the story differ from version to version, it appears that the Magdalene and her party were forced to flee from Palestine under less than perfect conditions – their boat was leaky, rudderless, oarless and without a sail, which is believed to have been the result of deliberate sabotage on the part of certain factions in their homeland. Even allowing for the inevitable exaggeration of myth-making – the ruinous state of their boat seems rather unlikely – given the Gnostic Gospels' depiction of the volatile situation between Mary and Simon Peter, it is not difficult to hazard a guess at the possible, even probable, identity of at least one of the plotters who would have wished her and her companions at the bottom of the sea. In the light of the legend of the leaky boat, it is chilling to recall Mary's words from the *Pistis Sophia*: 'I am afraid of Peter, because he threatened me and hateth our sex.'[1] But whoever sought to kill them, miraculously they survived, allegedly ending up on the wild coast of what is now

Provence, although in those far-off days it was far from the rustic backwater that might be imagined.

In the early years of the first century, Provence was a thriving province of the Roman Empire, enjoying all the joys of civilization: in fact, it was deemed so beautiful and restful that it boasted a colony of well-heeled Jewish ex-patriates – even Herod himself owned an estate there. Perhaps the independent and wealthy Magdalene herself boasted such a property in the area. It seems to have been that era's answer to today's holiday homes in Majorca or even, of course, modern Provence itself. Clearly the attractions of the area are timeless.

The story goes that they landed (no doubt very gratefully, after wallowing about in floods of seawater for weeks) at what is now the town of Saintes-Maries-de-la-Mer in the Camargue, in the wetlands where the Rhone meets the Mediterranean. Three Marys –.Magdalene, Mary Jacobi and Mary Salome – are the focus for great reverence in the grand church that rises like a stately sailing ship from the surrounding marshes, while in the crypt there is an altar dedicated to Sarah the Egyptian, allegedly the Magdalene's black servant girl, now the much-loved patron saint of the gypsies, who converge on the town for her annual feast day of 25 May. Surrounded by thousands of adoring devotees, Sarah's statue is paraded to the sea, where it is ceremoniously dipped. As medieval folk thought of gypsies as being from Egypt – 'egypsies' – it made sense for them to venerate this young woman who originated from that country. Indeed, the colour of her skin, and the fact that Egypt was known as the land of 'Khem', or blackness, may be very significant. Judging by the New Testament's division of one woman into three – the Magdalene, Mary of Bethany and the unnamed 'sinner' – perhaps the assorted women in the leaky boat were also merely different aspects of one woman . . .[2]

Meanwhile, the Magdalene is said to have lived the life of a penitent hermit – deliciously naked except for a mass of shaggy hair – for the biblically approved length of time of forty years, in a cave at Sainte Baume ('holy balm', a reference to her pot of spikenard). Unfortunately, this is a sanitized version of the fifth-century story of St Mary the Egyptian, a reformed prostitute who became a hermit in the deserts of the Holy Land for forty-seven years:

although, clearly a practical woman, she worked her passage by providing personal services for the sailors, for which – astonishingly – she was deemed to be nearer to God. But once again, the myth of Mary the Egyptian may hold some clues about the true nature of the Magdalene, which would otherwise have proved unacceptable to the masses – even, perhaps, to the heretics.

## A pagan sisterhood

In any case, Mary's cave at Ste Baume might have been rather crowded, for it was the centre for the worship of the goddess Diana Lucifera – Diana the Light Bringer, or *Illuminatrix*. But even though it is unlikely that Mary Magdalene made her home in that cave (even today's keeper of the Catholic shrine admits she was never there), it is interesting that the most famous account of the Magdalene in France, that of the Dominican Archbishop of Genoa, Jacobus de Voragine's *Golden Legend* (1250),[3] refers to her with the same titles accorded to the pagan goddess Diana: as both *Illuminata* and *Illuminatrix* – the enlightened one and the bestower of enlightenment. And the Gnostics claimed she was 'Mary Lucifera' – the Light Bringer, the highest honour they could accord.

It seems that she had much in common with that pagan goddess: indeed, when she preached on the steps of the temple to Diana at Marseilles there appears to have been no sense of outrage on behalf of the priestesses. Certainly, there was no move to make the Magdalene into a Christian martyr, or even, it seems, to threaten her in any way. Indeed, she appears to have been more threatened by Jesus' right-hand man Peter than by the pagans of southern France. She remained remarkably unscathed, even though it is said she preached against idolatry (but significantly, not against pagan goddesses). Perhaps she found sympathy with her largely female pagan audience, for why would a priestess need a graven image when she herself embodied the power of the goddess?

Although it is usually assumed that the Magdalene's message was indistinguishable from that of the New Testament, there are – as we shall see – good reasons to believe that was not so. We can also make an educated guess that she baptized her converts herself – perhaps in the many streams in the area of Provence and the Languedoc that bear her name, as in the Languedocian La Source

Madeleine (Magdalene Stream). Wherever she took her 'good news', now she was free of the repressive presence of Simon Peter, and among the congenial company of other priestesses, there would be no stopping her. And while Peter, James and Paul took their message to the big cities of the Roman Empire, the Apostle of the Apostles, Jesus' lover whom he called 'The Woman Who Knows All' – even his initiatrix and anointer – walked the wilderness of the south of France, eyes blazing with the glory of it all, inspiring her sisters in the Light. This is what may well have become of the woman who knew the inner secrets of both Jesus' mission and his private heart: although she built no cathedrals, convened no councils to enforce inflexible dogma – but somehow the sheer force of her personality and the power of her dreams inspired a line of 'heretics' who went underground to keep their secrets safe from the brutal attentions of Peter's dominant Roman Church.

The feud that had begun on a personal level now took on a wider, almost mythic quality, and the two movements – one masculine and exoteric and the other feminine and esoteric, one that demonized sexuality and the other that celebrated it as a sacrament – found themselves on either side of a line so deeply etched as to form a permanent scar in the flesh of Jesus' original movement. Which of the two would he have preferred? Given all we know of the 'forbidden' texts, it is not a difficult question to answer with something approaching certainty. 'Why do I not love *her* as I love *you*?' he had said to Peter and the men, incredulously.

## The continuation of the cult

It is evident that an important cult of an unorthodox, if not outright heretical, character dedicated to Mary Magdalene existed in southern France in the Middle Ages, connected with the mysterious Black Madonnas (which we will come to shortly) and with other heresies that flourished in the Languedoc and Provence, such as the Cathars. It may even have been connected with the Templars, whose heartland was in the same region and who (undoubtedly under the influence of their original patron, Bernard of Clairvaux) reserved a special veneration for the Magdalene.

Mary Magdalene still has a considerable cult following in the south of France, but this is the *Catholic* cult of St Mary Magdalene.

This conforms to the Church's accepted image of her as penitent whore and model for sinners who need Christ's (and the Church's) forgiveness. Even so, the fervour of the devotion that she arouses – particularly in Provence, and especially in her 'official' relic centre of Saint-Maximin-la-Sainte-Baume – shows how deeply engrained she is in the hearts and minds of the people there. If anything, the popularity of the Catholic cult stems from the hold that the Magdalene already had in the region, and from the ancient, heretical cult.

The existence of this cult is so plain that several researchers have even spoken of an 'Underground Church of Mary Magdalene' that existed in the south of France. These include Ean Begg (*The Cult of the Black Virgin*), Anthony Harris (*The Sacred Virgin and the Holy Whore*) and Peter Redgrove (*The Black Goddess and the Sixth Sense*).

But beyond establishing the existence of such a cult, and the fact that it was heretical and disapproved of by the Church, these authors have not really been able to pinpoint exactly what it was about and how and when it came to exist in that particular area.

Most commentators link the cult with the historical Mary Magdalene, through key legends, such as those of de Voragine. It is assumed that the French 'Church of the Magdalene' passed on teachings that derived from her, maybe even by her direct descendants. But this still fails to address the question of the nature of those teachings, or why the Church was so horrified by them.

And which came first? Were the legends the product of the cult, invented in order to establish a connection with the historical figure, or did the cult derive from a movement established by, or centred on, the real person?

It is a similar situation to the legends of Joseph of Arimathea's journey to Glastonbury. The two sets of traditions are related, as according to some versions the Magdalene and Joseph set out on the journey together, she remaining in France while he travelled on to England. And, both legends involve the Holy Grail.

The Church made strenuous efforts to suppress the Magdalene cult – which were largely successful, which is why it is so difficult to piece together at this distance in time the evidence about its true nature. But it does seem that her esoteric movement was already established in France before the Middle Ages, although how long before is hard to ascertain.

Whatever her cult was about, it was not one that had obvious associations with the lifestyle of a penitent hermit: there was little that smacked of the ascetic about the groups and individuals who accorded her great reverence. Instead, it found expression in the rich, vibrant and tolerant culture that existed in the Languedoc in the early Middle Ages – the most advanced and cultured part of Europe in the 11th and 12th centuries. (The Languedoc, then under the control of the Counts of Toulouse, was independent of France at that time.) Because of the depredations of the Albigensian Crusade, which decimated that culture and brought the Languedoc under the control of the King of France and the less cultured northern French lords, there is a unfortunate paucity of information about that golden age. Even so, its great respect for women and the feminine archetype – as exemplified by the courtly love and erotic poetry of the Troubadour movement – shone through, perhaps reflecting the proximity of the nearby Basques, who worshipped a female deity and had a tradition of equality of the sexes, especially in sexual matters.

Whatever the reason, the Languedocian culture was fertile ground for a cult centred on the Magdalene. The question is: did that culture single her out because she was a figure who would naturally have appealed to them, or was their veneration of the feminine a *result* of a movement dedicated to her?

First, there is the connection between the Cathars and the Magdalene cult.

As we have seen, the Gnostic doctrines of the Cathars can be traced to earlier heretical sects that existed in the Balkans – *except* for the Cathars' beliefs concerning Mary Magdalene and her relationship with Jesus. As Yuri Stoyanov and others have argued, this seems to be the result of the presence of these beliefs in the region *before* the arrival of the Cathars, and their assimilation into Cathar teaching. This suggests that the pre-existing Magdalene cult held doctrines that were similar to those of the Cathars, helping the process of assimilation. Therefore it seems that the Crusade against the Cathars, which continued for another thirty-five years, was to some extent a cover for the suppression of the Church of Mary

Magdalene. Both heresies were rooted out with unprecedented ferocity.

It was within a few years of the end of the Cathar Crusade that the most famous version of the legends of the Magdalene's life in France appeared, Jacobus de Voragine's *The Golden Legend*, which we have noted earlier. Significantly, Jacobus was a Dominican – and the Dominicans were the Inquisition. Coming so soon after the crusade in southern France, it seems that the purpose of his account was to subvert the popular French traditions about Mary Magdalene by producing a version that was more in keeping with the Church's image of her. They realized that although the crusade had eradicated her cult as a coherent movement or organization, her story would continue to circulate in the heretical subculture, so it had to be 'hijacked'. The process of taking control of the Magdalene cult was completed by establishing an 'official' cult and pilgrimage centre at Saint-Maximin-la-Sainte-Baume, the legendary scene of her death.

Until 1279 – again, in the wake of the Cathar Crusade – the Church's endorsement had been given to the relics of Mary Magdalene at Vézelay in Burgundy. Even these had a link with the south, as they had been taken from there to Vézelay by the Count of Roussillon in the 9th century. (It was from Vézelay that Bernard of Clairvaux had called for the Second Crusade.) But in 1279 a skeleton in an alabaster sarcophagus – allegedly of Mary Magdalene – was discovered beneath the crypt of the church in Saint-Maximin. A document found in the sarcophagus stated that her body had been reburied some 460 years before to protect it from invading 'Saracens'. (It is now known that this document is a fake – in part because there were no Saracen invasions in the 8th century – but it was believed at the time. Of course, if the document was faked, then undoubtedly so was the body.) The pope officially favoured these relics over those at Vézelay, and in 1295 authorized the building of the basilica that would serve as a centre for pilgrims. The skull was removed and is still displayed in the basilica today – which grins out of its ornate reliquary like a comment on human vanity and the ephemeral nature of mortality – and is paraded around the town annually to celebrate Mary Magdalene's feast day, encased in a handsome gold mask topped by a bandeau from which cascade shiny and ludicrously blonde locks.

The pope also placed the basilica under his direct control – not, as was customary, under that of the local archbishop – and replaced the Benedictine monks that were installed there with Dominicans. Effectively, the Magdalene cult and pilgrimage centre was placed under the control of the Inquisition. It is for this reason that St Mary Magdalene was made patron saint of the Dominicans (in 1297), and declared to be the 'daughter, sister and mother' to the Order.

Significantly, such was the local resistance to this move that a force of soldiers had to be sent with the Dominican master when he arrived to take charge of the basilica. Clearly, the people of Saint-Maximin were unhappy about the Inquisition taking over the Magdalene shrine.

As a result of the Cathar Crusade, a Church-endorsed version of the Magdalene's life was published in France, and a cult centre in Provence established under Inquisition control (in which the Dominicans took the lead). The heretical 'church' had been effectively contained and neutralized. The local people could continue to venerate her – but only on the Church's own terms, which raises two major questions: what was it about the earlier cult that had so alarmed the Church? And did the heretical cult survive? The answer to the first question must be that the Church feared the cult because it knew that it possessed something – some information or doctrine – that posed a very real threat to established Christian dogma and/or its own authority.

However, all that we know – that is, the little the Church has allowed us to know – about the southern French cult is that it held some unusual views about the relationship between Mary and Jesus (that they were 'concubines') and, because it blended so well with the Cathar beliefs, it must have been a form of Gnosticism. These two views are, of course, also true of the 'Gnostic Gospels' relating to Mary Magdalene that Mohammad Ali found at Nag Hammadi in 1945.

It can only be that copies of the Magdalene 'Gnostic Gospels' were circulating in France in the centuries before the Albigensian Crusade. In which case, it is not surprising that the Church wanted to eradicate the cult, destroy the texts, and claim the Magdalene as its own.

The question that it is impossible to answer at the moment is whether the heretical 'church' was founded purely on these books, in the same way that the Church of Rome was founded on the canonical Gospels, or whether it was founded by the Magdalene herself. However, the fact that these texts appear to have been in circulation in a region in which, according to legend, Mary Magdalene had lived, is particularly exciting. Did the Magdalene Church survive, driven underground by the Church's attempts to suppress it?

The very fact that even hints and echoes of the heretical cult have come down to us suggests that the Church was not entirely successful in eradicating it. But throughout history, the devotion to Mary Magdalene in France has retained an odd and decidedly unorthodox flavour.

## The Knights of Christ
By far the most successful – in worldly terms – of all the groups of French heretics was the Order of the Poor Knights of the Temple of Solomon, more commonly known as the Knights Templar. Founded in 1118 by Hugues de Payens, together with just eight other knights, the purpose of the Order was said to be to act as bodyguards for Christian pilgrims to the Holy Land, but as there were only nine of them for at least nine years, this seems to be a particularly weak cover story.

However, as this strange order of fighting monks grew in number and spread across Europe, the Templars soon earned a reputation for courage and skill on the battlefield that was second to none. They were the elite forces – the SAS – of their day, although they were bound by the usual religious rules of poverty, chastity and obedience. Recognized by the Council of Troyes in 1128 as a religious and military order, and their cause championed by the aggressively ambitious Bernard of Clairvaux (later canonized) – who wrote their Rule – the Templars soon achieved an extraordinary pinnacle of power. Officially only answerable to the pope, as their empire spread, their arrogance grew. Having been sent packing from the Holy Land in 1291 by the Saracens, they concentrated on expanding their European campaign, much to the chagrin of the pope and the French king, Philip the Fair. In 1307 nemesis caught up with them, and in a superbly orchestrated move, most of the Templars in France were rounded up. Many of them were tortured to elicit confessions of heresy and sexual misdemeanour, while others escaped. When Jacques de Molay, their Grand Master, was slowly roasted to death in Paris, it seemed it was all over for the Templars. While the subject of what happened to the Order after the Suppression is fascinating and complex – and is the subject of many well-researched books[4] – it is beyond the scope of this present work.

It is what the Templars *believed* that is most relevant here. On the surface they were simply 'the Knights of Christ', no more or less than celibate Christian monks, but there is considerable evidence[5] that a continuing inner circle kept alive a very much more heretical tradition. Although torture can prompt the most fevered and elaborate fantasies, created to accord with the torturers' own agenda, it does seem that certain of the knights did revere – perhaps even worship – a bearded, severed head or the replica of such a relic, which suggests the decapitated John the Baptist, who was especially revered by them. It was also said that they spat and trampled upon a cross in secret ceremonies – outright blasphemy – while one Fulk de Troyes told his accusers that he was shown a crucifix and told: 'Set not much faith in this, for it is too young.'[6]

Much of the Templars' symbolism conceals an unusually deep reverence for John the Baptist: for example, while most Christians think of the 'Lamb of God' as referring to Jesus himself – for the Baptist is believed to have announced at the sight of Jesus: 'Look, the Lamb of God, who takes away the sins of the world!'[7] – the Templars thought of the Lamb as John himself. They used the symbol of the Lamb of God on their seal, which was specific to the Order in the south of France.

This curiously Templar interpretation of the biblical image finds its way into Leonardo's works, reinforcing the suggestion of heretical undertones (if, indeed, they need reinforcing by now). In his famous *Cartoon* (now exhibited like a holy relic in a special, hushed room at London's National Gallery) we see the usually bland and oblivious Virgin sitting awkwardly on the lap of St Anne, her mother (who seems curiously masculine, with enormous hands), while an almost serpentine infant Jesus reaches over to bless the child John, who gazes innocently upwards. A cynic, or fellow heretic, might interpret the pudgy little hand that is raised to 'bless' John as a coming blow – his other hand is apparently steadying the future Baptist's head to receive it.

That this is not an interpretation that is far off the mark can be seen from the final version, for which the *Cartoon* was a preliminary sketch, the elegant *Virgin and Child with St Anne* (1501), in which young John has been replaced *by a lamb*, whose head appears to be about to be pulled off by a Jesus who grasps its ears, his arm cutting across the delicate neck like a sword. Here quite clearly John is equated with the Lamb of God, not Jesus – and this is a *Templar* symbol, although the Order had been officially annihilated for 200 years by the time Leonardo painted this work of art. And, once again, we see a distinctly Johannite bias to this picture: had Leonardo somehow been influenced by the secret remnants of the Order? And if so, clearly they must have been of the heretical Templar strand, not the mainstream Christian rank and file.

Even the name by which the Templars commonly went – the 'Knights of Christ' – may have been a clever deceit, for although 'Christ' (or *Christos* in Greek, meaning 'anointed one') is usually thought of as being unique to Jesus, in fact, the early Gnostics had a *christ-ening* ceremony in which all adult initiates became 'Christs'. Perhaps the Johannite Templars used the term 'Christ' as a covert reference to *John*, not Jesus: their intense interest in his life being reflected in many of their otherwise puzzling actions.

Certainly, the first waves of knights to arrive in the Middle East were unusually curious about the archaeological history of the area, which has suggested to some that they were searching for some religious treasure – perhaps a cache of documents similar to the Dead Sea Scrolls[8], or even the fabled lost Ark of the Covenant.[9] But while there is no convincing evidence that the Templars found a lost gospel or sacred artefact, there is evidence that they encountered a mysterious 'Church of John [the Baptist] of the East' while on their travels, which almost certainly inspired their un-Christian beliefs and apparently blasphemous practices.

A hint of the underlying Templar Johannitism can be seen from the warning of the Spanish visionary Raymond Lull[10] – previously a champion of the Order – who wrote during their suppression that their trials reveal 'dangers to the boat of St Peter' and 'There are perchance among Christians many secrets, from which a [particular] secret may cause an incredible revelation, just as that [which is] emerging from the Templars . . .'[11]

Yet the inner order of the Templars were not just secret devotees of the Baptist, but also – perhaps unexpectedly for such a masculine organization – possessors of a deep reverence for the Feminine. Bernard of Clairvaux, who played such a major part in the founding and promotion of the Order, was a passionate devotee of the Black Madonnas, which, as we will see, are inextricably linked to Mary Magdalene. He also preached many sermons about Mary of Bethany, who to him was the same as the Magdalene, and also the 'Bride' of the Old Testament book of erotic poetry, *The Song of Songs*, which the Church has always associated with Mary, to the point that certain passages from it are read out in churches on her feast day. And when Bernard preached to the Second Crusade, he did so from the great Mary Magdalene cult centre at Vézelay.[12]

The Feminine finds expression in many of the Templars' works, such as their idiosyncratic round churches, in this case symbolizing the rotundity of the Earth Mother, the big belly of the pregnant goddess. Significantly, after their suppression, there was an official ban on the building of round churches, although some have begun to reappear much more recently.[13] There were many other signs of reverence for the goddess: apart from the bearded severed head, the Templars were accused of worshipping a 'Baphomet', which the great New Testament scholar Hugh Schonfield has argued convincingly is the encoded version of 'Sophia', the Gnostics' goddess whom they equated with Mary Magdalene. (Schonfield also showed that the code utilized the 'Atbash cipher', which had been used by the authors of the Dead Sea Scrolls at least a millennium before the Order was founded, which shows that not only did the knights guard their secrets jealously and with ingenuity, but also that they had access to some ancient source of knowledge in the Middle East.) Sophia was also associated with the great pagan goddess Isis, who was sometimes specifically called by that name and of course, Sophia was the Gnostic's embodiment of the Sacred Light 'The All', with which the Magdalene is closely related.[14]

The Templars' exotic – and not always Christian – inclinations were symbolized in the great Gothic cathedrals, which they designed and organized from behind the scenes. (Even the stone-masons involved became lay brothers of the Order.) These astonishing architectural apotheoses included recognizably ancient Egyptian influences[15], being constructed with the harmony of proportion that epitomizes the concept of sacred geometry – the idea that geometrical proportion resonates with, and even represents, the divine mind. And these overtly Christian churches were crammed with pagan and specifically goddess-related images, from the labyrinth that decorates the floor at Chartres (symbol of the spider goddess, weaver of men's fate), to the many Black Madonnas,[16] and the jewel in the crown of Gothic cathedrals – the brilliant and evocative rose windows. As Barbara G. Walker writes:

> the Rose, which ancient Rome knew as the Flower of Venus, [was] the badge of the sacred prostitutes. Things spoken of 'under the rose' (sub rosa) were part of Venus' sexual mysteries, not to be revealed to the uninitiated . . .
>
> In the great age of cathedral building, when Mary [the Mother] was worshipped as a goddess in her 'Palaces of the Queen of Heaven' or Notres-Dames, she was often addressed as the Rose, Rose-bush, Rose-garland . . . Mystic Rose . . . Like a pagan temple, the Gothic cathedral represented the body of the Goddess who was also the universe, containing the essence of male godhead within herself . . .[17]

Yet the rose was not universally associated with the Virgin Mary, the Immaculate Conception, for hers is more usually the symbol of the austere and non-sexual Easter lily: it is the other Mary, the red-blooded Christian goddess figure who was revered in the Templar cathedrals through the image of the rose. And it had not escaped them that 'rose' is an anagram of 'eros', god of sexual love.

The Templars' passionate devotion to the Magdalene is most evident from their oath, which was sworn to 'God and Our Lady': that this particular 'Notre Dame' was *not* the Virgin, is suggested by the words of their Absolution: 'I pray God that he will pardon you your sins as he pardoned them to St Mary Magdalene and the thief who was put on the cross.'[18]

## Guardians of the Grail

Among their many legacies – which on a mundane level included the invention of the modern banking system[19] – the Templars influenced an opus of works that has seized the imagination of many generations and provided the basis for innumerable poems, plays, paintings and films.[20] It was, of course, the story of the Holy Grail, which first came to prominence through the work of Chrétien de Troyes' unfinished *Le Conte del Graal* (c.1190). Significantly, the town of Troyes, from which the author took his name, was home to the first Templar preceptory and its most impressive church is dedicated to Mary Magdalene.[21]

Although most people today think of the Grail as the cup Jesus used at the Last Supper, in its very first incarnation the relic was portrayed as a *platter*, being based on a much older Celtic tale about the adventures of Peredur, in which he encounters some form of ritual procession in a forest where he encountered a spear that dripped blood and a *severed head* on a platter. As in most Grail stories the action hinges on the key moment when the hero fails to ask a certain question, and as Malcolm Godwin says in his book *The Holy Grail* (1994): 'Here the question which is not asked concerns the nature of the head. If Peredur had asked *whose* head, and how it concerned him, he would have known how to lift the enchantments of the Wasteland.'[22] (As in many similar medieval tales, the land had been cursed: nothing would grow and winter ruled the land and the hearts of its inhabitants.)

The most overtly unorthodox of all the Grail romances was the Bavarian poet, Wolfram von Eschenbach's *Parzival*, written in about 1220. He claimed that he was improving on Chrétien's earlier version by taking it back to its source, allegedly one Guiot de Provins (Provence), a Troubadour and Templar sympathizer. In Wolfram's version, the Grail Castle is guarded by Templars, who are called 'baptized men', *not Christians* – surely a carefully worded reference to their Johannite status – and there is a significant love interest between a black queen and a European prince, whose mixed-race son and the Grail bearer, Repanse de Schoye, have a child who begets a line of mystical kings who always take the name 'John'. And the 'Messenger of the Grail', Cundrie, bears a jar of sweet-smelling ointment with which she washes the hero's feet and dries them with her hair. Once again, we find strongly Johannite and Magdalenian elements interwoven in the same heretical tapestry. But why? Where is Jesus in all this? Why did the inner cabal of the Templars ignore or even blaspheme him?

Clearly, the cult of the Magdalene – not to mention the more mysterious and interlinked one connected with the Baptist – survived in France, despite the best efforts of the Church.

## The village of the damned

Many readers will be very familiar with one particularly avid outbreak of Magdalene fever, which underpinned the strange events in the remote hilltop village of Rennes-le-Château, close to the town of Limoux in the ancient heart of Cathar country, the Languedoc. The mystery of Rennes-le-Château is by now something of a cliché in alternative history circles, and one about a great many words have been written – many of which, it must be said, are utterly wasted. There is a wide range of books, internet chat rooms and research groups for the Rennes enthusiast to choose from[23], but a brief summary of the story will suffice here.

Few people in the Anglo-Saxon world would have heard of Rennes-le-Château had it not been for the major alternative history book of the 1980s – indeed, perhaps the godfather of the recent genre as a whole – *The Holy Blood and the Holy Grail*, by Michael Baigent, Richard Leigh and Henry Lincoln, which had a profound and unsettling effect on many enquiring minds. With its heady mix of occult societies and deep secrets – and the astonishingly compelling idea of the sacred bloodline of Jesus and Mary Magdalene, upheld and protected by the shadowy Priory of Sion – it seized thousands, if not millions, of hearts and minds.

It began with the mystery of Rennes-le-Château, where in the late nineteenth century the parish priest François Bérenger Saunière discovered some encoded parchments while renovating his ancient church of Mary Magdalene. Perhaps he also discovered some booty – but, like the fabled Cathar treasure, its nature is open to a wide variety of interpretations – which made him a very wealthy man virtually overnight. He then began on a series of improvements for his own comfort and for the village, building himself a curious library called the *Tour Magdala* (Magdala Tower) complete with impressive ramparts, on the very edge of the conical hill on which the village is built. Saunière's new house was called the *Villa Béthanie* (Bethany House), reinforcing the underlying Magdalene theme that clearly obsessed him, which also prominently manifested inside the church in the form of a bas relief in front of the altar on which a fair-haired Magdalene kneels before a spindly sapling and a skull: it is said that Saunière himself lovingly put the finishing touches to this work of art. Among the many bizarre elements in the decorations of the church are a little black boy and a woman in a widow's veil – not to mention a man in a kilt – in the depictions of the Stations of the Cross, and a tableau in which John the Baptist towers over a kneeling Jesus, who in turn crouches in a mirror image of the alarming demon on whose head the stoup of holy water rests, just inside the door. Over the porch there is a Latin inscription that translates as 'This is a terrible place', an unlikely description, one might think, for a parish priest to set over the portal of his church.

Over the course of several years Saunière and his faithful housekeeper, the young local girl Marie Denarnaud, lived in great style, entertaining on a vast scale the many dignitaries who made the difficult journey to the remote village (even today, with decent roads, it is not a particularly easy place to reach), some of them from as far away as Paris. Among them was the famous opera singer Emma Calvé, whom it is said Saunière met (and possibly became the lover of) while in the French capital, and who was allegedly involved sexually – perhaps also in a ritual sense – with several men who were reputed to be occultists.

Saunière behaved strangely during this time: digging in the graveyard at night, defacing a tombstone – much to the outrage of the local bishop, among others – gathering sacks of stones from the valley below and engaging in a prolific, if mysterious, correspondence with people all over Europe. Although banned from officiating in his own church by the bishop, whose patience was at last exhausted by the growing scandal of Saunière's unorthodox behaviour, the local people refused to acknowledge his replacement and instead attended mass at Bethany House. Whatever else he might be, Saunière was always popular with the villagers, perhaps because he was set upon improving their lot. He had great plans, which involved building new roads, watch-towers – and a large open-air baptismal pool – besides a menagerie and other innovations, but most of them came to nothing, for it seems his wealth was inadequate for all his great ideas. Indeed, far from his receiving one lump sum through his mysterious initial discovery, it appears that he had regular cash-flow problems: sometimes he entertained like a minor Roman emperor, but at others it seemed as if he had to be careful with his money, although never returning to the financial status of the average parish priest. He was never again poor as the proverbial church mouse. So where did his money come from? Who paid him – and why?

Sceptics argue that Saunière was simply bringing in extra cash by trafficking in masses – being paid to say mass for the souls of the dead – and although he undoubtedly engaged in such an activity from time to time, this would hardly account for his undoubted vast wealth. Between 1896 and his death in 1917 he spent at least 160,000 francs a month, an incredible amount for a priest in the poorest area of France, once so rich and sophisticated, but since the fall of the Cathars which had been allowed to degenerate into poverty and despair.

Perhaps he was being paid to remain in Rennes-le-Château for some reason: even when he had the chance to leave – when banned by the bishop – he insisted on staying, and was almost ceaseless in his excavating and roaming around the countryside, as if searching for something specific. Add to this the curious link of a tomb on the road to nearby Arques with a painting by Nicholas Poussin (1593–1665), and the mysterious violent death of another local priest – not to mention the alleged fact that the priest who acted as confessor to Saunière on his deathbed fled in horror – there is a mystery that is ripe for milking. And milked it certainly has been, although the locals – and there are very few of them, for the village is almost deserted[24] – now maintain a curious blend of cynicism and pride in their homegrown celebrity, whose own tombstone in the graveyard has also been defaced.

Saunière's housekeeper, Marie Denarnaud, lived on in the village for about forty years after her master died, causing consternation by burning large quantities of banknotes and maintaining that Saunière had declared that if only the villagers knew they were walking on gold. She also announced, gnomically, that 'if you seek treasure, look around you'.

Recent research in France has shown that Saunière not only named his new buildings after his beloved Magdalene, but made many pilgrimages to her cult centres in Provence. If nothing else, he was determined to prove his love for her, and keep her cult going – single-handedly, if necessary. But the evidence shows that there were many others with the same adoration for the woman Jesus is said to have kissed.

## An enigmatic society

Such are the bare bones of the Rennes-le-Château story, now something of a cliché, although largely unknown outside France before it appeared in the work of Baigent, Leigh and Lincoln. However, even the Saunière mystery pales into insignificance in *The Holy Blood and the Holy Grail* compared to its revelations of the existence of an age-old secret society called the Prieuré de Sion (Priory of Sion), which was sworn to protect and uphold the descendants of Jesus and Mary Magdalene. Apparently, their children had given rise to the line of peculiar semi-mystical Frankish kings, the Merovingians, who, although usurped by the Carolingians, did not die out – and continue to this day, covertly. Was Saunière involved with the Priory of Sion? Had he discovered something spectacular in the crypt of his church, perhaps clues to the location of some great secret? Was it even, as certain authors have since suggested, the body of Christ that languishes in the cavernous nearby hillside called Peche Cardou?[25]

Unfortunately, it is extremely unlikely that Saunière was a member of the Priory of Sion, or even its hapless tool, for research shows that the organization has only existed since the 1950s. And the coded parchments that the priest was believed to have found were, it has been revealed, fabricated by two of its founders. Indeed, the Priory as a whole seems to have a penchant for fakery and elaborate practical jokes, which even includes smuggling faked documents into the Bibliothèque Nationale in order to impress the likes of Baigent, Leigh and Lincoln.

In that respect the organization has much in common with Leonardo, and therefore it comes as no surprise to discover that it lists him as one of the society's alleged Grand Masters – together with luminaries who also include Sir Isaac Newton, Victor Hugo and Jean Cocteau. It is as if they had trawled for the biggest names in history and claimed them for their own, although there are indications that they chose particularly appropriate personalities. It is significant that the alleged Grand Masters were also known to the Order as 'John' ('Jean') – Leonardo was, they claimed, John IX. Indeed, inexplicably, they call themselves the 'Swordbearers of the Church of John'.[26] Yet as there was no Priory of Sion in Leonardo's day, should we therefore forget the whole subject? Judging by Leonardo's undoubted Johannite sympathies, it seems as if the Priory chose at least one of its retrospective Grand Masters with particular care, and many of the others are known to have had similar interests.

The controversial texts, known as the *Dossiers secrets* (*Secret Files*) deposited by the Priory of Sion in the Bibliothèque Nationale in Paris, make repeated references to the Magdalene, whom they associate (without explanation) with Isis and the Black Madonnas. Then there is the curious – perhaps coincidental – associations with the woman whose grave seems to have been singled out by Saunière as being of particular importance, and which may be the key to the mystery. This was the last of the noble family to reside in the château that gives Rennes-le-Château its name, Marie de Nègre d'Ables, Dame d'Hautpoul de Blanchefort. She owes this grandiose title to the fact that she was of the de Nègre family from Ables, and was married to François d'Hautpoul, of the family who had been lords of Rennes-le-Château since the fifteenth century, and whose titles included that of Marquis de Blanchefort (a small fortification not far from the village).

Yet her name seems amazingly well chosen, as it embodies so many of the associations of the underground church of Mary Magdalene: Marie de Nègre means 'Mary the Black/Mary of Darkness' – and 'poule' is French slang for 'prostitute', making '*haut-poul*' into 'high prostitute'. If there were not documentary evidence that she really existed, one would be tempted to think her yet another joke of the Priory of Sion.

Dame Marie died on 17 January 1781, and was buried in the cemetery of St Mary Magdalene's church in Rennes-le-Château. Her gravestone was erected by her priest – Saunière's predecessor

– Abbé Antoine Bigou, to whom, it is claimed, she passed on some great secret. The inscription of the gravestone seems to lie at the heart of the mystery – particularly as it was erased by Saunière a century later (though not before it had been copied by visiting members of a local antiquarian society).

The inscription contains a great many errors – too many to be simply bad workmanship, which suggests it contains some kind of encoded message (presumably why Saunière tried to destroy it). One 'mistake' in particular is little short of outrageous. Instead of the Latin phrase 'RESQUIESCAT IN PACE' ('Rest in Peace'), the spacing renders it as: 'RESQUIES CATIN PACE'. 'Catin' is slang for 'whore', reinforcing the alternative meaning of 'Hautpoul'. (Even the misspelling of 'Ables' as ARLES on the tombstone has a special heretical resonance, as Arles – in 'Magdalene country' in Provence – was a famous cult centre for Isis in ancient times.)

Dame Marie's curious names and titles may be a bizarre coincidence, but there is no doubt about Saunière's devotion to Mary Magdalene and the importance accorded her by the Priory of Sion (though, typically, they never explain the reasons for this).

### The unknown 'Saunière'

The Saunière story is by now familiar to the point of obsession with many adherents of 'alternative history'. However, a remarkably parallel, and roughly contemporary, account – with identical themes – remains largely unknown, even in France. This is the story of the 'monastery' of Le Carol in the Ariège, some fifty miles from Rennes-le-Château, and the activities of another priest, an older contemporary of Saunière, Father Louis de Coma (1822–1911).[27]

When training for the priesthood, in 1842, de Coma was offered a place at the seminary of St Sulpice in Paris,[28] but his bishop ordered him instead to train in a seminary in the diocese. Nevertheless he chose a Sulpician house at Issy. Two years later, under the influence of his mentor, the Jesuit Gustave de Ravignan, he transferred to the Jesuit seminary at Amiens, and in 1846 studied theology in Belgium. He was ordained at Notre-Dame de Liesse in 1850, an important Black Madonna site with many other esoteric associations. As Ean Begg writes: 'Liesse was the most important place of pilgrimage for the French Royal Family from

1414 . . . Legend: Three Knights of St John (perhaps originally Templars) serving in the First Crusade . . . were captured and taken to Cairo. Resisting all attempts to seduce them into apostasy, they succeeded . . . in converting the Sultan's daughter Ismeria (Isis+Mary?) . . . The neighbouring castle of Marchais, where Royal pilgrims used to stay, still belongs to the Lorraine family (Merovingian blood-line) . . .'[29]

In the course of several subsequent postings, Father de Coma discovered a talent for preaching. On Christmas Day 1855 his father, Jean-Bonaventure de Coma, died, leaving a large estate of woodland and fields called Le Carol, near the village of Baulou in the foothills of the Pyrenees. (The parish church at Baulou, like that in Rennes-le-Château, is dedicated to St Mary Magdalene.)

From 1860 to 1885 (the year in which Saunière arrived at Rennes), de Coma devoted himself to building a religious centre at Le Carol – works that far eclipsed Saunière's constructions in scale and expense. When complete, the estate consisted of a sanctuary, inspired by the grotto in the Garden of Gethsemane, with an underground crypt, around which he planted olive trees and other exotic plants (where de Coma and members of his family were buried); a basilica – apparently modelled on the one at Lourdes; a church, which he named Gethsemane; and a monastery building, complete with cloisters. Up a wooded hill life-sized metal statues representing the Stations of the Cross terminated at a small chapel on the top. Most evocative of all, de Coma lovingly built an underground grotto, with a life-sized statue of Mary Magdalene gazing pensively into a pool into which splashed a fountain, believed by de Coma to be miraculous. The buildings were designed by Father de Coma's elder brother, Ferdinand, the diocesan architect.

The Gethsemane church was – unusually but deliberately – oriented to the north-east, rather than to the east. Its effect is to align all the major features of the estate – the church, the oratory of the crypt, the Magdalene grotto and the hill-top chapel at the head of the Stations of the Cross – not only with each other but also with St Mary Magdalene's church in Baulou.

In all, de Coma spent over half a million gold francs on his work – roughly the equivalent of £2 million today. But unlike the Saunière story, there is no mystery about the origins of his wealth:

he created a foundation called the Work of Gethsemane, which said masses for the souls of the deceased, being authorized to receive donations for doing so and for giving indulgences. A gifted preacher, he organized preaching tours throughout France.

Apart from the payments for masses, de Coma received large donations from individuals. Like Saunière, he was a monarchist who supported the claim to the throne of the Comte de Chambord. (And we have seen that Notre Dame de Liesse, where he was ordained, was a long-established centre of pilgrimage for the French Royal Family, and it has connections with the Merovingians.) The Comte donated 4,000 gold francs to de Coma's work, and his widow was later to make a similar gift – 3,000 francs – to Saunière, which funded the first restoration work of the church at Rennes-le-Château.

(The fact that the source of Father de Coma's wealth can be accounted for is the major difference between his story and Saunière. However, despite the obfuscation and later myth-making about treasure troves, the most likely explanation for Saunière's wealth lies similar donations, large and small. This is what Saunière himself told his bishop, naming his brother Alfred – also a priest and, like de Coma, a noted travelling preacher – as the intermediary for the donations. And Saunière was certainly trafficking in masses as well.)

De Coma intended the monastery to house a religious community, but he found considerable difficulty in finding a monastic Order that wanted it. The Fathers of the Holy Spirit finally accepted his offer, only stayed for a year – for reasons that remain obscure – after which the monastery and whole estate remained unused.

In 1890 de Coma, then in his late sixties, was appointed parish priest at St Mary Magdalene's in Baulou. The mayor complained to de Coma's superiors when he celebrated mass in the church at Le Carol, rather than in the parish church (just as Saunière had said mass in the Villa Béthanie). Gradually the estate fell into disrepair. In the last years of his life de Coma became the 'Hermit of Le Carol' – bizarrely often being seen tending the estate wearing dresses and hats that had belonged to his mother. He died on 14 November 1911, at the age of eighty-nine, and was buried, like other members of his family, in the crypt at Le Carol. The estate passed to his sister Claire, who in

1913 gave it to the Church. It remained unused and untended for over forty years. On several occasions, the tombs of de Coma and his family were desecrated, most seriously in 1956 when the coffins were broken open and the bones strewn about.

This act of outrage may have been what prompted the diocese to sell Le Carol. However, the Church demanded a curious condition from the new owner – that all the constructions, with the exception of the monastery, were to be completely demolished. Almost the entire site was duly *dynamited* in November 1956. (Perhaps coincidentally, 1956 was the year in which the Rennes-le-Château story began to move. The first newspaper stories on the Saunière affair appeared in the regional press in January, and the Priory of Sion officially registered itself in June.) Today all that remains is the monastery building, the hilltop chapel, and the subterranean grotto with its statue of the Magdalene.

Do the extraordinary stories of Rennes-le-Château and Le Carol show that the heretical 'church' of Mary Magdalene had survived, underground, for more than 600 years after the Inquisition had tried to wipe it out? Were both Saunière and de Coma – and possibly other unknown priests – intending to restore the Merovingian monarchy and with it, the old goddess-based, Templarist religion that revered the Magdalene and the Baptist while being lukewarm at best towards Jesus himself?

More research is needed, but the former existence of the Magdalene cult may go some way to resolving at least the Saunière affair. In *The Templar Revelation* we concluded that the source of Saunière's wealth was not the discovery of a treasure trove or the possession of a great secret that he was using to blackmail the Church, but the result of payments made to him – and other priests in neighbouring villages – to undertake explorations and research in the area. In other words, he had not actually *found* anything, but was being paid to look *for* something – something that he may never have found.

Saunière's day saw a great upsurge of interest in ancient texts and books relating to the origins and early days of Christianity not covered by the New Testament, many of which were only known through fragments. (This was the case with some of the Mary Magdalene 'Gospels' that were eventually discovered in a complete form at Nag Hammadi – there were a few fragments to show that they had once existed, but, until 1945, not enough to know what they contained.) Had someone realized that such books may once have existed in the south of France – and is that why Saunière showed such interest in the Magdalene and the legends and traditions associated with her?

In the absence of conclusive evidence, this has to remain conjecture. But this speculation did receive some curious support during the latest developments in the Rennes-le-Château affair. In 2000, the mayor of Rennes-le-Château received a letter from Jean-Louis Génibrel, an American of French descent who lives in California. Génibrel said that his uncle's grandfather had been in charge of the builders who constructed Saunière's *domaine* – and revealed that he had helped the priest bury a chest or casket beneath the foundations of the Tour Magdala.

As a result of Génibrel's claim, an American team, led by Dr Robert Eisenman, a leading professor of archaeology at the University of Long Beach in California – best known as the scholar who, in the 1980s, finally broke the academic embargo on the release of the Dead Sea Scrolls – came to Rennes-le-Château to carry out a survey using ground penetrating radar. The team was financed by an American organization, the Merril Foundation, which funds archaeological work connected with biblical sites.

Besides finding a crypt beneath the church (the existence of which was long suspected from old records), the team confirmed that there is indeed what appears to be a chest or box, some three feet square, buried around twelve feet (four metres) beneath the floor of the Tour Magdala.

Predictably, the discoveries created a great stir in the French press – along with much speculation that was encouraged by the lack of information coming from the team. Particular controversy was caused by the involvement of a theologian named Dr Serena Tajé and some of her alleged statements: newspaper reports quoted her as saying, 'Perhaps we will discover items concerning the foundation myth of the Church', and, more startlingly, 'It could concern a document that will challenge the history of the Catholic Church! . . . Unless it is a tangible sign of the presence in this place (a presence attested to by the holy texts) of Jesus's judge, of that same

Herod Antipas who stopped here, at Rennes-le-Château, on the path of exile, in the company of a certain Mary the Madgalenian.' (This is a rather odd form of words: Herod Antipas was not *Jesus'* 'judge', but John the Baptist's. Pontius Pilate would have been more appropriate. Perhaps in her original statement she did not say 'Jesus' at all, but, like the careful Templar wording, *'Christ'* . . .)

However, one of Dr Tajé's comments eclipsed even these statements. It was widely reported in the French press that, according to Rennes-le-Château's mayor, she had told him: 'The Church has given me the mission of destroying any compromising documents that we might find.' (This was later explained away as a joke made during a dinner at a local restaurant.) Plans were made for excavations to dig up the chest, at first to take place in September 2001, then in February 2002, but on both occasions the dig was postponed.

While Rennes-le-Château continues to work its strange magic, there are still many mysteries connected with the historical Magdalene to investigate: Mary who is associated with the cult surrounding the 'high prostitute' Marie de Négre, or Mary the Black/of Darkness, a black Egyptian, with the dark goddess Isis, and the strange Black Madonnas . . .

PART TWO

# Dark Secrets and Black Magic

## CHAPTER SIX

# 'Black, but Comely . . .'

Perhaps ironically for one who is believed to have so fervently rejected the frivolous and the superficial, the physical image of the Magdalene may well prove to be crucial in any analysis of her importance – and perhaps even provide the most disturbing insight into the Church's conspiracy of silence about her true role.

Some Christians and all members of the New Age movement think of Mary Magdalene as a ripe beauty, and – not without reason – a goddess figure, for according to the forbidden texts Jesus himself certainly saw her as at least semi-divine: to be the 'All' and intimately associated with Sophia, the incarnation of wisdom, elevated his *koinonos*, or sexual companion, yet further from the level of mere female humanity. Yet although it is believed she was a Jewish woman from Tarichea, it is interesting to note how she has been consistently portrayed by Christian artists over the centuries. Certainly, many over-heated imaginations have had her clothed – more usually, partly clothed – in scarlet, the red badge of sexual sin, of physical passion and the rawness of the pain that is concomitant with such a 'falling' from the grace of God. Sometimes (although rarely), she is shown as covered in shaggy hair and/or animal skins (it is hard to tell where one ends and the other begins) like a female John the Baptist, wild and shamanic, blurring the distinction between ordinary woman and mythical creature of the boundary places where Pan reigns supreme. But mostly, in Christian art, the penitents' unofficial patron saint is portrayed as fair-haired, in a full range of shades from mousy to outright – and often startling – blonde, as if in the depths of her agony of self-hatred she still finds the strength to reach through her sobs for the peroxide bottle. Although it is believed that her roots may be the same as those of David, Isaiah and Simon Peter, trichologically speaking, they will rarely be allowed to be *dark*.

As we have seen, on her feast day of 22 July, a grisly skull, believed to be that of Mary Magdalene herself, is paraded through the streets of the southern French town of St Maximin before rapturous crowds. But in order to present a more pleasing face to the throngs, it is encased in a mask of gold, and topped with an uncompromisingly blonde wig. This is very strange, for the blonding of the Magdalene is not a recent tradition, yet in medieval times there was a tendency to portray famous foreigners as local people, and the women of southern France would be just as likely to be as dark-haired as a Jewish woman from Palestine. Why did the clergy of St Maximin choose to make Mary Magdalene so blonde? Was this simply to reinforce the idea of her exotic nature? Perhaps, but the emphasis on such startling and unlikely blondeness raises certain suspicions: do they, perhaps, protest too much? Did they know that the real woman was very far from being blonde and were trying, however desperately, to cover up this (to them) unpalatable yet highly significant fact?

The Abbé Saunière, too, presented his beloved Magdalene as a notably fair young woman – certainly on the bas relief that decorated his altar, which he is said to have painted himself, she is hardly a typical Mediterranean beauty. Perhaps this represented nothing more significant than his personal predilection: no doubt his private devotions centred upon a Magdalene who appealed to him as a red-blooded man. (Although allegedly a celibate priest, he was probably the lover of both Emma Calvé and Marie Denarnaud, and in any case he was no stranger to the pleasures of the flesh.) And in this, for once, Saunière was merely following an age-old Church tradition. The Magdalene, it seems, must never be uncompromisingly and exotically dark.

However, it is not simply Mary who receives this treatment: in virtually every church in the west, Jesus himself is portrayed as fair or reddish-haired, with a thin, very white face. (The influential Pre-Raphaelites made him look like a consumptive girl with a fake beard, probably because that reflects the nature of the models they used.) In some churches, he is a strapping, blue-eyed, blond-haired Aryan hero: this is the preferred model, for example, in the Church of Jesus Christ of Latter Day Saints, otherwise known as the Mormons, where – although otherwise innocent of any 'popish' trappings such as statues or stained glass – a portrait of a sort of blond lumberjack Jesus hangs in every vestibule.

The Virgin Mary is also frequently portrayed as blonde – sometimes even the 'dizzy' variety, as in the curious tapestry that hangs above the altar in the church of Notre Dame de France in London. And this does not even have the excuse of the ignorance of the ages in its favour: this blonde Virgin is very modern, for the building was refurbished and rededicated in the 1960s. There is no trace of Semitism.

Of course it is human nature to make God in our own image, and if the prevailing apotheosis of physical female beauty is a slim blonde, then it is only natural that the Mother of God – not to mention a very good friend of his – should reflect the prevailing standards of loveliness. But this licence only works one way: while no one takes the Church to task for westernizing Jesus' womenfolk, depictions of them as obviously Jewish are still seen as distasteful. (A friend who lovingly painted a beautiful and very Jewish Virgin in art class at convent school had her work torn up in a fury by a nun, who accused her of 'blasphemy'. This happened as recently as the 1980s.)

As we have seen – and will discuss further – there are distinct possibilities that the Magdalene did *not* come from Tarichea, but from beyond the borders of Palestine, perhaps from a distant and more exotic land. Not only because of her gender, intelligence, independence and closeness to Jesus, but also as a result of her very appearance, could she possibly have offended the Church's racial sensibilities yet further? Although political correctness allows – or positively demands – that the actress playing Mary Magdalene in *Jesus Christ Superstar* should be dark-skinned, and the Church has long permitted African Christians to portray Jesus and his family in their own image, there is still a distinct element of condescension, the underlying feeling that it is all right for them to do so as long as no one really believes – no one who really *counts,* that is – that the living saints were anything other than blatantly and comfortingly Caucasian. Michael Jackson's desperate attempts to be white may inspire ridicule or pity, but they may well be as nothing compared to the Church's literal whitewashing of Mary Magdalene, the woman whose name they have always been so keen – paradoxically – to blacken. For there are clues – admittedly fragmentary and scattered – that instead of being an olive-skinned Levantine, she may well have been a woman of colour. (It may be difficult for an African woman to dry a man's feet with her hair, but it is certainly not impossible.) The implications of this, even as a hypothetical idea, are interesting, to say the least. Was Mary Magdalene, the woman Jesus kissed and who was hated and feared by Simon Peter, originally from either Egypt or Ethiopia, a real child of the dark continent? Could that explain why she has been the subject of such remorseless misrepresentation, and why her relationship with Jesus has been obscured and denied for so long? After all, as far as the Church was and is concerned, it is bad enough to be faced with a Jesus who loved this woman so much he made her his Apostle of the Apostles, and with whom he united sexually in a sacred rite, but the possibility that there were offspring of this mixed-race union would be too terrible to contemplate. African icons of Jesus may be black-skinned, but that is the limit of the Church's skin-thin tolerance: it has always been a thorn in the side of the Vatican that Jesus chose not to be a comfortingly born Caucasian – providing the sick-minded *raison d'être* for countless pogroms against the 'God-murdering Jews' – so the very notion that he may have ignored the implicit rules of apartheid and loved a black woman is an idea for burning. But was Mary Magdalene really dark-skinned? What are the hints and clues that still lie scattered among the surviving gems of the heretics?

## Madonnas with dirty faces

Scattered across Europe are little cult centres that blur the line between pagan and Christian, and which contain clues not only to the true origins of Christianity, but also to the real nature of the Magdalene. These are the homes of the Black Madonnas or Black Virgins – in most regards exactly similar to other statues of the Madonna and child, except that both the Lady and her holy infant are depicted with black faces and hands. Wherever they are found, they are the focus of enormous veneration, real passion, among the local people, who regard them as something other than the usual array of pale-faced Christian saints – even as something quite different from the usual Virgin and Child. This difference in emphasis has not been lost on the Catholic Church, which has always maintained a careful distance from the Black Madonnas.

In the 1980s British writer Ean Begg travelled extensively to research the Black Madonnas, producing his now-classic book *The Cult of the Black Virgin* in 1985, in which he states: 'there was no mistaking the hostility, when, on 28 December 1952, as [papers were presented] on Black Virgins to the American Association for the Advancement of Science, every priest and nun in the audience walked out'.[1] The 1950s were a very long time ago, especially where cultural attitudes are concerned, so it might reasonably be supposed that these strange statues have since been welcomed into the wider Catholic fold, alongside the likes of St Thérèse of Lisieux and St Bernadette of Lourdes. But although Pope John Paul is known to make private visits to certain Black madonnas, not one of these cults has yet been officially recognized, nor has their veneration even been tacitly encouraged. What could possibly be so *wrong* about the Black Madonnas that the clergy continue to find them so distasteful? Is it simply that they have always represented the idiosyncratic worship of rural backwaters that seem a little too independent-minded for the Catholic hierarchy – or is there still some other, deeper issue involved?

As he moved around Europe from site to site, Begg noted a curious phenomenon: although the Madonnas were often prominently displayed in local churches, even their own parish priests frequently professed no knowledge of them. When challenged on the subject, while finally admitting that their church had actually had a Black Madonna for over 500 years, many responded with the ludicrous suggestion that the blackness was simply the accumulation of the dirt of ages, which – apart from casting generations of church cleaners in a particularly inefficient light – is very odd because many of the statues in question were actually painted black. In any case, why would a few especially grimy and discoloured statues have inspired such passion for hundreds of years?

Begg told of how one colleague asked a priest why the Black

Madonnas are black, only to be told: 'My son, she is black because she is black.'[2] In *The Templar Revelation*, we mentioned this episode to illustrate the Church's consistently dismissive attitude on the subject. Although the priest may well have shrugged away an uncomfortable question in this manner, ironically his words were to initiate this current investigation, for it is possible to interpret them quite differently. It may be that once again, the theory of Occam's Razor – in which the simplest and most obvious answer is often the correct one – triumphs. Instead of being the equivalent of the mindless answer 'Because it is' to questions such as 'Why is that horse white?', there is an alternative way of framing the priests' words: she (the statue) is black because she (the Madonna herself) was black.

There is another layer to the phenomenon of the Black Madonna, however: wherever she is found, she is intimately, and specifically, connected with ancient pagan sites. It was common for the Church to Christianize ancient holy wells or sacred groves that had once been the site of nature rites and goddess worship. Canny Church elders realized that the people still loved these places and would honour them despite official condemnation, so they took over these magical locations, just as they had metamorphosed pagan gods into purely mythical saints. Although on the whole much later, across Europe, the most sacred of the pagan sites began to boast Black Madonnas – depictions of dark-faced Virgins with their children that are so nearly Catholic images, while so obviously still, essentially, pagan idols.

The majority of the Black Madonna sites have traditionally been associated with the old goddesses such as Cybele, Diana and Isis, all of whom were often depicted as black-skinned. These, with other similar deities, were originally Moon goddesses, divine feminine archetypes whose three manifestations mirrored the main phases of the Moon: the New Moon, or Virgin phase; the Full Moon, or fertile phase of motherhood, and the Dark of the Moon, when the goddess reaches her apotheosis as embodiment of wisdom, as the old woman, hag or crone.

In her *The Woman's Encyclopedia of Myths and Secrets*, Barbara G. Walker writes of the universality of belief in the power of the female deity that was embodied in the Moon:

*The Crucifixion.* A grief-stricken Mary Magdalene clutches at Jesus' feet in a typical representation of her role at his death. She is still widely seen as a prostitute whom Jesus converted, but who – oddly, one might think – nevertheless remained overwhelmed by the enormity of her past sinfulness. This image, for which there is not a shred of evidence, has been very useful to the Church in its campaign to repress its female flock over the centuries.

*St John the Baptist.* Leonardo's depiction of John the Baptist, which, together with the *Mona Lisa* – which may represent Mary Magdalene – hung in his room as he died, in northern France in 1519. The subject of both pictures have the same knowing smile: indeed, to the heretical Templarist groups of which Leonardo was clearly a member, both these marginalized Biblical figures were of supreme importance as the embodiment of great mystical secrets.

*The Last Supper.* In Leonardo da Vinci's famous wall-painting, we see the young St John, who is described in the Bible as leaning against Jesus' chest shown here leaning as far away as possible from him, forming a spreadeagled 'M' shape. But this 'St John' has breasts and a necklace – is 'he' really supposed to represent Mary Magdalene? Or is the hermaphrodite-like figure both the Magdalene and the young John? And why would either Mary or John wish to lean so far away from Jesus as if trying to distance themselves from him?

In the Louvre version of Leonardo's *The Virgin of the Rocks*, apparently we see the young Jesus blessing a kneeling John the Baptist as a child. Yet the children are with the wrong guardians: surely Jesus should be with his mother and John with his traditional guide, the archangel Uriel? If seen this way, Jesus is kneeling to John – another of Leonardo's clear Johannite allusions. His caustic view of Mary's sexual status can be understood in the extraordinary object – shaped out of the rocks – that rises from her head to the skyline.

Although the Magdalene is usually portrayed as fair-haired, even sometimes an unlikely blonde (as in the bewigged skull, said to be hers, in the basilica of St Maximin in Provence, France: above left), she is associated with both the Black Madonnas (above right) and ancient pagan goddesses (such as Isis, below), who are sometimes portrayed as dark-skinned. Is this merely because of some metaphorical darkness such as the mysterious wisdom of the Moon goddesses, or simply because Mary Magdalene was herself a black woman?

The heretical Cathars of medieval southern France were so convinced that Jesus and Mary Magdalene were unmarried lovers that they willingly went to their deaths at the hands of the Crusaders. The annihilation of the Cathars was the first instance of genocide in Europe.

The Languedoc maintained its extreme love for the Magdalene: in the late 19th century the mysterious priest Francois Saunière of Rennes-le-Chateau was clearly a devotee (his altar bas relief shows her kneeling before a book and a skull). Not far away and at much the same time, the unknown Father de Coma, whose curious life mirrored Saunière's, also created a Magdalene centre. Her statue (below) is all that remains after it was dynamited by the Church.

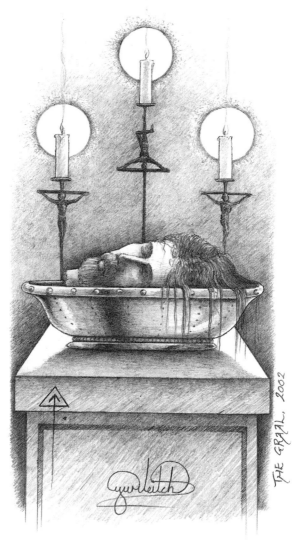

The early stories about the Holy Grail describe it as being a bearded, severed head, not a cup. Other research indicates that it may have been both – the head of John the Baptist used as a sacramental drinking vessel. Drawing by the Glastonbury-based researcher and artist Yuri Leitch.

Ashanti people had a generic term for all deities, Boshun, 'Moon'. In the Basque language, the words for 'deity' and 'moon' were the same. Sioux Indians called the moon 'The Old Woman Who Never Dies'. Iroquois called her 'The Eternal One'. Rulers in the Eritrean zone of South Africa bore the Goddess's name, 'Moon'. The Gaelic name of the moon, *gealach*, came from Gala or Galata, original Moon-mother of Gaelic and Gaulish tribes. Britain used to be called Albion, the Milk-white Moon goddess. Persians called the moon Metra (Matra, mother), 'whose love penetrated everywhere'.[3]

Priestesses of goddess cults celebrated the female mysteries at the appropriate phase of the Moon, sharing and passing on the secrets of menstruation, lovemaking, childbirth – and death, for women, as bringers of life, have always also been recognized as the guardians of the mysteries of death. Like Mary Magdalene with her jar of spikenard, they tend the mortal remains of those they love and grieve for the loss of physical presence, while recognizing at a primeval level that life will return, as spring follows winter.

Walker goes on:

Wearing the [lunar] crescent was 'visible worship' of the Goddess. That was why the prophet Isaiah denounced the women of Zion for wearing lunar amulets (Isaiah 3:18). 'The crescent moon worn by Diana and used in the worship of other Goddesses is said to be the Ark or vessel of boat-like shape, symbol of fertility, in the Container of the Germ of all life.' The same Ark, carried gods, like Osiris, into death . . .[4]

Of all the lunar goddesses, however, one that has the most direct bearing on the Black Madonnas – and, ultimately, on Mary Magdalene – is the famous Egyptian mother goddess Isis, who ruled healing and the magical arts. Like the Magdalene, she is connected with ships: she rode in her barque or great heavenly boat, ferrying the souls of humankind, and for ever seeking and mourning her lost love, Osiris. Like Jesus' lover, Isis is closely associated with France: it is believed that Paris, the city of love – originally *Para Isidos* (Greek for 'near Isis') – was dedicated to her, as was the temple on which the famous cathedral of Notre Dame was built. Indeed, a statue of her survived in the church of St Germain-des-Prés, only to be smashed by the fifteenth-century Cardinal Briçonnet, incensed that women were still lighting candles to her, just as they reverenced the Virgin Mary.[5]

It might be thought that a goddess from far-off Egypt would have had little effect on the pagan cult centres of France, but it is surprising how far her religion spread, especially during the years of Roman dominance. Martin Bernal, in his scholarly work *Black Athena* (1991) describes the spread of the cult of Isis in the ancient world:

> The Egyptian mother goddess Isis . . . had been worshipped in Athens since the 5th century, not merely by resident Egyptians but by native Athenians. By the 2nd century BC there was a temple of Isis near the Akropolis and Athens was officially encouraging its dependencies to take up Egyptian cults. Even on Delos, especially sanctified to Apollo, cults of Isis and Anubis [her companion, the jackal-headed god] were made official in a move that was in no way connected to the Ptolemaic kingdom which had lost control of the island by that time. Indeed, by the 2nd century AD Pausanias, who made no mention of other Oriental cults, reported Egyptian temples or shrines in Athens, Corinth, Thebes and many places in the Argolid, Messenia, Achaia and Phokis.[6]

However, as Bernal puts it: 'Greece had experienced only part of a wave that had spread throughout the Roman Empire. For instance, the most important shrines discovered at Pompeii from 79 AD – when it was overwhelmed by the eruption of Vesuvius – were "Egyptian" . . . [the] later emperors . . . were passionately devoted to the Egyptian gods.'[7]

Isis was frequently portrayed as a nubile young black woman, her statuettes unequivocally carved from ebony-coloured stone. There was no doubt about her dark skin, no hasty pseudo-explanations involving incompetent cleaners and candle smoke. In one of her aspects, the great Egyptian goddess was black and beautiful and her majesty was supreme.

128

Although Isis was worshipped as a holy virgin – indeed, scholars recognize that she was the prototype for the Church's part-invention of Mary the Mother – she was understood by her many thousands of devotees to be considerably more than that. All ancient goddesses were seen as a mysterious, fluid feminine essence that could be Virgin, could even be a Virgin Mother – seen to represent the impossible, the paradoxical nature of the all-powerful – but also a natural mother, a knowing sexual initiatrix and an aged wise-woman.

However, when the men of the Church came to adapt and marginalize the feminine aspects of Christianity – having discovered that nothing they could do or threaten would prevent ordinary people from loving a goddess figure – they rejected utterly the obvious 'Christian Isis', Mary Magdalene. She was too subversive, too obviously sexual, too powerful and possibly far too black. Either she had to go or – because she was too well known and loved to be excised from the story altogether – turned into something pitiable, totally power*less*.

### The new Isis

It is particularly strange that Jesus' mother is honoured with semi-deification,[8] for as Professor Morton Smith observes wryly in his *Jesus the Magician* (1978): 'It is not said [Jesus] loved her. Any hero who speaks to his mother only twice, and on both occasions addresses her as "Woman", is a difficult figure for sentimental biographers.'[9] Yet the early Church was so desperate to include the requisite touch of goddess worship into its practice to placate the masses – and pander to those who were tempted by the more egalitarian Gnosticism – that they chose as her new representative the safely anodyne woman whom Jesus did *not* appear to love, rather than the more dangerous priestess whom he was well known to have adored.

Of the two central women in Jesus' life it is Mary the Mother who was given not only the style, but also the titles of the goddess Isis. (And the deification of the mother becomes even more disquieting when the many rumours about her true status are taken into account, as we shall see later. Perhaps Leonardo's *Virgin of the Rocks* was not too far off the mark.) Whereas the Roman world was familiar with statues representing Isis with her holy child Horus in her arms or on her lap, gradually the first-millennial Church began to present Mary the Mother in exactly the same mould, quite deliberately. And, like Isis, she was called 'Queen of Heaven' and 'Star of the Sea' (*stella maris*), represented with stars around her head and a crescent Moon at her feet. But unlike Isis, she was exclusively, and for ever, a Virgin, despite the fact that this is not only highly unlikely for a real mother, but impossible even in the context of the New Testament – for Jesus quite clearly had siblings. Catholic apologists may claim that this is a misunderstanding, and that his so-called brothers and sisters were actually his disciples, but one passage makes the differentiation very plain:

> When Jesus was still talking to the crowd, his mother and brothers stood outside, wanting to speak to him. Someone told him, 'Your mother and brothers are waiting outside, wanting to speak to you.'
> He replied to them, 'Who is my mother, and who are my brothers?' Pointing to his disciples he said, 'Here are my mother and my brothers. For whoever does the will of my Father in heaven is my brother and sister and mother.'[10]

Here he is not only tacitly admitting the existence of his family, but taking pride in ignoring them in favour of his disciples. At least one of his blood brothers, 'James, the Brother of Jesus', was famous in his own right, going on to become the first Bishop of Jerusalem.[11] (And there is the distinct possibility that he had a twin.) Yet even today, Catholic writers denounce such an interpretation of Holy Writ: theologian Karl Barth speaks for many millions when he declares: 'It is essential to the true Christian faith to accept the doctrine of the virgin birth'. To challenge the idea that Mary was never less than a virgin is considered 'an insult to our Lady', ironically echoing the heretic Cathars' extreme distaste for sexuality and procreation.

However, this often passionate defence of Mary the Mother's status overlooks the fact that the Hebrew word *almah* originally translated as 'Virgin' in the King James Version of the Bible simply meant 'young woman'. Of course, even if the word had been correctly translated, until the nineteenth century, few would have known the difference: apart from among the ranks of the clergy, it was very rare to find anything like widespread literacy, and in any case the Church carefully kept its scriptures in Latin – unintelligible to the masses. These days, Catholics are still not encouraged to read the Bible for themselves (Bible discussion groups tend to be the province of the Protestants and independent churches), but even when they do, the psychological blindness that is the reward of life-long conditioning – the phenomenon that Leonardo understood so well – prevents them from seeing what is staring them in the face. The brain skids on concepts that the eyes innocently pick out – and instantly rejects them. How can Jesus have had brothers and sisters when his mother was always a holy Virgin? The offending passages are subconsciously deleted, and the little flurry of panic that arises out of confronting inconvenient facts gratefully subsides, without the conscious mind being aware of any of it.

## Another Templar legacy

It might be supposed that the Black Madonna cults had been a feature of religious life in France since the time the Isian religion had held sway there, or at least from the first two centuries of the Church, when its rules and orthodoxy were still being established, but on the whole this is not so. There were few cult statues that can be said to have been 'Black Madonnas' in France before the coming of the Knights Templar – but of that handful, it is significant that one was said to have been brought over by the Magdalene herself, although this may be a retrospective attempt to add a more authoritative gloss. Or the statue of the black woman and her child may simply have been a representation of Isis and Horus. In fact, the Black Madonna phenomenon coincided approximately with the heyday of the Knights Templar in the mid to late thirteenth century, almost certainly the product of their influence.

The rank and file of the Order may have been enthusiastic worshippers of the Virgin and Jesus – embodiments, it was believed, of sexual purity – but the inner, esoteric group were, it seems, Johannite and more inclined towards the Magdalene. As it was this shadowy esoteric circle that were keepers of the Order's secrets – which they chose to hide in the decorations of the great Gothic cathedrals such as Chartres – what esoteric Templar traditions did the Black Madonnas embody?

It is now recognized that Isis/the Black Madonnas were intimately linked to one of the Christian Marys: not to Mary the Mother, but rather Mary the lover – the Magdalene: Ean Begg discovered that no fewer than fifty centres dedicated to the alleged former prostitute also contain shrines to a Black Madonna. In *The Templar Revelation* we noted: 'For example, the famous black statue of St Sarah the Egyptian is found at Saintes-Maries-de-la-Mer – the very place where the Magdalene is said to have disembarked after her journey from Palestine. And in Marseilles there are no fewer than three Black Madonnas, one in the crypt of the basilica of St Victor, immediately outside the underground chapel that is dedicated to Mary Magdalene. There is another in "her" church in Aix-en-Provence (close to the place where she is believed to have been buried) and yet another in that town's main church of St Saveur.'[12] There are also two in the parish church of the village of Montségur, in the shadow of the Cathar's last great stronghold.

Ean Begg's investigations revealed an astonishing concentration of Black Madonnas in the area of Lyons/Vichy/Clermont-Ferrand, focussed on the hills known as the Monts de la Madeleine (the Magdalene's Hills). And all around the eastern Pyrenees and Provence, where there are enduring legends connected with her physical presence, there are also high concentrations of statues of Black-faced Virgins and their children. Clearly, the French have long believed – or perhaps even *known* – something to connect the Magdalene with pagan goddesses and with blackness.

Yet although these statues are specifically associated with the Magdalene and not the Virgin Mary, it is also an uncomfortable fact that these statues are of a *mother and child*. They do not depict a woman alone, as might be expected in representations of the Magdalene, almost certainly a visual confirmation of the heretical belief that she bore Christ's children. That alone is a good enough reason for the Church to stand aloof from this cult.

While it no longer seems unlikely to most non-Christians (and even to some liberal-minded churchgoers) that Jesus and the Magdalene had children, it is no doubt a new challenge to consider that she may have been a black woman, and therefore their family would be of mixed race.

There is one other intriguing traditional association with the

Black Madonnas that may have a bearing on this investigation: according to Ean Begg, the important Roman god Janus, whose 'two faces illustrate not only his role as deity of beginnings, looking to past and future, but his essential duality as the original bisexual chaos and the form which emerged from it' may have been transmuted by time and custom into Jean (John), 'one of the companions of the Black Virgin'.[13] Once again, we find the curious link in the underground stream of the Magdalene and a figure called John, just as it is striking how many churches dedicated to both Mary and the Baptist are situated close to each other in the south of France – and also to a lesser extent elsewhere, such as the west of England. The wild man of the wilderness, too, has some tangential associations with blackness: the feast of his beheading, on 29 August, is the day after that of the Ethiopian robber-turned-monk, St Moses the Black, who ended his days in the Nile delta: besides, the Baptist's executioner is traditionally shown as being black.[14]

Of course in themselves these associations may be meaningless: it could be pure coincidence that the two feast days fall a day apart, and perhaps it is simply a fact that the Baptist's executioner was black – or if not, the Church may have tried to 'smear' the anonymous man who committed this sin against Jesus' forerunner by portraying him as dark-skinned (to their way of thinking physical or symbolic darkness being equated with blackness of soul).

If there were no other reasons to raise suspicions, these examples could be easily dismissed, but – as we will see later – the Church has committed at least as grave a crime against the Baptist as they have against the Magdalene. Both have been deliberately marginalized and rewritten for the purposes of propaganda, yet great care has been taken to ensure the readers of the gospels never associate the two. Why? What possible relationship could the Magdalene and the Baptist have had – especially one that was in some way threatening to the emergent Church – when according to the New Testament there is no evidence that they ever even met?

Yet repeatedly there are clues that something profoundly disquieting did link them together, something about which the Gospels writers and the Church elders behave like guilty men presenting a highly sanitized version of their crime to the police. We have seen how Leonardo revered, perhaps even loved, both the

Magdalene and the Baptist, while despising Mary the Mother and Jesus himself, which seems to reflect the secret allegiance of the inner circle of the Knights Templar. And although the Priory of Sion is a modern invention, much given to tricks and jokes – rather like Leonardo himself – the Masonic and quasi-Masonic groups that operate under the umbrella name of the Order are also extremely passionate about both the Magdalene and the Baptist, while maintaining an equivocal attitude to the Holy Family itself.

Now we find that there is a strong, if partly submerged, tradition linking Mary with blackness, and even a few hints to place the Baptist in the same category. We have seen how time and time again the Magdalene is linked with black Isis, the great Egyptian goddess of erotic love and magic, who presided over the obsequies of her consort Osiris – a dying-and-rising-god *who was also often depicted as black* – and even magically conceived by his dead body. This presupposes a major connection with Egypt, where Jesus and his family were known to have lived (allegedly fleeing from Herod's massacre of the innocents), and where there was a town called Magdolum.

Although technically a north African country, Egypt is rarely thought of as part of the dark continent, but of course it has always maintained strong trading links with the surrounding – to our eyes, much more 'African' – countries, such as Ethiopia, where for many years there was a fortress called *Magdala* . . .

### 'Dark am I, yet lovely'

The earliest Christian commentary – dating from the second century – on that curious book of erotic poetry in the Old Testament, the *Song of Songs*, associates the central character of the legendary Queen of Sheba, Queen of Ethiopia (which means 'burnt faces') with Mary Magdalene,[15] and this link has remained: evocative, potent, but barely understood. Bizarrely, given the explicitly sensual nature of this ancient book, this extract is read to the congregation in Catholic churches every year on the Magdalene's feast day:

> All night long on my bed
> I looked for the one my heart loves;
> I looked for him but did not find him.
> I will get up now and go about the city,

through its streets and squares;
I will search for the one my heart loves,
So I looked for him but did not find him.
The watchmen found me
as they made their rounds in the city,
'Have you seen the one my heart loves?'
Scarcely had I passed them
when I found the one my heart loves.
I held him and would not let him go
till I had brought him to my mother's house,
to the room of the one who conceived me.[16]

What is the connection between the alleged Jewish penitent and this lamenting lover? Is the bridge between them once again the goddess Isis? For the legend of the great Egyptian lover/mother tells how her beloved Osiris, god of the underworld (born at the time of the Winter Solstice) was brutally murdered and dismembered, his body scattered. Isis searched throughout the whole of Egypt for him, all the while lamenting with her whole soul. The priestess who assumed the role of the goddess in the annual Isian mystery plays wandered distraught, crying: 'They have taken him! They have removed him from my sight! Pray tell me where his body lies!' – just as Mary Magdalene was to tell the 'gardener' that they had stolen her Lord, and taken him to an unknown place. (Interestingly, the priests of Osiris were sometimes known as 'gardeners'.)

Yet there is another subtext in this otherwise mysterious link between the erotic Old Testament *Song of Songs* and the New Testament disciple Mary Magdalene. The 'bride' in *Song of Songs* describes herself as 'dark am I, yet lovely' ('Black but comely' in the more familiar King James version): but although there is some controversy among the black communities about the original wording – some claim it should have read less offensively: 'dark am I, *and* lovely' – it does appear that the translation as it stands is correct.[17] However, in itself that means little: the Hebrew for the conjunctions 'and' and 'but' is the same, and the alternative interpretations are therefore interchangeable. It is possible, of course, that the writer was guilty as charged, his intention being to imply that it was unusual for a black woman to be attractive – 'black *but* comely' – despite the fact that Moses himself had an Ethiopian (or 'Cushite') wife.[18] Indeed, the Jewish chronicler Josephus claimed that the great prophet had once lived in Ethiopia,[19] although he also described the Queen of Sheba as 'Queen of Egypt and Ethiopia', referring to the significant fact that ancient Ethiopia was a vast empire that covered most of the Nile valley, stretching from the Mediterranean Sea to the much smaller area now occupied by the present-day Ethiopia, much of which once belonged to the Egyptian Empire.

Ethiopia had a long history of being ruled by powerful black female monarchs, Virgin Queens, of whom several were called 'Candace', including a legendary warrior-queen, a formidable military tactician, who in the year 332 BCE so challenged Alexander the Great's unbroken string of victories – not to mention his masculine ego – that he halted at the borders of the country rather than be humiliated by a woman. Another Queen Candace waged war against the Romans and was finally routed by Petronius at her capital of Napata in 22 BCE, while Pliny records that when Nero's expedition was travelling through Nubia, a Queen Candace reigned over the island of Meroe, adding that 'this name was a title common to all the queens of that country'.[20] And much later, the *Acts of the Apostles*[21] tells how St Philip converted and baptized the black high treasurer of a Queen Candace of Ethiopia, thus paving the way for Christianity to enter that country.

The 'bride' of the *Song of Songs* is believed to be the Queen of Sheba, the Shulamite Virgin Queen who was seduced by King Solomon, and who is enjoying something of a surge in popularity at the time of writing.[22] But why should this Old Testament monarch be so intimately linked with the New Testament Mary Magdalene? Clearly there is a perception, albeit presumably at an unconscious level on the part of the Church, that the extreme eroticism of the *Song of Songs* – allegedly describing the passion of the Queen of Sheba for Solomon – finds an echo in the relationship between the Magdalene and Jesus. However, as this is clearly unacceptable, Church apologists virtually tie themselves in knots trying to explain this away – some claim that Solomon represents Jesus, while the 'bride' symbolizes his Church, although why the imagery should be quite so fevered is not addressed. (Is it really necessary for Jesus to kiss his Church on the lips, or rhapsodize about its breasts being 'like two fauns, like twin fauns of a gazelle that browse among the lilies'?) And, as we have seen, there is also a clear echo in the Shulamite's words of the lines spoken in the mysteries of the goddess Isis, who searches desperately for her missing lover, just as – to complete the circle of connections – the Magdalene tells the risen Jesus that she has no knowledge where they have taken his body.

There is also that undercurrent of blackness, a suspicion that Mary's ethnic identity was something else that has been assiduously covered up by those who do not want the image of the Saviour that has proved so useful to them to be 'tainted' by association with her. What are the other possible links with the powerful and enigmatic Queen of Sheba, lover of Solomon and mother of his child?

## Queen of the South

The story of how the 'black but comely' queen met and fell in love with King Solomon (or, at least, was uncomplainingly seduced by him, depending upon the version of the story) in his magnificent palace at Jerusalem is told in the Old Testament books of the *Song of Songs, I Kings* and *Chronicles,* and in the fourteenth-century CE Ethiopian saga, the *Kebra Negast (Glory of Kings).*

The earliest version is preserved in the Old Testament, describing how the Queen was attracted by Solomon's already legendary reputation, travelling to his palace with a magnificent caravan made up of 797 camels, each piled high with the perfumes and spices for which Ethiopia was much prized, and carrying glittering presents with which she dazzled both king and court.[23] It is estimated that the gold alone was the equivalent of $3,690,000 today.[24]

This glamorous queen, dripping jewels and exuding costly perfume, together with her spectacular retinue, was clearly a sensation, rapidly becoming a legend not only among the members of Solomon's court, but also entering into other Middle Eastern chronicles. (Such is her timeless appeal that to this day her name is still used to sell thousands of beauty products to millions of women worldwide, eager as ever to possess their own piece of her special magic.)

Testimony to her breath-taking charisma is the fact that she appears in the Koran and her name is even invoked by Jesus, and at least four modern countries squabble about evidence that may suggest that she belongs to their own past. Even now, the Queen of Sheba has men fighting over her.

The general consensus among archaeologists and historians is that Sheba was not a personal name, but a reference to her place of origin – Saba, in south-west Yemen, where a great queen is known to have ruled during the tenth century BCE. Some even claim to have found the ruins of her ancient Sabaean city, the fabled Marib, in the desert, although political tension in the area has made excavation near-impossible for any protracted period. Certainly there is abundant evidence of the rule of a legendary woman in the area, whose empire dates from around the time of the biblical character – and whose name may have been 'Bilqis', although this is by no means certain. The fact that the Queen of Sheba was commonly associated with the Arabian peninsula in the first century CE is reflected in Jesus' prophecy about her: 'The Queen of the South shall rise up in judgement with this generation, and shall condemn it; for she came from the uttermost parts of the earth to hear the wisdom of Solomon; and behold, a greater than Solomon is here.'[25] The references to Solomon make it easy enough to identify the queen in question, and 'the South' commonly referred to the Yemen in Jesus' time and place.

Yet even if her kingdom radiated its might from amid the deserts of Arabia, the Queen of Sheba was fated to travel further afield, and not only north to Solomon's court. According to the *Kebra Negast*[26] – in which she is called 'Makeda', or, significantly, *Magda,* which may simply mean 'Great One' – she *returned* to Ethiopia, where she discovered she was carrying Solomon's child, whom in due course she named Menelik ('son of the wise man'). Even in the Arabian version, it is admitted that a few years afterwards they left the Yemen and travelled to Ethiopia, where although they disappeared from written record, it is believed they founded the Davidic dynasty, held by many to be sacred. Usurped in the thirteenth century by the semi-pagan Adous – who traced their ancestry to Moses[27] – the Davidic/Solomonic line was restored within years by the great King Lalibela, the most celebrated monarch of the dynasty, who built an astonishing cluster of churches hewn out of solid rock in the city that now bears his name.

All that was in the distant future when Sheba disappeared into the dust of Ethiopia. Mystery surrounds her subsequent fate, although a team of British scientists from Bournemouth University, working with archaeologist Dr Patrick Darling believe they may have discovered her possible burial place – hidden in the Nigerian rainforest at Eredo, not far from the capital of Lagos and close to the ruins of some impressive ancient monuments.[28] While not so elaborate as the world-famous monuments of Giza, these earthworks required the builders to move an estimated 3.5 million cubic metres of earth in order to construct massive ramparts – 1 million cubic metres more than was used in the construction of the Great Pyramid.

Patrick Darling enthused to the BBC about the discovery, saying 'We are not linking what we found to a city, but to a vast kingdom boundary rampart.' The kingdom in question was that of ancient Ijebu, once ruled by the 'Awujale', a great spiritual leader whose word was law. Clearly, the sheer size of the site is breathtaking: Dr Darling says: 'The vertical sided ditches go round the area for 100 miles and it is more than 1000 years old. That makes it the earliest proof of a kingdom founded in the African rainforest.'[29]

However, the Bournemouth team have made an exciting historical link – if it can be substantiated – between these ruins in the Nigerian jungle and the legendary Queen of Sheba, or Bilqis. Patrick Darling says that local people who live near the Eredo site associate the area with Bilikisu Sungbo, their name for the Queen of Sheba – and local tradition tells of a great queen constructing a vast memorial nearby. Even now, thousands of people make an annual pilgrimage to what is believed to be the Queen of Sheba's grave, described as 'a magical shrine grove under tall trees'.[30]

Africa may figure prominently in the legends about Sheba's ultimate fate, but they provide no proof that she herself was black. The inhabitants of Nigeria are, of course, unambiguously black-skinned, and the people of Ethiopia are dark (actually a sort of deep bronze colour), but if her homeland was Saba in Arabia, this suggests that she herself was Semitic in appearance: typically with luxuriant, glossy dark hair, an aquiline nose, voluptuous figure, and olive- or light brown-coloured skin. Yet the *Song of Songs* has her uncompromising in her autoeroticism, describing herself as 'black but comely'/'dark . . . but lovely'. And the Queen of Sheba is – for

139

reasons that are yet to be clarified – linked to the Black Madonnas through Mary Magdalene. How could this Arabian queen be black – did the writers of the Old Testament book confuse her later association with Ethiopia with her place of origin? And in any case, scholars have always categorically stated that the Sabaeans influenced Ethiopia, and not the other way round (although this may be another example of the state of denial that exists in academia about the achievements of black Africa).

There is, however, evidence that, although Sabaeans were originally from Arabia, they had emigrated in large numbers to Ethiopia between 690 and 590 BCE[31] and returned in at least two waves, having presumably intermarried in the interim years. Of course the dates are wrong for the Queen of Sheba – who lived approximately 500 years previously – to have been involved in that particular wave of emigration, but even a cursory glance at the map shows that the straits of Bab el Mandeb, the narrowest point of the Red Sea between the Yemen and Ethiopia, would have presented no obstacle to determined traders and emigrants. So despite the attitude of Western scholars that the traffic between the two countries went only in one direction, if nothing else common sense dictates that there must have been mutual commerce for centuries. Based on geographical proximity alone, the Queen of Sheba could easily have been black.

## Evidence of the Grail stories

Clues also abound in the Grail story *Parzival* by the thirteenth-century Wolfram von Eschenbach, the most explicitly Templar of all the genre. But, as Graham Hancock discovered as he searched for the fabled Ark of the Covenant in Ethiopia in the 1980s, *Parzival* also appears to contain veiled references to the Sheba legend. In *The Sign and the Seal* (1992) the British author points out that an early chapter of the Grail story spoke of a far-off land called 'Zazamanc' where the people 'were as dark as night'.[32] The story tells how the French nobleman Gahmuret of Anjou travelled to this exotic country and fell in love with its queen, Belacane, whose name seems to Hancock to be a blend of the names Makeda and Bilqis, perhaps an example of Wolfram's penchant for neologisms. In any case, as Hancock points out, 'the poet describes her as a "dusky queen"'.[33]

Wolfram constantly stresses the difference in race between the hero and his beloved. The French knight is 'fair complexioned', a fact that seems to worry Belacane slightly, for she says to her maids: 'His skin is a different colour from ours. I only hope this is no sore point with him.' If her black skin was ever a problem, it was resolved once and for all when she 'disarmed him with her own dark hands' on a great fur-strewn bed, and they united in passionate love 'little though their skins matched in colour'.[34]

But although the lovers married and 'the dusky lady was dearer to him than life', Gahmuret abandoned her when she was pregnant, allegedly because she was not a Christian. Clearly on the defensive, he declares: 'Now many an ignorant fellow may think that it was her black skin I ran away from, but in my eyes she was as bright as the sun!' The boy-child that was born of their union was described as having a 'pied' skin, for 'it pleased God to make a marvel of him, for he was both black and white . . .' The tale describes how Belacane kissed her son's 'white spots', and how 'His hair and all his skin were particoloured like a magpie' – a particularly vivid metaphorical way of describing a child with mixed race characteristics. The boy's name underlines this: he is called Feirefiz, deriving from the French *vair fils*, which may carry the loaded double meaning of 'true son' and 'piebald son', both of which are appropriate. The hero Parzival is Feirefiz's half-brother, the child of Gahmuret and a French (and therefore fair-skinned) queen, which may be a sop to the racial sensibilities of Wolfram's European readers. As Hancock says wryly:

I was . . . undisturbed by the fact that it was not Feirefiz himself who was depicted as being on a quest for the Grail – nor Feirefiz who was eventually accorded the honour of finding the precious relic. Such an outcome would have provided much too *direct* and obvious a pointer. And, besides, Wolfram could not have afforded to allow the heathen half-caste son of a black queen to become the hero of a romance written for the amusement of medieval European Christians.[35]

Like much of the Templar-inspired Grail literature, Wolfram's heroic tale can be read on several different levels. Clearly, the first layer is the exoteric adventure story, the search for the Grail by the hero Parzival – an early Indiana Jones – and his adventures along the way. But of course the otherwise irrelevant secondary tale, of his parents' love, is an obvious echo of the legend of Solomon and the Queen of Sheba's union, and the birth of their son, Menelik, the founder of a great royal dynasty in Ethiopia.

Although the Queen of Sheba was known as a biblical character in Europe before the thirteenth century – when Wolfram's romance began to circulate among the literate classes – it was only after that time that her connection with Ethiopia was known in France and elsewhere. This was almost certainly because, as Graham Hancock conclusively demonstrated in *The Sign and the Seal*, the Knights Templar had travelled widely in that remote country, searching for the Ark and other sacred treasures. If they left behind them evidence of their presence in the form of several examples of their characteristically round churches, they returned the complement by transporting Ethiopian imagery to Europe. Two statues of the Queen of Sheba decorate the exterior of the great Gothic cathedral at Chartres, the finest flower of Templar-influenced sacred architecture in the west – one, above the south porch, shows her with a flower in her left hand, while the other at the north porch depicts her standing over a crouching 'negroid' or 'Ethiopian' slave,[36] although she herself appears to be of European appearance, almost certainly, once again, for reasons of racial diplomacy.

At more or less the same time that Chartres was being constructed, statues of the Black Madonnas were beginning to appear in France . . . It seems that during their sojourn in north Africa, the Templars had discovered that the Queen of Sheba was not only a black Ethiopian, but also a major figure in esoteric lore in some way – and that she had links with both pagan goddesses, specifically Isis, and with Mary Magdalene.

Embedded in the 'alternative' literature and the writings of the heretics are other clues about the link between the Sheba legend and the mystery of the Church's distaste for the family at Bethany. Significantly, the authors of *The Holy Blood and the Holy Grail* draw our attention to the entangled lineage of Parzival's descendants, although they note that according to *Perlesvaus* it leads back to 'Laziliez', 'whose parents are Mazadan and Terdelaschoye

[Chosen Land]'. This certainly draws us into deeper waters, for to a new eye it appears that not only is 'Mazadan' almost an anagram of Wolfram's 'Zazamanc', the country of dark-skinned people where Gahmuret encountered his beloved black bride, but 'Mazadan' – especially when read aloud – also bears a striking resemblance to 'Makeda', the Ethiopian name for the Queen of Sheba.

Laziliez's mother Mazadan seems to represent a black country – which, if reflecting the legend of Solomon and Sheba, would be consistent with his father's name of 'the chosen land'. However, there may be something even more intriguing lurking between the lines: Mazadan and Terdelaschoye's son is called *Laziliez*, suggesting another layer of significance. Surely this is an obvious blend of the Hebrew name 'Eliezer' and its Greek version 'Lazarus' – in other words, a coded reference to John the Beloved, Mary Magdalene's brother who lived with her at Bethany, and whose true identity the Church has long sought to obscure. Yet even today John's alternative names (especially in the Hebrew version) tend only to be known to theologians, students and researchers who devote time to unearthing out-of-the-way facts, so in the days of the Grail stories, when the disciplines of historical research were unknown, how were those authors familiar with them? Is this further evidence of the existence of 'lost' gospels, suppressed texts – or at least exciting secret information – circulating among 'those with eyes to see'? The fact that even the heretics obscured John's name in this way suggests they realized that there was something about him and his family that could not be presented openly.

It is wise not to forget that Wolfram's Grail legend was essentially Templar propaganda, and as such he would hardly have wasted the smallest opportunity to present, however subtly and subliminally, the Order's own particular understanding of myth and religion. Knowing the Templars' travels in Ethiopia and the Holy Land, and their fascination with the hidden Christian goddess, is Wolfram's evocative medieval romance a clever blend of *both* the Sheba/Solomon legend and the Jesus/Magdalene story? Or was he deviously employing the Old Testament legend as a more overtly acceptable vehicle, a taut literary device with which to present profoundly heretical ideas about two quite different religious figures? Concealed behind the richly attractive Sheba story is the underground stream of the Templars' secret knowledge: Christ, the prince from the Chosen Land, had a bride or lover from a country where the people were black. And this was no ordinary woman: she was the queen, or at least an aristocrat. Were Wolfram and his Templar associates hinting heavily at Mary's superior status? A queenly background would certainly explain her independent wealth, her unusual assertiveness in the presence of men and apparent inability to suffer fools gladly. Implicit in the story there is another suggestion: if Mary really were black and aristocratic, then her brother John the Beloved/Lazarus/Eliezer would also share the same racial characteristics and blue blood.

Even in the New Testament there are clues about the Magdalene's status. Just as the Queen of Sheba was called 'Makeda' or 'Magda' in Ethiopia, the Bible employs the curious phrasing 'Mary (called *Magda*lene)'. Did the two women, separated by a millennium, essentially share the same title, bestowed on Ethiopian women of rank or 'greatness'? We know that the Magdalene and the other women funded Jesus' mission, which implies that they were wealthy in their own right. Indeed, in that hierarchically minded culture, Mary's name is always given precedence, even though another in the list, Joanna, is married to Herod's chief steward Chuza,[37] from which we might infer that the Magdalene was not only socially superior to the spouse of a major court official, but also financially independent of any man. And it seems she was generous to her lover, for although Jesus famously 'took no thought for tomorrow' and lived off the hospitality of his followers as he travelled around, the fact that the centurions played dice for his clothes in the shadow of the cross suggests they were more costly and covetable than itinerants' rags.

Certainly, Jesus was impressed with the legend of the Queen of Sheba and saw its relevance to his own mission, saying: 'The Queen of the South [Sheba] shall rise up in judgement with this generation, and shall condemn it; for she came from the uttermost parts of the earth to hear the wisdom of Solomon; and behold, a greater than Solomon is here.'[38] If, as seems to be the case, Jesus is referring to himself as 'a greater than Solomon', who among the disciples represented the Queen of Sheba? Who, like Sheba visiting

Solomon, had come 'from the uttermost parts of the earth' to hear his wisdom? It is possible that the comparison with Sheba was not intended to be merely flattering to his beloved companion – presumably sitting on his right hand as he spoke: did Jesus really see Mary as another Queen of the South? If the Gnostic Gospels are to be believed, the male disciples needed a sharp reminder that she was to be taken seriously. Was Jesus really talking about the legendary queen, or threatening the male disciples with 'judgement' by the Magdalene? And on another occasion, he refers to himself as 'the bridegroom', which his Jewish audience would instantly recognize as a reference to Solomon in the *Song of Songs*. Once again, he is deliberately associating himself not only with a king, but also through him with a black queen.

The Gnostics supplied other clues about the nature of Jesus' relationship with Mary, and perhaps also her ethnicity. One of the most infamous names in the history of the early Church was Simon Magus, who was condemned as 'the first heretic', the charlatan who tried to buy the Holy Spirit and whose cheap pagan magic was overwhelmed by the godly power of St Peter. However, this may be yet another example of an early Christian smear campaign, for Simon was in many respects a mirror image of Jesus, performing miracles and being worshipped as a god. At all costs they had to separate the two men in the eyes of the masses – Jesus the Son of God, and Simon the evil one.

The Magus notoriously travelled with a woman called Helen, said to have been a prostitute, whom he called 'First Thought' (*Ennoia*), the Mother of All, or the bodily incarnation of Sophia – just as Mary Magdalene was given the title of 'the All' by Jesus and revered as the embodiment of wisdom in the Gnostic book, the *Pistis Sophia*. Indeed, John Romer in his book *Testament* is explicit about the parallel relationship: 'Helen the Harlot, as the Christians called her, was Simon Magus' Mary Magdalene.'[39]

Simon founded his own sect, based on the concept that Wisdom was a woman – and a whore at that – and through the sacrament of ritual sex, a man might find salvation. But Simon's Helen is also interesting to us for other reasons. As Hugh Schonfield writes: 'the Simonians worshipped Helen as Athena (Goddess of Wisdom), who in turn was identified in Egypt with Isis.'[40] And in this he is joined by Professor Karl Luckert, who states unequivocally that Simon's concept of the First Thought, as incarnated in Helen, can be traced back to Isis.[41]

There is more: an apocryphal source (dated around 185 CE), describes Helen, this mirror image of Mary – in a particularly sexually evocative and tantalizing glimpse – as 'dancing in chains . . .'[42] (Such a spectacle would certainly have brought some excitement to the drab and repressed villages of the first-century Middle East, and it is tempting to speculate that Jesus' group employed similar methods of attracting attention.) More to the point, however, she is specifically described as being '*black as an Ethiopian*',[43] which raises the question as to how exact the parallel was between Helen and the Magdalene. Given the accumulation of other hints and suggestions, there is a case for believing it may have extended to the colour of their skin.

(And according to strictly non-canonical sources, the Magus had another surprise – some might consider it a shock – up his sleeve, which will be discussed in a later chapter.)

## Mari of Magdala
Centuries of Church propaganda have conditioned generations never to question what they believe to be God's word, the scriptures, which cannot therefore lie or even bend the truth a little. But once it is understood that the New Testament is just as much political and religious propaganda as any other set of ancient texts – or modern books for that matter – possible alternative interpretations immediately begin to be suggested. From the fragmentary and often obscure clues already examined, it seems that there is a highly thought-provoking case to be made for an Ethiopian Magdalene, not a prostitute from the shores of Lake Galilee as is generally believed.

The Queen of Sheba's great Arabian city was called Marib, which encompasses the core name for the great goddess – *Mari* – a favourite girl's name in the Near and Middle East. Perhaps the great queen named her city after the goddess of the sea – or it may even have been one of her own forenames or titles, just as Roman emperors appropriated those of the gods. But the link between the name 'Mari/Miriam/Mary' and the classic female deity is too obvious for some: Barbara G. Walker believed that neither Mary

the Mother nor Mary Magdalene really existed because they fit too
neatly into the mythic requirements of the goddess:

> Fathers of the Christian church strongly opposed the worship of
> Mary because they were all aware that she was only a composite
> of Marianne, the Semitic God-Mother and Queen of Heaven;
> Aphrodite-Mari, the Syrian version of Ishtar; Juno the Blessed
> Virgin. Isis as Stella Maris, Star of the Sea; Maya the Oriental
> Virgin Mother of the Redeemer; the Moerae or trinity of Fates,
> and many other versions of the Great Goddess.[44]

But clearly the Magdalene *did* exist, for why should myth-makers
create such an unusually feisty woman and set her in the repressive
background of first-century Palestine, against all their cultural
expectations? Why should the Gnostics invent the awkward fact of
the hostility of Simon Peter? It seems perfectly comprehensible that
a real woman should not only be named Mari after the goddess, but
also be accorded the honour of 'Magda-lene', the 'great' or
'magnificent' one because of her own memorable words and deeds.

But where did Mari the goddess figure, Mary the black Queen of
the South, 'Mary (called Magdalene)' actually come from? As we
have already noted, there is another, perhaps peripheral, link
between Mary Magdalene and Ethiopia. For years a remote rocky
hilltop in the Amhara region of central Ethiopia was called
*Magdala* – and even when it was renamed, the distant flavour of
Jesus' lover remains, for it is now known as Amba *Mariam*. While
the modern Ethiopians are generally devoted to Mary the Mother,
the juxtaposition of both the hill's ancient and modern names
suggest a connection with another Mary altogether. Although it is
extremely difficult to uncover any history of that area before the
mid nineteenth century,[45] it does seem to have had a long association with the Magdalene: raising the question as to whether this was
the original home of Jesus' 'Queen of the South', which she left for
reasons of her own to travel to Bethany – via Egypt – with her
brother 'Lazarus' and her sister Martha.

The process of gradually coaxing a coherent picture out of long-
censored material and half-hidden heresies can be very satisfying,
but it is equally full of pitfalls and only too liable to lead to dead

ends. Tantalizing though it is to piece together a persuasive Ethiopian/Magdalene connection with Grail romances, the Sheba legend and the often elusive magic of toponyms, there are certain annoyingly loose ends. The Black Madonnas may provide pointers to Mary's racial background, but their cult also possesses intimate links with pagan goddesses, especially the Egyptian Isis. Yet the Ethiopian legends – although, perhaps significantly, not the Old Testament – are firm on the point that Solomon persuaded Sheba to convert from her pagan religion to Judaism, so how could an Ethiopian Magdalene, with so many awkward associations with Judaism and Judaea, have become the heretics' much-loved representative of Isis? Although ancient Ethiopia included parts of what we would call Egypt, it is hard to see how the worship of a pagan goddess can be reconciled with the tradition that describes the Queen of Sheba as a Judaic convert.

The Ethiopian legends about her, such as the *Kebra Negast,* state unequivocally that she was originally a worshipper of the sun and moon, but was converted to Solomon's religion.

Superficially, this appears to demolish at a stroke the tentative theory that the Magdalene was part of an Ethiopian goddess-worshipping tradition inspired – or even embodied – by Makeda/Magda, the great Queen of Sheba, ruling out any spiritual trafficking with the Egyptian cult of Isis. However, yet again, all is not quite what it seems, for delving a little deeper reveals an astonishing fact: even the great King Solomon himself was in fact a goddess worshipper . . .

## CHAPTER SEVEN

# The Rise and Fall of God's Wife

The picture of the hidden Magdalene, which is gradually building up from various threads – Gnostic and heretical sources, French legends and Grail stories, the Queen of Sheba, the Black Madonnas and even the Church's own tradition – may be intriguing, even disturbing, but it is also contradictory. While she appears to be some kind of pagan priestess, linked in the minds of the well-travelled Templars and her cult-followers in France with ancient deities, particularly with the Egyptian goddess Isis, she also, undoubtedly, has a Judaic background. Indeed, her role as sexual initiatrix and central participant in the *hieros gamos* seems distinctly at odds with the Ethiopians' legend in which the Queen of Sheba is described as being converted by Solomon to Judaism – and, of course, with the concept of the Magdalene as the Apostle of Jesus' Judaean mission, in the heart of the land of the Jerusalem Temple. How can a pagan, goddess-worshipping Magdalene be reconciled with such a fiercely patriarchal religion?

First, it must be said that the Queen of Sheba's conversion is not explicitly described in the Old Testament, where it might be expected to take pride of place, as evidence of Yahweh's superiority to the pagan worship of the sun and moon – although in *Kings* we read: 'And when the Queen of Sheba heard of the fame of Solomon, concerning the Name of the Lord, she came to prove him with hard questions.'[1] This implies that the whole point of her journey was to seek his religious wisdom, and learn of the ways of Yahweh – and in this, she was not disappointed, for Solomon 'answered all her questions: there was not anything hid from the King, which he told her not'.[2] Clearly, Sheba had been given religious instruction and was initiated into Solomon's form of Judaism, for we read in the *Kebra Negast*, how the king waxed lyrical about his God to the foreign pagan queen, in a paean of personal testimony:

> Verily, it is right that a man should worship God, Who created the Universe, the Heavens and the Earth, the Sea and the Dry Land, the Sun and the Moon, the Stars and the brilliant bodies of the Heavens, the trees and the stones, the beast and the feathered fowls, the GOOD and the EVIL. Him alone we should worship in fear and trembling, with joy and gladness. For He is the Lord of the Universe, the Creator of Angels and Men. It is He who killeth and maketh to live, and inflicteth punishment and showeth compassion, who raiseth up from the ground and who bringeth down. No one can rebuke Him, for He is the Lord of the Universe, and there is no one who can say unto Him: 'What hast thou done?' And unto Him it is right that there should be praise and thanksgiving from angels and men. And verily there hath been given unto us the Tabernacle of the God of Israel, which was created before all Creation be His glorious counsel. And He hath made to come down to us His commandment done in writing so that we may know his decrees and the judgement that He hast ordained in the mountain of his Holiness.[3]

The sincerity and pride rings out clear and strong: no Imam could praise Allah so fulsomely, no fundamentalist Christian laud Jesus Christ to the heavens with more heartfelt fervour. Moreover, the Queen of Sheba's response seems unequivocal:

> From this moment I will not worship the sun, but will worship the Creator of the sun, the God of Israel. And that Tabernacle of the God of Israel shall be unto me My Lady, and my seed after me, and unto all my kingdoms that are under my dominions. And because of this I have found favour before thee, and before the

God of Israel my Creator, who hast brought me unto thee, hast made me to hear thy voice, hast shown me thy face and hast made to understand thy commandments.[4]

Judging from the tone of both Solomon and Sheba's undiluted praise for the God of Israel any putative connection between the foreign queen and a pagan Magdalene seems to recede rapidly into middle distance. But where this particular line of investigation is concerned, perhaps all is not yet lost. Indeed, the possibility swims back into sharp focus with the discovery that, for all his mono-theistic protestations, even the great King Solomon *was also a goddess worshipper,* and by no means such a fervent devotee of the 'one true God' as either the Old Testament or the *Kebra Negast* would have us believe. It seems that the much later Gospel writers did not possess the monopoly of the tendency to embroider, elaborate and use the written word for purposes of religious and political 'spin'.

## The forgotten Feminine
It appears that just as mainstream Christianity rejected the feminine (except for their reluctant and sanitized goddess, the ultimate female eunuch in the form of the Virgin Mary), so Judaism has taken active steps to excise or subsume its own ancient female deities. In his ground-breaking book *The Hebrew Goddess* (enlarged edition, 1990) the American academic Raphael Patai sums up the suspicion of many objective researchers when faced with the apparent anomaly of an ancient religion without a goddess: 'In view of the general human psychologically determined predis-position to believe in and worship goddesses, it would be strange if the Hebrew-Jewish religion, which flourished for centuries in a region of intensive goddess cults, had remained immune to them.'[5] Faced with the image with which Judaism prefers to present itself, Patai continues:

Yet this is precisely the picture one gets when one views Hebrew religion through the polarising prisms of Mosaic legislation and prophetic teaching. God, this view maintains, revealed himself in successive stages to Adam, Noah, Abraham, Isaac and Jacob, and

151

gave his Law to Moses on Mount Sinai. Biblical religion, in this perspective, is universal monotheism, cast in a virtual-legal form.[6]

Patai points out[7] that although God, being pure spirit, is beyond the earthly confines of gender, the Israelites were careful to frame the nature of Yahweh in aggressively and uncompromisingly masculine terms. The One True God became 'Master of the Universe', 'Lord of Hosts' and 'Man of War' and as a result, the role of women in religious observance dwindled into insignificance, and – because love and respect for a great feminine archetype encourages similar feelings for ordinary women – as a result of the departure of the goddess, all things female became suspect and unclean. When Moses sought to prepare the Israelites for the immanence of God's word, he gave them the unequivocal order: 'do not go near any woman',[8,9] which, apart from reinforcing the concept that women are inherently taboo, also implies that the Lord's revelations were not intended for the ears of female members of the tribe. As Karen Armstrong writes in her *The End of Silence: Women and the Priesthood* (1993): 'The holiness of God was deemed incompatible with a woman's presence' and asks the loaded question: 'Have Jewish women never truly been included in the covenant at all?'[10]

However, judging from the discoveries at excavations at Ugarit (modern Ras Shamra), in the north-eastern corner of the Mediterranean, against all expectation women may once have taken pride of place in early Jewish religious practice – for according to inscriptions on fourteenth-century BCE tablets, it was believed that *Yahweh had a bride*. Called unequivocally 'the wife of El' (the Lord) , and even 'Progenitress of the God' – which implies that she preceded him, both chronologically and even metaphorically, in terms of status – the fertility goddess Asherath (or Asherah) appeared to have had a special place in the hearts and minds of her Jewish flock. Certainly, she reigned beside her consort as joint supreme deity for 600 years after the arrival of the Israelite tribes in Canaan,[11] although there were also other unashamedly pagan divinities in the pantheon – including the god Baal, who is so often represented in the Old Testament as a foreign abomination.

Asherah ruled many nearby lands under different names: fourteenth-century BCE tablets from Amarna (comprising of letters from a Canaanite functionary to his overlord, the King of Egypt) reveal that she and the more famous goddess Astarte were interchangeable.[12] Indeed, so entrenched was she in the culture of the time that Elath, on the southern coast of the Gulf of Aqaba may have been named after her,[13] and she even creeps insidiously into the Yahweh-loving Old Testament – for example, in Genesis Leah names her handmaid Zilpah's son *Asher*,[14] although the associations with the great goddess are deliberately left obscure.

## The secret of Solomon

Far from being the proselytizing Yahwist of Judaic propaganda (be it Israelite or Ethiopian in origin), Solomon himself was clearly beguiled by the mysteries of the pagan deities, including the great goddess. The chronicler of his reign rebukes him for having a heart 'that was not whole with Yahweh his god',[15] becoming exercised because the king 'did what was evil in the eyes of Yahweh, and went not fully after Yahweh as did David his father'[16] – a rather different image from that promulgated by either the *Kebra Negast* or Orthodox Jews today. And far from Solomon converting his lover, the Queen of Sheba, to a monotheistic religion, it seems that one of his pagan wives reversed the process: for it was his 'most politically ambitious marriage',[17] to the daughter of a Pharaoh and a Sidonian, that seems to have introduced him to the delights of worshipping 'the Goddess of the Sidonians' – or Asherah, soon to rule beside her spouse, Yahweh. As the American academic William G. Denver writes:

> Recent archaeological discoveries provide both texts and pictorial representations that for the first time clearly identify 'Asherah' as the consort of Yahweh, at least in some circles in ancient Israel . . . We cannot avoid the conclusion that in Israel Yahweh could be closely identified with the cult of Asherah, and in some circles the goddess was actually personified as his consort.[18]

That the ordinary people were familiar with the concept of God's wife is reflected in the common blessing from around the time of Solomon: 'Blessed be [name] by Yahweh and his Asherah',[19] which suggests that the goddess' cult was both widespread and close to the hearts of the Israelites at that time. Even several centuries later, 'ninth-century [BCE] kings set up official fertility cults in her honour, complete with the sacred priestesses'.[20]

However, evidence – if it were now needed – that Solomon himself revered other gods, and especially Asherah, is even found in accounts of the decoration of his legendary Temple, which most people still believe was built to celebrate the glories of Yahweh alone. While private individuals kept small votive statues of the great fertility goddess in their homes or in shrines on hilltops and sacred groves, she entered into the official pantheon through her great stone pillars inside the Temple, which also boasted images of the sacred sun and many 'strange altars'.[21] Despite his carefully honed image, Solomon, it appears, was neither a monotheist nor averse to the psychologically and spiritually balancing love for the supreme goddess.

So powerful a deity was Asherah that it has even been conjectured that the two sacred stones said to be contained by the legendary Ark of the Covenant originally 'represented Yahweh and . . . his female companion'.[22]

Removed in fury by the zealous Yahwist King Asa, these evidences of goddess worship sprang up again, even in the Temple, only to be destroyed more finally by King Hezekiah (727–698 BCE) a century later. Yet for all the repeated attacks on God's wife by zealous misogynists, she managed to survive for a surprising length of time, as Raphael Patai notes:

Of the 370 years during which the Solomonic Temple stood in Jerusalem, for no less than 236 years . . . the statue of Asherah was present in the Temple, and her worship was part of the legitimate religion approved and led by the king, the court, and the priesthood and opposed by only a few prophetic voices crying out against it at relatively long intervals.[23]

Astonishingly, Solomon's Temple also harboured an exotic group of sacred male prostitutes – presumably eunuchs or an alternative form of the more usual female 'temple prostitutes' – who were also destined to be denounced and relegated to the scrapheap of history, together with their Mother Goddess, by the fanatical Yahwist King Asa. The Old Testament describes how:

> Asa did what was right in the eyes of the Lord, as his father David had done. He expelled the male shrine-prostitutes from the land and got rid of all the idols his fathers had made. He even deposed his own grandmother Maacah because she had made a repulsive Asherah pole [a fertility symbol]. Asa cut the pole down and burnt it . . . Although he did not remove the high places [the hilltop shrines to the goddess], Asa's heart was fully committed to the Lord of all his life.[24]

Even the over-zealous Asa baulked at tearing down the people's much-loved nature shrines, just as the Christians of the future millennium would build their churches on the age-old sacred sites of European pagans. (And surely there are other possible reasons for wanting to 'depose' a grandmother, always supposing she had political power and position, as is hinted here.)

## The Queen of Sheba and the night-hag

While mainstream Jews worked hard at banishing the goddess, heretics sought ways to re-establish her, in a process analogous to that whereby the Christian outcasts maintained the significance of Mary Magdalene. A central figure in this campaign was Lilith, believed to be Adam's first wife, who although rapidly relegated to the role of night-hag and succubus by Yahwists, achieved her apotheosis as God's wife in the hands of the medieval Kabbalists. Raphael Patai declares: 'No she-demon has ever achieved as fantastic a career as Lilith, who started out from the lowliest of origins, was a failure as Adam's intended wife, became the paramour of lascivious spirits, rose to be the bride of Samael the Demon King, ruled as Queen of Zemargad and *Sheba* [my emphasis] and ended up as the consort of God himself.'[25]

This fantastic and muddled curriculum vitae suggests some knowledge of a connection between the Queen of Sheba and pagan mysteries, although they are given the usual Judaeo-Christian gloss of devil worship. Indeed, Lilith turns up in the heretics' heartland of the south of France in a particularly thought-provoking context.

155

As A.T. Mann and Jane Lyle write in their cult classic *Sacred Sexuality* (1995): 'In the Pyrenean cathedral of St Bernard-de-Comminges, Lilith has found her way into a church: a carving there depicts a winged, bird-footed woman giving birth to a Dionysian figure, a Green Man.'[26]

According to Flavius Josephus, the first-century Jewish chronicler, the small town of St Bernard-de-Comminges was also the final destination of a clutch of New Testament 'baddies' – including Herod, his harridan wife Herodias and the aristocratic stripper, his stepdaughter Salome, who demanded the head of John the Baptist on a platter. Indeed, there may be a kernel of truth in this, for many rich Judaeans had estates in southern Gaul. Banished to the then Gaulish town of Lugdunum Convenarum, Herod disappeared from history, Salome drowned in a mountain stream (appropriately enough for one who brought about the destruction of the Baptist), and Herodias transmuted into a particularly virulent form of night-hag – in other words, a Lilith. In *The Templar Revelation* we wrote: 'Another colourful Languedocian legend concerns the "Queen of the South" (*Reine du Midi*), a title of the countesses of Toulouse. In folklore, the protectrix of Toulouse is *La Reine Pédaque* (the Goose-foot Queen). This may be a reference in the punning, esoteric "language of the birds" to the Pays d'Oc, but French researchers have identified this figure with the Syrian goddess Anath, who is in turn closely linked with Isis.[27] And there is the obvious association with the bird-footed Lilith.'[28]

There is also the association with that other 'Queen of the South' – the Queen of Sheba – who appears in the external decoration of Chartres cathedral, and who is linked through the Black Madonnas with Mary Magdalene . . . With its background in heretical secrets, coded language and esoteric symbolism, the Languedoc never espoused any historical character without a profound reason. The complex but tantalizing chain of associations – Lilith–Herodias–Sheba–Magdalene – appears to reflect some inside knowledge about goddess worship in the area, involving powerful women with African backgrounds and the tormentors of John the Baptist.

### God's playmate
Even though officially condemned, the goddess refused to go quietly, being metamorphosed into 'angels' or the *shekhina*, a term

found in the Jewish Talmud to denote the manifestation of God on Earth in tangible form, although originally, in the Midrash literature, the Shekhina were separate, *female* entities who embodied wisdom. In this, they were the equivalent of the Greek *Sophia*, who transmutes into Mary Magdalene in the Gnostic Gospels. And like the empowered female Apostle of the Apostles in the *Pistis Sophia*, where she closely questions Jesus on his teaching about those destined for heaven or hell, one of the functions of the Shekhina was to argue 'with God in defense of man', 'prompted by her compassionate nature'.[29] Perhaps curiously, in this at least the Magdalene can be seen to follow a Jewish tradition, although not one that is widely promoted or discussed among orthodox circles.

Although the term 'Shekhina' does not appear in the Bible, similar figures appear in different form, for example, as the character 'Wisdom', who declares ecstatically: 'The Lord brought me forth as the first of his works/before his deeds of old/I was appointed from eternity, from the beginning, before the world began . . . Then I was the craftsman at his side/I was filled with delight in his presence/rejoicing in the whole world and delighting in mankind.'[30]

Described exquisitely as Yahweh's 'playmate',[31] the Shekhina frolicked and skipped through God's realm like a troupe of heavenly Tinkerbells, considered 'to have an opinion, a mind, a will, and a personality of [their] own'.[32] The Shekhina's role is essentially that of Devil's advocate, trying to influence God and change his mind, just as according to the Gnostics, Mary Magdalene persuaded Jesus to be more compassionate towards sinners condemned to hell.[33] These female companions are much beloved by the male divinities, whose doctrines are first tested in the fire of their unique logic. That this age-old tradition was dropped by both the Jewish and Christian patriarchs may imply an underlying fear that God's male ego was being terminally threatened by his too tolerant acceptance of the aggressive harridan by his side. Perhaps her constant questioning seemed rather too much like nagging – after all, it would not do for God to seem hen-pecked. But with the marginalization of the Goddess, God himself lost much of his uniqueness: how could it be otherwise when he was subjected to a determined process in which he was ruthlessly created in man's image?

Paradoxically, without the counter balance of his feminine side God was effectively emasculated, for as the medieval Indian ode has it: 'If Shiva is united with Shakti, he is able to exert his prowess as Lord; if not, the god is not able to stir.'

Once his wife had gone, God became a stressed lone parent, given to fits of uncouth rage and tyrannical demands. Instead of love and compassion, there was fear and trembling, as in the hearts of cowering children who, in the midst of their games, suddenly hear the dread step of their drunken father with his belt in his hand.

Yet the Shekhina survived as the 'Holy Spirit' – of both Judaism and Christianity – implicitly adding a feminine dimension to the otherwise all-male triad of 'The Father, the Son and the Holy Spirit'. And more immediately, where the early Israelites were concerned, she transmuted into the Cherubim, whose image as morbidly obese winged babies in wispy underwear so beloved of the sentimental Victorians owed nothing to their real origins. Indeed, if their true image was more widely known, attitudes to the Judaic roots – and even the origins – of Christianity might be rather different.

## Under their wing

The word Cherubim (Hebrew: *K'rubh*) is now thought to derive from the Akkadian *karibu*, meaning intermediary between God and humankind, although Patai may be nearer the mark with his description of 'female genii', with the implication of slightly wayward sentient entities. Traditionally, Yahweh rode on the Cherubim – especially in their manifestation as feisty mares – a perfect example of pre-Freudian, but nevertheless unequivocal, erotic imagery. Indeed, the Cherubim were intimately associated with sexuality, for even in Solomon's temple there existed the 'graven image' of two Cherubim locked in such a graphically passionate embrace – as representatives of a great sacred mystery – that their very presence acted as quasi-pornographic titillation to the populace, who were reported to have fornicated orgiastically after catching a glimpse of such unashamed sexual licence, when the Cherubim were paraded through the streets in what clearly amounts to pagan ritual. As the American academic Nelson Glueck writes of similar magico-religious scenarios: 'The excitement of pagan worship and participation in feasts of sacrificial offerings apparently often led male and female worshippers to join together in feverish consummation of fertility rites.'[34]

However, representations of the Cherubim often bore striking similarities to other deities whose presence constantly bubbles under the surface of this investigation. Excavations of the palace of King Ahab of Israel (873–852 BCE) in Samaria have uncovered an ivory plaque showing two crouching female forms – allegedly 'Cherubim' – apparently holding lotuses and wearing *Egyptian collars and headcloths*. More significantly, these figures bear solar discs on their heads and have winged arms, exactly the same artistic style as the iconography of the great Egyptian goddess Isis. We already know that Asherah was worshipped in Egypt as Anath, although academics habitually imply that the Egyptians were inspired by the Hebrew goddess, and not the other way round.

In fact, this blindness to the extent of Egypt's influence in the ancient world is so entrenched among historians and archaeologists – even, incredibly, Egyptologists – that it has not only cast a pall over Academe, but also over modern attitudes to race. Surprising and disturbing though this may seem, the widespread state of denial about ancient Egypt's true place in the world has indirectly brought about the complete misunderstanding of Christianity in general and of Jesus, John the Baptist and Mary Magdalene in particular, besides the repression of healthy sexual instincts and the rise of white supremacy across the world.

And much of this profoundly dangerous error concerns the marginalization of the 'Mother of God', the first 'Star of the Sea', 'Queen of Heaven' and the original 'Black Madonna' – Isis, consort and sister of the dying-and-rising god Osiris and mother of the magical child-god Horus. Intimately associated with the dark goddess Nepthys, the goddess of love and motherhood Hathor and the supreme ruler of eternal justice Ma'at, Isis was the direct precursor of the Virgin Mary, whose sanctity was decided – or even invented – by a Vatican council. Embedded in the story of the hijacking of Isis and the denial of the power of Egypt is the lone figure of Mary Magdalene, fighting like the goddess herself for recognition in a cold-hearted, white European patriarchy.

CHAPTER EIGHT

# Resurrecting Egypt

In the minds of virtually all educated people today civilization as we know it came from ancient Greece, with its proto-democracy, famous philosophers, great poets, writers and orators and of course its highly influential and, indeed, beautiful language. The glories that were Greece formed an integral part of the aristocratic Grand Tour, and even now we think of that ancient culture as so rarefied and intrinsically admirable as to be almost beyond question. Yet this golden age did not leap fully formed from the mind of the gods: as even the Greeks themselves admitted, their own culture had arisen only because of colonization by Phoenicians and Egyptians around 1500 BCE – indeed, the Greek language contains clear evidence of 'borrowings' from Egyptian, and references to the original mother land appear in several Greek plays.[1]

The historical realm of the Pharaohs, with its enduring wonders of the ancient world, the Pyramids of Giza, is still widely seen as having been a backward country (who nevertheless managed to build the pyramids with the most primitive of tools), without any lasting legacy – and a rather embarrassing religion, with its pathetic emphasis on death and the afterlife – although, as we have seen, it clearly influenced the more obviously seminal Judaism with the Isis-like Cherubim and the associated female deities that decorated Solomon's Temple for so many years. Indeed, as many writers have pointed out,[2] Judaism owes a much more enduring debt to its

161

former slave-masters, for when Yahweh gave Moses[3] the Ten Commandments he had clearly been reading *The Egyptian Book of the Dead* (more properly known as *Chapters of Coming Forth By Day*). Spell 125 contains the so-called 'Negative Confession', or 'Declaration of Innocence', which the post-mortem spirit speaks before the gods in the Hall of Judgement, and which includes the familiar words:

I have done no falsehood . . . I have not robbed . . . I have not killed men . . . I have not committed perjury . . . I have not [sexually] misconducted myself... I have done no wrong. I have seen no evil . . . I have not reviled God . . . I am not wealthy except with my own property . . . I have not blasphemed God in my city . . .[4]

Clearly, God had decided to improve on the Egyptians' voluntary statement of innocence by turning it into commandments from on high. Yet there is a general feeling among academics that although Egypt may still yield up many treasures from its shifting sands, only gullible New Agers and inconsequential alternative writers are really interested in what people of that ancient land had to say.

Despite the low opinion of Egypt's culture, its religion in its purest form, that of the priesthood at Heliopolis,[5] contained many astounding secrets – a fact that is barely acknowledged even among those whose unwillingness to accept unquestioningly the academic certainties propel them unerringly in the direction of ancient Egypt. As Clive and I wrote in *The Stargate Conspiracy* (1999):

The priesthood of Heliopolis was famed for its learning and wisdom. Two of its greatest achievements were in the fields of medicine and astronomy – its high priests held the title 'Greatest of Seers', generally understood to mean 'Chief Astronomer'.[6] Its priests were still regarded as the wisest and most learned in Egypt at the time of Herodotus (fifth century BCE) and even remembered in Strabo's day, as late as the first century CE. The priesthood was even famed among the Greeks, and it is said that, among others, Pythagoras, Plato, Eudoxus and Thales went to Heliopolis to study. And although we know few of the names of the great Egyptians who were its graduates, we do know that Imhotep, the genius who designed the first pyramid – the Step Pyramid of Djoser at Saqqara – and was venerated as a god for his medical knowledge, was a High Priest there.[7,8]

We added: 'Significantly, the priesthood probably included women. An inscription of the Fourth Dynasty, roughly contemporary with the Giza pyramids, refers to a woman in the Temple of Thoth holding the title "Mistress of the House of Books".[9] In fact, although by today's standards still constrained, the women of ancient Egypt were the freest in the known world, being seen as separate entities – both legally and morally – from the menfolk in their lives, and were permitted to own property and obtain divorces. It was an ideally suited milieu in which intelligent and independent women such as the Magdalene might live and move and have their being, and represented a diametrically opposed attitude to that of even relatively relaxed areas such as cosmopolitan Galilee.

The priests and priestesses of Heliopolis saw all knowledge as not only desirable but God-given. To them – as to their later admirers in Renaissance Europe – there was essentially no difference between what we would call the study of magic and that of theology and science. All categories of information blended fluidly together to the greater glory of both man and gods. From this swirling mass of potential came great astronomical knowledge, which found expression in the Pyramid Texts (the first of which, in the pyramid of Unas, dates from around 2350 BCE, although there is evidence that a version of them existed as early as 3100 BCE[10]), making them the oldest surviving scriptures in the world.[11]

Central to the Heliopolitan theology was the story of creation, in which the first god Atum masturbated himself to an explosive ejaculation, which caused the birth of the stars and planets. Long dismissed as a primitive – not to say embarrassing – myth, to objective modern eyes it contains more than a hint of intelligent deduction, or even astonishing secret knowledge. As we pointed out in our previous book:

An objective reading of the Pyramid Texts reveals much more than poetic symbolism. For example, its system of creation is a remarkable parallel to modern physicists' conception of the creation and evolution of the Universe. It literally describes the 'Big Bang', in which all matter explodes from a point of singularity and then expands and unfolds, becoming more complex as fundamental forces come into being and interact, finally reaching the level of elemental matter ... The system also includes the concept of a multidimensional universe, represented by the different levels of creation as embodied in the god forms.[12]

That these insights represented more than a coincidental reflection of modern cosmological knowledge was revealed when the NASA team led by Lou Allamandola published its findings into the origins and requirements of life in the universe in the late 1990s.[13] Whereas it had always proved impossible to assemble the basic ingredients with which to create even the most primitive form of life in laboratory conditions on earth, it was exceptionally easy to create some of the complex molecules necessary for the process in laboratory conditions similar to those found inside clouds of interstellar gas. Did the myth of Atum's explosive orgasm conceal sophisticated knowledge about the 'seeding' of the universe from a point of singularity in which all the necessary ingredients were already present?[14] Were the allegedly primitive and embarrassing Egyptians in fact extremely sophisticated cosmologists and inspired thinkers? Certainly, this seems to be the case, but instead of celebrating their remarkable ancient wisdom, academics ignore them in favour of the prolix literary Greeks, despite the fact that the construction of the pyramids remains largely unexplained – and certainly unmatched. Why? What is the reason for this underlying distaste for Egypt and all its wondrous works?

## A disturbing secret

Despite the unavoidable majesty of the pyramids, as soon as archaeology became a recognized discipline – a process that began in late eighteenth-century Europe – Egypt has failed to win praise and admiration for its achievements among academics for one simple, if profoundly distasteful, reason. As Martin Bernal writes in his monumental and inspired tome *Black Athena: Volume I* (1987): 'For 18th- and 19th-century Romantics and racists it was simply intolerable for Greece, which was seen not merely as the epitome of Europe but also its pure childhood, to have been the result of the mixture of native Europeans and colonizing Africans and Semites . . .'[15]

In other words, because Egypt was essentially *African*, it could not be allowed to have any intellectual achievements worth studying – whereas white patriarchal Greece seemed like a home from home to the European historians, a culture worthy of giving birth to *us*. (And even though most modern academics would furiously deny there was even the slightest element of racial undertones in their work, the fact remains that modern scholarship is built on hundreds of years of blatant racial prejudice.) Whatever the truth, because of this bias, the facts were revised to be racially acceptable, even though, as Bernal states: 'Egyptian civilisation is clearly based on the rich Pre-dynastic cultures of Upper Egypt and Nubia, whose African origin is uncontested.'[16]

Even when Egypt is taken seriously, its black roots are sanitized for public consumption, as in the case of R. A. Schwaller de Lubicz, the Alsatian Egyptologist who is still so revered among alternative writers and their public. In the 1920s he wrote in *Les Veilleurs* (*The Watchers*), the journal he founded: 'there is an insurmountable partition between one race and another',[17] and denied vehemently that apart from a few notable exceptions, 'there are no *blacks* [his emphasis] properly so called [in dynastic Egypt]'.[18] This is absurd, for archaeological evidence has demonstrated conclusively that the ancient Egyptian people boasted several different races, including those who were undeniably black.[19] Objective visitors can even discern distinctly African features on the face of the Sphinx.

In fact, Schwaller de Lubicz was a fervent fascist who went on to inspire Hitler's mystically-minded deputy, Rudolf Hess – and even helped design the uniform of the SA, the forerunners of the SS, who were instrumental in the Führer's rise to power. Yet de Lubicz and his associates have had immense influence on modern thinking about ancient Egypt – with the implicit rubric that the country can only be worthy of study if those inconvenient black faces are denied their place in the ancient world's hall of fame.

Elements of Egyptian life and thought that should be seen as noble have been dragged in the dirt by racist academics who see any black African influence as contaminating. Although even relatively cursory attention to the Egyptian religion reveals that despite the many gods (some of them curiously animal-headed) it was actually a monotheistic system, this 'zoolatry' was dismissed with an arrogant shudder as 'Negro fetishism',[20] although as Martin Bernal points out, he could find no 'eighteenth- or, for that matter, twentieth-century references suggesting the obvious thought that the "Negro fetishes" themselves could have had symbolic or allegorical functions . . .' He adds sadly, or perhaps incredulously, 'Such is the power of racism!'[21]

(Even here the Egyptians were by no means as unsophisticated as they might appear to be, for their many gods were merely different aspects of the One True God, just as the pantheon of Catholic saints are patrons of various forms of human endeavour. While calling upon several gods – some extremely obscure – the central character of the *Egyptian Book of the Dead* liberally peppers his posthumous invocations with phrases such as 'Sole Lord . . . the Great God who lives by truth' and 'the Great God', and, in the Confession of Innocence given above, he declares that he has 'not blasphemed God in the city'. Clearly, the average Egyptian had no difficulty in reconciling the apparently over-stuffed pantheon with one absolute deity.)

Up until relatively recently, scholars took for granted the white supremacist opinion of the likes of Count J.A. de Gobineau, the nineteenth-century precursor of de Lubicz, who wrote:

The black variety [of humankind] is the lowest and lies at the bottom of the ladder. The animal character lent to its basic form imposes its destiny from the moment of conception. It never leaves the most restricted intellectual zones . . . If its faculties for thinking are mediocre or even nonexistent, it possesses in its desire and as a consequence in its will an intensity that is often terrible. Many of the senses are developed with a vigour unknown in the other two races: principally taste and smell. It is precisely in the greed for sensations that the most striking mark of its inferiority is found.[22]

Bernal applies a psychological rule of thumb to the situation that existed between the pre-twentieth century scholars and the idea of a black Egypt, writing: 'If Europeans were treating Blacks as badly as they did throughout the nineteenth century, Blacks had to be turned into animals or, at best, sub-humans; the noble Caucasian was incapable of treating other full humans in such ways.'[23] Just as the 'noble' Aryan Nazis tortured, starved and massacred millions of Jews, gypsies, Slavs and other allegedly racially impure groups on the grounds that they were 'sub-human' and therefore undeserving of the slightest humanity or compassion, so the Europeans felt they could treat black Africans in ways that still cry out for justice because they, too, were deemed not really human.

Bernal then goes in for the kill, brilliantly summarizing the perverse logic of the racist scholars in these words [his emphasis throughout]: *'If it had been scientifically "proved" that Blacks were biologically incapable of civilization, how could one explain Ancient Egypt – which was inconveniently placed on the African continent?'* [24/25] Faced with this problem of Egyptian blackness, there were – according to Bernal – three solutions for the scholars:

> The first was to deny that the Ancient Egyptians were black; the second was to deny that the Ancient Egyptians had created a 'true' civilization; the third was to make doubly sure by denying both. The last has been preferred by most nineteenth- and twentieth-century historians.[26]

Things are changing slowly, and with a sense of wonderment, as the great achievements of the African continent begin to emerge from the long winter of European denial. Just as the native people of Australia were said not to have noticed Captain Cook's ships because their brains had no frame of reference with which to interpret the sight (and similarly, visitors to Leonardo's great works fail to spot even the strangest anomalies), so Academe failed to notice that there was such a thing as black civilization.

It is heartening to notice that Dr Patrick Darling, who led the British team on its excavations of the putative burial place of the Queen of Sheba at Eredo in Nigeria, remarked: 'What is exciting about this for me is that we are beginning to bring out the tremendous political and cultural achievements of black Africa',[27] adding that Eredo could become Nigeria's first world heritage site, joining monuments like Stonehenge in the UK and the pyramids of Egypt.

The Queen of Sheba was linked not only to Arabia, but also to both Ethiopia and Nigeria (and some even believe she could have had a palace in Zimbabwe). And of course the first-century Jewish chronicler Flavius Josephus in which he describes Solomon's lover as 'Queen of Egypt and Ethiopia' – if nothing else, providing a double connection with sophisticated blackness, which seems to be reflected, once again, in the life of the Magdalene . . . From snippets and hints, from tiny clues and ancient traditions, we find all roads ultimately leading to magnificent but maligned Egypt in the tumultuous first century.

## The Egyptian mission

The New Testament tells how Mary, Joseph and the infant Jesus fled Herod's persecution into the nearby country of Egypt. We know nothing of their lives there, but they would certainly have felt at home, for as we have seen, there were several flourishing Jewish communities scattered around the country – indeed, the only Temple outside Jerusalem was built at Leontopolis in the Nile delta – particularly in the great melting pot of the ancient seaport of Alexandria, where Jews occupied two of its five major districts. It was a bustling, cosmopolitan city, a typical theatre audience there being described by Dion Chrystostom the Orator as including: '. . . not only Greeks and Italians, but also Syrians, Libyans, Cilicians and yet others from farther countries – Ethiopians, Arabs, as well as Bactrians, Scythians, Persians and a few Indians'. The Jewish colony lived in the east of the city, and included – surprisingly, perhaps – the alleged forerunner of Christ himself, John the Baptist. Perhaps one of the Ethiopians who made their home in Alexandria was 'Mary (called Magdalene)', finding fulfilment and excitement among fellow black priestesses such as Simon Magus' Helen, who danced so spectacularly – and distinctly shamanically – in chains.

Yet the religion of Roman Egypt was very different from that of the pyramid age, for on the whole its magic and majesty had been long lost, its resounding invocations dwindling to so much meaningless verbiage. That there was a deeply embedded sense that in future time the ancient religion would fall apart is evidenced from the *Lament*, from one of the *Hermetic Texts:*

There will come a time when it will be seen that in vain have the Egyptians honoured the divinity with pious minds and with assiduous service. All their holy worship will become inefficacious. The gods leaving the earth will go back to heaven; they will abandon Egypt; this land, once the home of religion, will be widowed of its gods and left destitute. Strangers will fill this country, and not only will there no longer be care for religious observances but, a yet more painful thing, it will be laid down under so-called laws, under pain of punishments, that all must abstain from acts of piety or cult towards the gods . . . The Scythian or the Indian, or some such barbarous neighbour, will establish himself in Egypt.

Clearly, there was a great fear of a time when the beloved old gods would no longer be welcomed in Egypt, although the writer of the *Lament* could not possibly have known that the reign of new, hybrid gods would straddle the time of the ancient deities and the unimaginably different future. In the years following the death of Alexander the Great in 323 BCE, Ptolemy I Soter – the first of the Macedonian kings to rule Egypt (323–283 BCE) – introduced a new god, a blend of Osiris and the bull-god Apis, who had a cult centre at ancient Memphis. This new creation was Serapis, who also came to be associated with the god of healing, Asclepius, and with the underworld dying-and -rising gods Pluto and Dionysus. Although Serapis was a cynical invention whose purpose was to unite the Greek and Egyptian population of Alexandria under the patronage of a new god, he soon had a devoted following, mainly because he was seen as the companion of the beloved ancient goddess Isis. With her an intrinsic part of the new religion, he could hardly fail. Indeed, the author Macrobius wrote: 'In the city on the borders of Egypt which boasts Alexander of Macedonia as its founder, Serapis and Isis are worshipped with a reverence that is almost fanatical . . . '[28]

Serapis was pictured as a very masculine riverine god, with abundant curly hair and beard, and a basket – exoterically said to be of grain, but actually of mysteries – balanced on his head, from which the initiate might pluck great and rapturous secrets. On a more mundane level, Serapis became inseparably associated with the glories of knowledge, for the great Serapeum that dominated the narrow lanes of Rakotis, the native quarter of Alexandria, contained the world-famous library that was said to contain more than 42,000 scrolls on a huge variety of subjects. This undoubted wonder of the world fell victim to the conflict between Christians and pagans, which in 389 CE caused the Temple of Serapis at Canopus (Abou-Qir) to be destroyed, followed in 391 by the annihilation of the Alexandrian temple/library on the orders of the Roman Emperor Theodosius, who saw it as the last stand of the Egyptian pagans. Fourteen years later, the Neo-Platonist mathematician and the last person known to have taught at the Library School (the Mouseion), a gifted woman named Hypatia, was murdered, marking the end of paganism in the city of Alexandria.

The reaction against the association between learning and paganism – and, incidentally, with learned women like Hypatia – was to underpin the long bleak years of the Dark Ages, when ignorance was encouraged and the institutionalized repression of women was to give way to the active horrors of the medieval witch hysteria. It is interesting to note that it was the late nineteenth century before the first European women were legally permitted to enjoy a college education, and – in Britain, certainly – well into the twentieth century before they could graduate from university. We had fallen a long way since the days of Hypatia, and even before her, since the era of the anonymous 'Mistress of the House of Books' at the theological college of pagan Heliopolis. When the Serapeum went up in smoke, it signalled the death of hope for many future generations.

Yet all that was a mere black spot on the distant horizon when Serapis was first invented (in a move with remarkable parallels with the Church's progressive creation of various aspects of Jesus' life). The new god and his female companion were allowed their moment of glory first. Both Serapis and Isis were believed to appear to their followers in ecstatic dreams. Lucius Apuleius, a passionate devotee of the goddess, describes how he was blessed by a dream of rapture:

All the perfumes of Arabia floated into my nostrils as the Goddess deigned to address me: 'You see me here, Lucius, in answer to your prayer. I am Nature, the universal Mother, mistress of all the elements, primordial child of time, sovereign of all things spiritual, queen of the dead, queen also of the immortals, the single manifestation of all gods and goddesses that are . . . Though I am worshipped in many aspects, known by countless names, and propitiated with all manner of different rites, yet the whole round earth venerates me . . . call me by my true name, namely, Queen Isis.'[29]

Buried in this speech – which, although allegedly spoken by the goddess herself in dream-form, may be taken to encompass traditional concepts about her – are two points worth noting. She describes herself as the 'single manifestation of all gods and goddesses that are' – which may simply be a manifestation of divine vanity, but it is also an expression of basic Egyptian monotheism. Clearly, this female archetype would suit the most demanding of today's feminist worshippers, presenting God as Mother with power and pride and not the semi-apologetic tones of the Church of England's 'inclusive language' prayer book.

But Isis also declares that she is 'queen of the dead', an age-old function that finds an echo in the Magdalene's visit to the dead Jesus with her spices to anoint his body for burial. And of course she had already anointed him as sacred king with her jar of costly spikenard in a ritual that was beyond the understanding of the male disciples. *The Egyptian Book of the Dead* has Isis declaring 'I am mistress of the Enneads [the nine major gods], the Lady of All';[30] 'the woman who lightens darkness'[31] and 'the Lady of Light',[32] prefiguring the titles and attributes of Mary Magdalene in her role as Christianity's black goddess.

Paradoxically, the new cult of Serapis revivified the ancient worship of Isis, and inspired an entirely new approach to religion in Egypt – for missionaries were sent out beyond its borders for the first time in history at that time, spreading the word about Serapis and the Mother Goddess. As R. Merkelbach, writing in the seminal 1970s' partwork *Man, Myth & Magic,* says: 'It is clear that the "church" of Isis had a mission during the imperial period . . . There is therefore no doubt that propaganda was being spread.'[33] It is no accident that this religious phenomenon coincided precisely with the era of the missions of Jesus, the Magdalene and the Baptist, all of whom had some connection with Egypt.

Jesus, in particular, was supposed to be linked with that country, for did Yahweh not state that 'out of Egypt have I called my son'?[34] This resonant phrase surfaced again in Matthew's gospel to support the significance of the Holy Family's flight into Egypt,[35] and underline Jesus' role as chosen one, the long-prophesied Messiah – despite the fact that even just the use of the past tense reveals it was never intended to be a prophecy. Was the passage some kind of a hint about a deeper Egyptian connection? American academic Professor Karl Luckert asks:

Has this brief addendum to the nativity tradition of Christ Jesus been intended to hint at the broader nativity of Christian theology in Egypt? Did some of the first Christians actually sense the Egyptian direction into which their theologizing tended to move? A turning point in sacred Jewish history, an exodus in reverse from Palestine to Egypt, is implied even in the surface meaning of the story.[36]

But even if Matthew had fabricated the flight into Egypt to give Jesus an Old Testament pedigree, there is abundant evidence that the fledgling Christ had spent quite some time in that country – even to suggest that, although ethically he may well have been a Jew, his whole mind-set was not Judaean as widely believed, but basically Egyptian. When he writes in sand, walks on water and raises the dead; when he says 'Come to me all you who are burdened, and I will refresh you', or speaks of his 'father's house' having 'many mansions', and when he is portrayed as dying and rising again, there is no doubt that Jesus is echoing the beliefs and practices of Egypt, not the traditions of the Jerusalem Temple.

In tracing Christ's true background, piecing it together from the usual fragmentary clues and the sterling work of certain ground-breaking scholars, some astonishing – and even profoundly shocking – secrets are revealed. Suddenly the man who may have been God, or at least the embodiment of human love and compassion, is seen as someone less than laudable, and certainly no universal role model. If we thought we knew Christ, the man that emerges from this deconstruction is unrecognizable, yet the sources that yield him up are very largely the same that have persuaded millions of devout Christians that he is the god to die for. What is different is that while believers are conditioned not to see what threatens their position, we will acknowledge the uncomfortable nuances that change the sunlit Sunday School pictures into something much darker and more disturbing. Be prepared to discover Jesus the stranger.

## CHAPTER NINE

# The Jesus Myth Exposed

Liberal Christians may be gradually returning to a form of goddess worship with the advent of 'inclusive language' Bibles and prayer books, and many educated churchgoers no longer believe in a literal Virgin Birth and Christ's resurrection from the dead, but it would be wrong to claim that the same general picture pertains among the universal Church. To millions of Christians – especially Roman Catholics – essentially nothing has changed over the centuries: Jesus is still god incarnate, born of a life-long Virgin, who was incarnated as a Jew; whose coming made sense of John the Baptist's entire life up to the point at which they met on the banks of the River Jordan. Jesus called twelve male disciples to him; was betrayed, denied and killed on the cross to atone for our sins, and miraculously rose again two days later. It is axiomatic that he never had sex, married or fathered children and embodied the apotheosis of opposition to paganism, occultism and magic tricks. Questions are not encouraged, even the more obvious ones such as those that arise from the problem with the Christian concept of Atonement: if Jesus died to save us from our sins, why do we still have to be baptized to wash them away and even then answer for them on the terrible Day of Judgement? Just what effect did Jesus' death have on our personal burden of guilt? Yet the entire edifice of Christianity is built on foundations that are just as shaky as the Atonement 'logic', and on what amounts to the most blatant propaganda on behalf of certain vested interests.

## A question of history

Although it might be thought that the so-called heretical books are the only repository of an alternative view of Christ, in fact the four New Testament Gospels themselves provide many clues as to the true background of the man they call Lord, beginning with the beguiling story of the Nativity, one of the most familiar – and best loved – in the world. It describes how Joseph and his young wife Mary (who was on the brink of giving birth) travelled to Bethlehem to take part in a Roman tax census, but, finding all the inns were fully occupied, had to make do with a stable, in which Jesus was born. Angels alerted shepherds to the birth of the holy child, and three wise men followed a new star to the stable, where they fell down in adoration, presenting their gifts of gold (except in Leonardo's *Adoration of the Magi* in which it is conspicuous by its absence), frankincense and myrrh. They then left, taking a different route in order to avoid the attentions of Herod. This cosy tale never fails to lighten the depressing dank days of late December, with its message of renewed hope and joy expressed in the simple poetry and poignant melodies of the time-honoured Christmas carols. Who among Christians can forget the strange sense of wonderment as a child when confronted with the Nativity scene at church, the straw-strewn stable with the serene veiled Virgin and swaddled child, the token Joseph inscrutable behind his beard, the uniquely fragrant and docile animals and the shepherds and magi kneeling in adoration? Candles, incense and a profound feeling of calm tinged with a feeling of magic remain the abiding memory for many, and a sense of time standing still, as if sharing in that story momentarily unites all Christians across the ages in a kind of happy innocence. A halo shines protectively over the whole scene and lights up something ancient, trusting and longing inside. Unfortunately, there is not a word of truth in any of it.

As Desmond Stewart remarks drily in his 1981 work *The Foreigner*: 'A guiding star may work on a Christmas card but could conduct no travellers on real land to a particular house. Other details, whether charming, bizarre or contradictory, illustrate temperament or editorial purpose in these gospel writers.'[1] And, as we have seen, all the many other dying-and-rising gods also shared Jesus' birthday at the Winter Solstice, although when the pope finally announced that Jesus was not born on that day after all, this caused widespread astonishment. The fact that this amendment came as late as 1994 is breath-taking. However, the pope did not elaborate on this theme for obvious reasons: it would not have appealed to his flock to know that Osiris, Tammuz Adonis, Dionysus, Attis, Orpheus and (some versions of) Serapis were not only born on the Winter Solstice, but clearly their mothers, too, had problems with over-booked hotels, for their births also took place in humble circumstances, such as caves, where they were attended by shepherds and wise men bringing expensive symbolic gifts. These pagan gods were given very familiar titles such as 'Saviour of Mankind' and 'Good Shepherd' – although these were not the sole preserve of male deities, for Isis also bore these titles, besides those later appropriated for the Virgin Mary. Some of the elements in the Nativity story were even taken from the birth-myths of the Emperor-god Nero.[2]

Such clear and plentiful correspondences between the Christian story and the myths of many other ancient gods inevitably raise suspicions about the intrinsic authenticity of Jesus and his mission. There are those – such as authors Timothy Freke and Peter Gandy[3] – who see the myriad pagan associations in the Jesus/Virgin story as clear evidence that it was all a fabrication, purely and simply a new version of the usual dying-and-rising god story. However, this is by no means a new idea. The concept of the 'Jesus myth' was popular among nineteenth-century German scholars, and continues to resurface from time to time. One of the most learned expositions of this argument was J. M. Robertson's book *Pagan Christs*, originally published in 1903, although recently relaunched in an abridged version with an introduction by Hector Hawton, who writes: 'no one seriously claims that Adonis, Attis and Osiris were historical characters . . . why, then, is an exception made of the alleged founder of Christianity?'[4]

Robertson writes:

> The Christian myth grew by absorbing details from pagan cults . . .
> Like the image of the child-god in the cult of Dionysus, he was
> pictured in swaddling clothes in a basket manger. He was born in a
> stable like Horus – the stable-temple of the Virgin goddess Isis,

queen of heaven. Again like Dionysus, he turned water into wine; like Aesculapius, he raised men from the dead and gave sight to the blind; and like Attis and Adonis, he is mourned and rejoiced over by women. His resurrection took place, like that of Mithras, from a rock-tomb . . .[5]

Although it is astonishing that Robertson's radical ideas did not cause a furore among the English-speaking world in the more god-fearing and reverential era of the 1900s, they still have the power to unsettle and destabilize the old certainties about Jesus' divine uniqueness. He writes: 'Like Christ, and like Adonis and Attis, Osiris and Dionysus also suffer and rise again. To become one with them is the mystical passion of their worshippers. They are all alike in that their mysteries give immortality. From Mithraism Christ takes the symbolic keys of heaven and assumes the function of the virgin-born Saoshayant, the destroyer of the Evil One . . . In fundamentals, therefore, Christism is but paganism reshaped.'[6]

Robertson then twists the knife in the wound, declaring categorically that: 'There is not a concept associated with Christ that is not common to some or all of the Saviour cults of antiquity.' Indeed, he might have added that even in Solomon's temple in the days of Ezekiel, the women sat by the northern gate weeping for the dying-and-rising god Tammuz,[7] who was so revered centuries later that even one of Jesus' disciples, and possibly even his own twin brother – 'Thomas' – was named after him.

Authors Timothy Freke and Peter Gandy begin their 1999 book *The Jesus Mysteries*, subtitled: *Was the Original Jesus a Pagan God?* with a list of the similarities between Jesus' life and teachings and those of the archetypal dying-and-rising god to whom they given the composite name 'Osiris-Dionysus', which include:

• His father is God and his mother a mortal virgin.
[. . .]
• He rides triumphantly into town on a donkey while people wave palm leaves to honour him.
• He dies at Eastertime as a sacrifice for the sins of the world.[8]

To those authors the associations between Jesus and all those other

178

gods is too close to allow any other explanation than the idea that he never existed, but was created from the myths of pagan gods.

On the surface it does seem as if the pagan links militate against a historical Jesus – the ultimate dying-and-rising god who was born of a goddess in her Virgin phase, and whose birth and subsequent life and death mirrored almost exactly those of the gods of antiquity. However, there are several arguments against this theory: first, why invent yet another dying-and-rising god when the new Scrapis cult had successfully fulfilled that need? Why create a god whose disciples were known to exist, some of whom professed to have met him? Not all of them were liars and cynical myth-makers. Why invent the only dying-and-rising god without a female consort? Although the Magdalene is associated with Sophia in the Gnostic texts, the first Christian propaganda was the androcentric writings of Paul, who is credited with the invention of much of the religion – and there is nothing there that can possibly be construed as a goddess figure. And finally, those who wished to fabricate a god would hardly make him so contradictory and – as we will see – also the possessor of a rather unpleasant streak.

Although undoubtedly Jesus was in most respects interchangeable with other dying-and rising gods, an acquaintance with pagan myths might have inspired him to borrow their trappings in order to seem more powerful and appealing – for he had spent some time in Egypt and was presumably well-informed on the subject. Besides, his disciples – perhaps the shadowy Bethany family – seemed keen to promote him in this way, ensuring that the donkey was waiting for him on which he would ride into Jerusalem. It seems both Jesus and those closest to him in his movement – and all the evidence suggests that the usual twelve disciples are not that inner circle – was basically *pagan* in their attitude, which may owe much to the Egyptian connection. The real Jesus and the pagan god appear to take turns to speak in the pages of the Bible, often with disturbing results.

In some passages of the New Testament the ancient god speaks, but in others it is the voice of a very human, and not particularly admirable, itinerant cult leader. A real man is hidden among the morass of pagan associations, and that man became – wittingly or unwittingly – the human incarnation of the divine. While the god is what is remembered, loved and worshipped, the man is ignored for fear he will destroy the carefully constructed power-base of the Church. Yet he is still there, hidden in the words of the New Testament, flatly contradicting the gloss of the divine image time and time again. The Christ of faith is alarmingly at odds with the Jesus of history.

Besides, a certain group who honoured John the Baptist, who himself figures in Josephus' chronicles, knew of the real Jesus (Yeshu/Yeshua) and clearly was not impressed: as we shall see in the next chapter, its descendants loathe him to this day . . . It does seem as if, even against the odds, there *was* a man called Jesus whose life did match in certain curious ways those of the mythical gods. Rejecting the Christian apologists' pronouncement that this was so because he came to fulfil the role of saviour god – which, up to that time had, according to them, suffered from the grotesque parody of the likes of Osiris – as profoundly unlikely and distinctly pathetic, there are other reasons for Jesus' suspiciously pagan words and deeds. And foremost among which is the probability that *he was a pagan himself,* and deliberately working to the script of non-Jewish mystery plays, the time-honoured story of the lives of the gods, just as there is evidence that he also incorporated certain Messianic elements into his *modus operandi* (such as riding into Jerusalem on a donkey, to fulfil the Old Testament prophecy.) This was a man who was not a god, but seems to be determined to make his life reflect the ancient myths of gods.

Why he would choose to do this and thereby put not only his own life but those of his followers in danger is, and can only ever be, a matter for conjecture. Perhaps he was acting on the orders of a shadowy group who essentially set him up as sacred king/sacrificial god/Messiah – an agenda that may have been that of the wealthy and influential Bethany family, as some researchers have suggested.[9] Or the historical Jesus may have suffered from the same Messianic delusion as the hundreds of others who ended up stoned by the Jews or crucified by the Romans, a form of mental illness that combined a *folie de grandeur* with a desire for martyrdom. He may have come out of Egypt as a missionary for Serapis/Isis – many did, but only in that little window of history – together with his 'goddess' Mary Magdalene and others. Once back in the country of his ancestors the temptation to impress his personality on the people may have been too great, and he may have found himself caught up in a heady mix of Messianic expectation and religious glory from which there was, ultimately, no escape. As God he has demanded our love and worship, but as a man he may well deserve our pity and compassion.

## Mary the outcast

Absolutely central to the Catholic faith is the belief that Jesus' mother was a virgin who miraculously conceived through the means of the Holy Spirit (which is interesting in itself, for as we have seen, the Holy Spirit is a form of the Judaic Shekhina, which is *female*), but this, too, was not unique in the annals of divine nativities. As many Greek myths described how gods took a perverse delight in 'slumming it' with mortal women, this aspect of the story would have come as no surprise to most contemporary pagans, although they might have been taken aback by the concept that Mary was a real woman, so real that she might be pointed out across the street. If Jesus really existed, and it seems that he did, he must have had a mother and her name could well have been Mary (Mari or Miriam). But was this living, breathing woman also a real – and, as the Church asserts – life-long, virgin?

Her allegedly unique sexual status was useful in establishing her son's divinity, for Isaiah seems to lay this down as a prophetic prerequisite for the birth of the Chosen One: 'Therefore the Lord himself will give you a sign: the virgin will be with child and will give birth to a son, and will call him Immanuel[10] [or "God with us"]'. But as Desmond Stewart points out, both the Old and New Testaments' translation is incorrect: neither should be 'virgin', but 'young woman' or 'maiden'.[11] And of course, as we have already noted, not only does the Nag Hammadi *Gospel of Thomas* state that Jesus had a twin brother, but Mary went on to have other children,[12,13] presumably by Joseph, the older man who was said to have married her while she was pregnant with Jesus in order to conceal her 'shame' – for the average Jew could not be expected to know about God's involvement in her increasingly obvious bump, and clearly thought the worst of her for it. In fact, the average Jew may well have been right in his or her assumption, for in the cold light of historical reality, Jesus may well have been a *mamzer*, or bastard. (The mind's eye is irresistibly recalled to Mary's surprising form of headgear in Leonardo's *Virgin of the Rocks*.) Indeed, even the New Testament contains heavy hints about this, when the Jews confronted Jesus with the interesting words: '*We* [my emphasis] are not illegitimate children',[14] and the Gospel of Mark tells how the townspeople referred to him as 'son of Mary',[15] implying his father's identity was uncertain. To be 'son of a woman' or 'born of women' was – and indeed still is – an unequivocal insult in the Middle East, and one that has a peculiar relevance to this investigation, as we will see.

(If, as appears to be the case, Mary the Mother was not only not a virgin when she conceived and gave birth to Jesus but also an adulteress, her portrayal as the Virgin goddess by the Gospel writers is both morally indefensible and an extraordinary example of literary overkill, not to mention virtually a sick joke. Yet how were they to know that in allying her with an ancient goddess tradition and whitewashing her human frailties they would effectively condemn generations of women to be measured against impossible standards of purity? Mary the Mother was at one stroke removed from any taint of adultery and set upon a distant cloud, just as Mary Magdalene was divided into three New Testament characters to remove her from any suggestion of sexual relations with Jesus – and any obvious association with John the Baptist and young John – but in doing so the Gospel writers and Church Fathers did real women no favours. It would come as a terrible shock to many good Christians that the 'Virgin' may well have been a woman of morals almost as dubious as those of the traditional Magdalene. And of course such a revelation would no doubt add the gravest insult to the injuries inflicted on the women of the Magdalen laundries.)

Although there were rumours – no doubt fuelled by anti-Christian feeling – that Mary had borne a child by her own brother when living in Alexandria,[16] either this was completely untrue or Jesus was not that son. The *Talmud* suggests that his 'father was a gentile, an archer from Tyre called Panthera' who was attached to the Roman army,[17] whose tombstone may have been found in Germany. Bearing dates that roughly correspond with what is usually taken to be Jesus' date of birth, the name reads: 'Tiberius

Julius Abdes Pantera' – and perhaps significantly, 'Abdes', a version of 'Abd Shem', means 'servant of the sun'.[18] (Presumably meaning he was a member of the sun-worshipping Mithras cult, very popular among the Roman military.)

## The Egyptian cult leader

Because most people assume that Jesus was a Galilean Jew they never search for evidence that suggests otherwise – yet if they did, they would not be disappointed. Apart from John the Baptist and almost certainly the Magdalene, there were others in his retinue who appear to have hailed from across the border in Egypt; the mid second-century Jewish-Christian Hegesippus identifies the New Testament 'Clopas' – whose wife (or daughter) Mary is described as attending the crucifixion – with the brother of Joseph, Mary's husband. Desmond Stewart points out that 'Clopas' is the Aramaic form of 'Cleopatros', the male form of Cleopatra – an unlikely name for a Judaean Jew. If true, this would place Jesus' uncle on his step-father's side in Egypt, suggesting a family link with that country that went back at least a generation, to the time of that relative's birth and naming.

There are even clues about Jesus' true status as a foreigner hidden among his own words, which are not exclusively those of a home-grown Jew, for as Stewart points out, he seems to employ metaphors that would be unfamiliar to his Galilean audience, and which certainly do not reflect a rural upbringing. In Matthew (5: 14–16) he declares: 'You are the light of the world . . . A city built on a hill-top cannot be hidden', but Stewart notes that 'The city set on a hill hardly suggests Galilee, whose most imposing cities were by the lake shore.'[19] Moreover, the fact that Jesus fails to mention any of the larger Galilean towns shows he was basically unfamiliar with the area, possibly even with Palestine as a whole. Certainly, he seems different from the other Galileans, for although Simon Peter was ridiculed for his rustic accent, this never happened to Christ – and certain key first-century texts definitely place him elsewhere. The *Talmud* described him as 'an Egyptian sorcerer',[20] and Jesus' own words often reveal a familiarity with Egyptian concepts and modes of expression.

The famous passage – often seen on posters outside churches – 'Jesus said: "Come to me all you who are burdened and I will refresh you"', while engendering comforting feelings of divine love, disappointingly did not actually originate with Christ. If he did say it, then he was quoting: for that passage was inscribed, word for word, over the entrance to a Nile-side temple of Isis, which predated Jesus by hundreds of years. Similarly, his metaphor of the grain of wheat: '. . . unless a grain of wheat falls to the ground and dies, it remains only a single seed. But if it dies, it produces many seeds',[21] while an example of dubious horticultural theory, comes undeniably from Osirian imagery.[22] And that most puzzling of statements: 'In my father's house are many mansions',[23] which although translated in more modern versions of the Bible as 'rooms', was a turn of phrase taken directly from the Egyptian *Book of the Dead*.[24,25]

There is also another example of Jesus' Egyptian background, although one with a surprising twist. According to the accepted story, Jesus only gave the form of words for one prayer to his disciples, which is known and loved as the 'Lord's Prayer' today – 'Our Father Who Art in Heaven, Hallowed be Thy Name' and so on, in the familiar words of the King James Bible. Yet this most solidly Christian prayer has an unexpected history: despite the universal belief to the contrary, Jesus did not invent that form of words, for it is an only slightly altered version of an ancient prayer to Osiris-Amon, which began: 'Amon, Amon, who art in heaven . . .'[26] and the Christian mode of ending each prayer with 'Amen' although encompassing the Hebrew for 'certainly', originates from the Egyptian custom of doing so with three repetitions of the name of the god – 'Amon, Amon, Amon . . .' The demoralizing deconstruction of the Lord's Prayer does not even end there, for there is another complication: in fact, the words do not come down to us at just one remove, but actually at two, for the Bible implies that in the form it was presented to the disciples it came directly from *John the Baptist*. (The implications of this will be examined in the next chapter.) Who is the real 'Lord' of the 'Lord's Prayer'? Is it Jesus, the pagan god Amon – or John the Baptist?

Clearly, this is a rather different picture of Jesus from that of the object of the Church's adoring and unquestioning worship. But are these calumnies merely libel, the usual result of ignorance and hostility to the arrival of a new and vibrant teacher on the scene? After all, enemies are always happy to condemn the most innocent people in roundly vile terms, so perhaps Jesus the god, Christ the divine, was the faultless subject of a heartless smear campaign by those who sought to denigrate his memory. Yet there are not just one or two isolated hostile comments about the real man, but a whole raft of them, which invites further investigation. On closer inspection, and allowing for the over-emphasis of prejudice, these suggest that he was indeed both a foreigner – from Egypt, even if ethnically a Jew – but incredibly and shockingly, perhaps also a rather unpleasant man.

Central to Jesus' mission were the miracles – the instant cures, walking on water and raising the dead – which acted as curtain-raisers for his teaching and deification, 'hooking' the multitudes. (Significantly, dealing with corpses was distinctly un-Jewish, for anything connected with the tomb was deemed unclean and anathema. On the other hand, Egyptians are well known to have practised solemn rites for the dead.) Perhaps preceded by an impressive black Magdalene whirling and dancing in chains, like her ethnic sister Helen, the Jesus group would enter a village and, for a short time, provide the greatest show on earth, spectacularly casting out demons and making the lame to walk. Yet every one of these miracles – and some of Jesus' more arcane behaviour, such as writing in the sand – came from the same magical tradition as the hosts of Egyptian sorcerers that enthralled the masses across the border, and who occasionally strayed across it.

Morton Smith, in his *Jesus the Magician* (1978) points out that even Jesus' own family were sceptical of his powers – to the point that they tried to have him restrained as a lunatic.[27] Surely there can be fewer more novel concepts than that of the Blessed Virgin Mary trying to have her son, the Christ, God's chosen Messiah, effectively *sectioned* as a danger to himself and others! No wonder Jesus retaliated by snubbing her whenever possible, saying for example when told she and his siblings wanted to see him: 'My mother and brothers are those who hear God's word and put it into practice'.[28] This is ironic, considering that he is seen as the ultimate examplar of filial love, for which there is not a shred of evidence –

185

if anything, quite the reverse. He also urges his followers to have less than the respect required of children for their parents by Mosaic Law, saying: 'If anyone comes to me and does not hate his father and mother, his wife and children, his brothers and sisters – yes, even his own life – he cannot be my disciple.'[29]

It is interesting that he urges us all to hate our own lives – also a grave Gnostic failing – which besides being rather ungrateful to God the creator, is at odds with his instruction to 'love your neighbour as yourself'. Such love is clearly not worth much.

Yet Jesus is still seen as the champion of the poor and oppressed, promising that the 'poor in spirit' shall be 'blessed . . . for theirs is the kingdom of heaven',[30] which is cheering for the billions who have never had any recourse against injustice, but has the drawback of being safely in a vague future. Flippancy aside, there is also the inevitable thought that even if the advent of the Kingdom were tomorrow, the poor in spirit – the 'meek' in the King James Bible – are of course the last people who would complain if the promised rewards never materialized.

This strangely off-putting character, who was somehow transmuted into the insipid milksop 'Gentle Jesus, Meek and Mild' so beloved of sentimental Victorians, also appears to be the staunch defender of children, stating sternly: '. . . if anyone causes one of these little ones who believe in me to sin, it would be better for him to be thrown into the sea with a large millstone around his neck'.[31] Superficially, this sounds reasonable, not to say caring and compassionate, for surely he is promising terrible retribution to those who harm innocent children, perhaps – reading between the lines – even child molesters? Of course if that were a fair summary, it would indeed be laudable and comforting, but there is a catch: note the phrase 'these little ones *who believe in me*': in other words, he will defend the cult's children, but does not promise to extend that offer to any other child. Similarly, Mark tells how Jesus gathered up a small child in his arms, and said: 'Whoever welcomes one of these little children *in my name* welcomes me . . .'[32] implying that welcoming children for any other reason is not notably laudable.

Indeed, once the blinkers of Christian conditioning are removed, it is surprisingly easy to see Jesus himself as a typical cult leader – ironically fulfilling many of the requirements set out by modern

Christian cult-busters. The generally agreed characteristics by which outsiders can recognize dangerous cult leaders include their possessing dominant or unusually charismatic personalities, whose commandments include severing family ties and sharing all property and money in common. The leader may also claim to be God or the son of God, asserting that although he may be martyred he will rise again/return in glory, and will prepare his followers for a similar fate, although promising a blissful reunion in an afterlife. It seems they have no sense of irony, these Christian cult-busters. But while David Koresh may be beyond the pale, Jesus himself – arguably the most successful cult leader in history, if only posthumously – is deemed to be beyond question.

Theologians have long argued over the vexed question of whether Jesus intended to be worshipped as God, or whether this was purely a construct of the later Paul's highly successful propaganda campaign. Yet judging by the New Testament there is little doubt that Jesus never underestimated his own status: there does seem to be a marked lack of anything that was truly humble or modest about him. As we have seen, even children only qualify for his protection if they believe in his divinity, and the following passages reinforce these suspicions: 'I am the gate, whoever enters through me will be saved';[33] '. . . in the future you will see the Son of Man sitting at the right hand of the Mighty One and coming on the clouds of heaven';[34] and 'For the Father loves the Son and shows him all he does . . . even so, the Son gives life to whom he is pleased to give it . . .'[35] 'He who does not honour the Son does not honour the Father, who sent him.'[36] Jesus may give the disciples teaching about their own dealings with the world, but he never seems to waste an opportunity to emphasize his own divine status. Of course such grandiose words would only be right and fitting in the mouth of a genuine god, but if he was merely the fatherless son of Mary the adulteress and a former Egyptian swine-herd[37] (see below) they do seem rather excessive.

And Jesus' words also betray a political agenda – associating with zealots and *sicarii* or terrorists, and declaring: 'I have not come to bring peace, but a sword.' He – or the family at Bethany – ensured that he fulfilled certain Old Testament messianic prophecies: he came out of Egypt, rode into Jerusalem on a donkey and so on, although as the long-awaited Jewish Messiah it must be said that he was a complete débâcle, for being crucified as a criminal was certainly never envisaged as the culmination of that role. The Messiah was seen as a major religious and military figure who would rise up and annihilate the Roman occupiers at the head of a massive and glorious army, and here was a pretender who consorted with sinners and travelled with women (at least one of whom was probably a black pagan), causing grave scandal wherever he went.

It may be objected that the proud and insular Jews would never have massed behind an Egyptian, even one of their own religion. The very practices of Judaism are designed to prolong a horror of the time of slavery in Egypt, and induce a sense of great relief at the Exodus that delivered them from it. Even the words and gestures of the annual Passover recall the distant day when Yahweh smote their masters with plagues and terror, and when Moses led them to freedom in the desert. Yet curiously, there is evidence – admittedly slight, but extremely tantalizing – that an Egyptian actually did lead a rebellion within Palestine in the first century CE. In his *The Jewish War*, Josephus gives an account of a figure known only as 'the Egyptian' who raised a large army of Jews with the intention of overthrowing the occupying Roman force. Describing this mystery man as 'a false prophet', the chronicler writes:

Arriving in the country this man, a fraud who posed as a seer, collected about 30,000 dupes, led them round by the wild country to the Mount of Olives, and from there was ready to force an entry into Jerusalem, overwhelm the Roman garrison, and seize supreme power with his fellow-raiders as bodyguards.[38]

Although it is tempting to try to shoehorn this character into the shoes of Jesus Christ, the dates are wrong: the Egyptian led his army against the hated Romans about twenty years after Jesus was said to have died. But there are still intriguing links with Christianity, for when Paul was rescued from an angry mob and put under the protection of the Romans, the captain of the guard asked him: 'Aren't you the Egyptian who started a revolt and led 4,000 terrorists out into the desert some time ago?'[39] (Note that the Egyptians' army has dwindled somewhat, compared to Josephus' clearly inflated account.)

Nervously, Paul answers: 'I am a Jew, from Tarsus ...'[40] But the word 'terrorists' is actually *sicarii*, the group that included Judas, and with whom Jesus seemed to feel at home. There is nothing in the New Testament to suggest that he persuaded the *sicarii* or the Zealots among his followers to renounce their violent ways, or even that he saw their causes as unacceptable.

The more-or-less contemporary accounts of Jesus also cut him down to size in more immediate ways. To us, he has always been a towering figure, both metaphorically and literally – a noble and strapping version of the young Leonardo da Vinci – so it comes as a shock to discover that he had a quite different reputation. Indeed, the Platonist Celsus described Jesus as: 'they say ... small and ugly and undistinguished',[41] although clearly he must have been possessed of the cult-leader's characteristics of enormous charisma and a dominant personality. And several accounts condemn him as a glutton and a drunkard[42] – although this may merely reflect a negative comparison with the much more ascetic John the Baptist.[43]

But was this hostility to Jesus due to first-century attitudes to *mamzers,* a social stigma that attached to illegitimate children? Many similar outsiders across the centuries – from Leonardo da Vinci to Lawrence of Arabia – have fought against prejudice and succeeded in making a unique contribution to both contemporary and future culture. Was the historical Jesus another victim of this ignorant attitude to offspring whose parentage was uncertain? Perhaps, but there was a twist: in that time and place if a bastard was deemed to live a decent and honourable life his birth status was not an issue, but if he transgressed the Jewish laws, became an apostate, or behaved in ways that brought his culture into disrespect his illegitimacy was stigmatized publicly and unstintingly.[44] It was not Jesus' lack of a legal father but his perceived immorality that inspired such gall.

Perhaps Celsus had no more idea of the real Jesus than we do today, but it is still worth quoting him and his contemporaries, in order to help balance the traditional picture of the perfect god-man. Origen, who called Jesus 'a bandit', declared that he had: 'many true things I could say about ... Jesus that bore no resemblance to those written by his disciples',[45] while Tertullian (*c.* 200) sums up the Jewish account of Jesus' life and work in these words: 'Son of a carpenter or a prostitute, profaner of the Sabbath, a Samaritan and one who had a demon . . . bought [by the high priests] from Judas . . . beaten with a reed and slapped, disgraced with spittle, given gall and vinegar to drink . . . [a man] whom his disciples spirited away [from the tomb] so they could say he had risen, or whom the gardener hauled off, lest his lettuces be damaged by the crowd of sightseers'.[46]

The writer's bile is only too clear, and obviously he was no friend of the first-century sect. In the essentials, however, Tertullian agreed with Celsus, who declared that the 'Virgin' Mary had been thrown out by Joseph as an adulteress, before giving birth to Jesus, son of Panthera. After growing up in Galilee, Jesus went as a hired labourer to Egypt, where he learned magic, then returned to Palestine where 'he set up as a god'.[47]

This is interesting because Jesus' famous parable of the Prodigal Son seems to reflect his own bitter experience, and is set in a country liable to famine and where there is no taboo against pigs (and, seemingly, the young man's Jewish sensibilities do not prevent him from working with 'unclean' animals, about which he has a choice),[48] which seems to suggest Egypt.

From these fragments and clues it is easy enough to phrase the pertinent questions: was Jesus a god, a madman or a devious schemer? Assuming that he could not have been a god – or, if he was, his attitude to his family, children and the role of terrorists makes him curiously unattractive to modern sensibilities – he emerges as a cult leader, a man with a somewhat confused mission and a tendency to self-aggrandisement. But if he was so very human and not particularly appealing, why did the heretics' beloved Magdalene consort with him so intimately? And why did John the Baptist retract his famous categorical pronouncement that Jesus was the chosen one, whose shoes he was unworthy to unlatch?

## CHAPTER TEN

# *Jesus and the Death of the Baptist*

While only the more extreme sceptics would deny that miracles do occasionally happen – although, it must be said, rarely – even many of the relatively unsophisticated people of the first-century Roman Empire had their doubts about the alleged powers of Jesus Christ. Like the Jewish Talmud, the Babylonian Talmud describes him unambiguously as an 'Egyptian sorcerer' who was 'to be stoned because he practised magic and incited Jews to worship alien gods and as a false prophet, led Israel astray.'[1] In this light it is significant that Jesus was arraigned before Pilate as a 'doer of evil', which is not the vague term it appears to be, but a specific reference to sorcery, a charge that followed the early Christians to Rome. Those condemned to a horrendous death as human torches by Nero were accused of 'hatred of the human race',[2] which Morton Smith interprets 'most plausibly . . . as referring to magic'.[3]

It is possible to deduce even from the writings of apologists such as Justin Martyr (100–65 CE) that Jesus' miracle cures were fake, or perhaps hallucinations that lasted only as long as he was physically present – Egyptian magi were renowned for their startling abilities as master hypnotists. There are many other hints about the real nature of the miracles, disillusioning though they may be: Jesus made food grow in enormous abundance,[4] which is a common trick that features in ancient magical papyri; he calms the storm[5] – magical talismans were believed, even by Christians, to have

191

similar properties (and indeed the ability to *cause* storms was always attributed to witches, as in *Macbeth*); and when Jesus cursed the fig tree,[6] he was merely continuing the time-honoured and dishonourable practice in which the magus 'consumed', 'burnt' or 'withered' a living thing.[7]

Although devout Catholics would be horrified to think in these terms, the Church has continued the age-old, atavistic magical tradition with its transubstantiation (the turning of mere bread and wine into Jesus' *actual* body and blood, a curiously overt form of esoteric cannibalism and vampirism), relics that confer blessings and miracle cures, and bleeding and weeping statues.

In the Gospel of John[8] Jesus promises to send the 'spirit of truth' into his followers, which he accomplished by blowing on them: Celsus described Egyptian magicians driving out demons and curing illnesses by blowing them away. And among the more currently unacceptable declarations of Jesus is this: 'I have come to set a man against his father, and daughter against her mother, and daughter-in-law against her mother-in-law, so that a man's enemies shall be those of his own household.'[9] Christian apologists claim that this is merely a precognitive summary of the circumstances that would pertain in the future, when the religion would cause bitter division among members of the same family. But even if he was simply preparing his cult realistically for a strife-torn future, need he seem so *pleased* about it? It is almost as if he is boasting about the coming wave of domestic hatred. Isn't it a curious thing for a teacher of peace to focus on, and for the Gospel writers to choose to include? Sad to say, it seems more likely – given the many other examples of similar incitements – that this passage means what it says: indeed, stirring up hatred was a well known characteristic of the magi, who not only exorcized those in the grip of demonic possession, but could also conjure malevolent entities to do their bidding, as unholy 'servitors'. (These creatures are also mentioned in the *Pistis Sophia*,[10] reflecting the then-current image of Jesus as a magus.)

Significantly, driving out one demon through the power of another was common practice among first-century Egyptian sorcerers: the philosopher Porphyry recorded his praise for the new god Serapis as 'the ruler of demons, who gives spells for their expulsion'.[11] Once again, there is a clear connection with the contemporary beliefs and practices of the Egyptian magicians, and a link with the inspirational Serapis, companion of the queen of magic, Isis – whose role in the Jesus mission was fulfilled by the black 'goddess' Magdalene.

Naturally the people were in awe of this authority over demons, and feared the magus' powers enormously. As Morton Smith notes, 'This was the blackest sort of magic, so it is not surprising that the gospels minimize Jesus' practice of it. He does not "send" the legions of demons into the Gadarene swine,[12] he just "permits" them to enter and destroy them.'[13]

Another of Jesus' apparently less-than-pleasant actions was to curse the fig tree that inconveniently bore no fruit when he was hungry. In a fit of petulance, he cried: 'May you never bear fruit again!'[14] The tree withered immediately, amazing the disciples with the speed of its demise. When asked how this could happen, Jesus replies: 'if you have faith and do not doubt, not only can you do what was done to the fig-tree, but also you can say to this mountain "Go, throw yourself into the sea," and it will be done. If you believe, you will receive whatever you ask for in prayer.'[15] But why give way to such a display of spite when – presumably – his powers would have permitted him to *bless* the fig tree so that it was suddenly weighed down with fruit, not just for Jesus' stomach, but also for the benefit of other hungry travellers? It is easy to sympathize with J.R. Ackerley who, in a letter to the occult historian Francis King, fumed: 'when you come to look into him, was he not a thoroughly nasty man? How can one excuse the barren fig-tree?'[16] Perhaps it is unsurprising that theologians have tried to minimize the sense of outrage, if only by putting forward the unconvincing explanation that this episode was really meant to be a symbol of the system that was out to destroy Jesus, although it is only through some considerable intellectual contortions that it even begins to approach a comprehensible meaning.

Was Jesus really an itinerant Egyptian sorcerer, duping the masses with miracles and wonders? Professor Smith believes that much of the evidence has been destroyed when the believers 'not only wrote the texts but formed an organization, the Church', which was then used to 'suppress those who disagreed'.[17] Yet the fact remains that what prompted so many to follow Jesus was the *coup de théâtre* of the marvels, the wonderworking – and undoubtedly in his entire story the greatest wonder was the resurrection of the dead Saviour in the tomb. Although, as we have seen, this ultimate miracle was an intrinsic part of the usual dying-and-rising god's curriculum vitae – especially for Osiris, black god of a culture formerly obsessed with physical immortality – it also became suspect as an act of black magic, of necromancy. An obscure rabbinical curse from the third century CE says: 'Woe to him who makes himself alive by the Name of God', which implies that the uttering of the secret name of God in order to conjure life into one's own corpse was seen as the most terrible of all spells.[18]

From the internal evidence of the Gospels, it is clear that what Judas actually sold for his thirty pieces of silver was a description of the rite of the raising of Lazarus at Bethany, which was seen not only as a disgusting example of necromancy, but also a threat to destroy the Temple.[19] According to the Gospel of John it is because crowds gathered to ogle the revivified Lazarus that 'the priests made plans to kill Lazarus as well [as Jesus]',[20] while the other Gospels have Judas' betrayal coming immediately after the Magdalene's anointing ceremony.[21] Either way, something that happened at Bethany was deemed so repugnant that it was ultimately the cause of Jesus being delivered to his enemies. Desmond Stewart (referring to the first-century Isian mystic) writes: '. . . the evidence of Bethany indicates that Jesus practised a species of mystery akin to what Lucius Apuleius experienced in the cult of Isis'.[22]

The devoted Isian initiate himself wrote of this life-changing experience: 'I approached the very gates of death and set foot on Proserpine's threshold, yet was permitted to return, rapt through all the elements. At midnight I saw the sun shining as if it were noon; I entered the presence of the gods of the underworld and the gods of the upper world, stood near and worshipped them.'[23]

To the outsider – and certainly to the later Gospel writers – it must have seemed as if Lazarus/John had really died and been resurrected by Jesus' magical powers. Being unfamiliar with the Isian mysteries, the onlookers, and even many of the disciples, would not have realized they were seeing – or hearing of – a symbolic death only, and word would have spread that Jesus was a necromancer (especially if they used a real tomb for the ritual). To a culture that abhorred anything connected with the physical detritus of death,[24] this immediately put him outside the Law.

If Lazarus' death was symbolic, what of the crucifixion? There are odd features in the story: it took place without crowds of spectators and at a distance from the few there were; Jesus died very quickly for a young man – crucifixion was designed to last many hours, even days, yet he died within a few hours, and did not even require the customary *coup de grace* of having his legs broken. It has been speculated that the vinegar-laden sponge he was given as he hung on the cross contained some kind of drug that would make him comatose, aping death for long enough to have him wake in the tomb. If so, was this pre-arranged with the Roman guards, or even Pilate? Perhaps the crucifixion was designed as the ultimate initiation, an ordeal of terrible agony that would set his soul free temporarily to encounter the gods, just as shamans use pain and drugs to visit the otherworld and learn great secrets – a sort of 'flatlining', or deliberately induced near-death experience. Perhaps the Magdalene, with all her money and status, bribed the Romans to allow the crucifixion to take place under Jesus' own terms.

Or maybe he was simply executed and his body stolen by the disciples, and the entire resurrection story added later to give the necessary noble and divine gloss to a sordid end at the hands of the hated Romans, just as some French criminals and collaborators during the Second World War suddenly became heroes of the Resistance in later accounts. And it should be remembered that the Gospels were written several decades after the events they described and by that time there was a marked lack of the promised Second Coming in glory, which Jesus' first disciples had firmly believed would happen within their own lifetimes. A Messiah who died a shameful death *and* did not return as promised was transmuted into an atoning, sacrificial god who rose from the dead after the usual two days in the tomb and, after working yet more miracles in his resurrected state, then ascended into heaven. (This physical 'translating' to heaven was also, it is claimed, the fate of the 'Virgin' Mary, although there are certain intriguing possibilities for the location of her tomb.)[25] Perhaps even the Gospel writers would be amazed that their more desperate 'spin' is still the current dogma even in the sophisticated twenty-first century, and that to question it is deemed to approach blasphemy.

What really happened to Jesus on the cross – whether he died as in the accepted story, saw a substitute die for him, as certain groups within the Priory of Sion believe, or fell into a death-like coma from which he later awakened – is beyond the scope of this book. Clearly, though, something drastic happened that removed him from the Magdalene's life, for the French legends have her fleeing in the leaky boat shortly after the crucifixion – presumably forced to escape from Simon Peter's hostility. The catalyst may not have been Jesus' death, however: her departure may even have been due to a terminal rift between them . . .

The events in and around the tomb are also murky. Even the believers hinted that the disciples stole his body, claiming that he had risen from the dead. In fact, the resurrection myth – familiar to most people in those days as part of the Tammuz, Osiris and Dionysus stories – was hastily cobbled on as damage limitation, for as no one expected the Jewish Messiah to be executed as a common criminal, an element had to be introduced to raise the profile of this humiliating tragedy, which cleverly elevated Jesus to the status of a king, for Jesus, like Lazarus/John could be reborn in the manner of the Osirian mystery school, and all dead pharaohs became an 'Osiris'. The story of the risen Jesus encountering two disciples on the road to Emmaus was taken from the ancient myths that inspired Lucius Apuleius' hymn to Isis, *The Golden Ass*.[26]

As the events of Jesus' life and death became increasingly miraculous – or, depending upon one's viewpoint, wilder and more fantastical – the suspicion grows that this was such mythical overkill as to smack of 'protesting too much', as if the Gospel writers and early Christians were collectively very much on the defensive. It is as if they were saying: '*your* teacher or even god may be powerful, but no human could possibly be so wondrous as ours'. Yet this putative rival was not, as might be expected, Serapis, nor the Roman favourite Mithras, but a figure that was much closer to Jesus – and one whose significance has repeatedly surfaced throughout this investigation. This worrisome competitor was, of course, Leonardo's beloved John the Baptist, the curious figurehead of whose church the Priory of Sion[27] declare themselves 'sword-bearers'.

But why should this intimidating puritan – who only apparently existed to kneel at Jesus' feet before baptizing him – have such enduring power over so many heretical hearts and minds? John in his camel-hair garments, living frugally off locusts and honey in the wilderness, from which he emerged to call the people to 'repent and be baptized' seems hardly the sort of enduring charismatic charmer who would be able to persuade a hard-boiled cynic like Leonardo – or the tough men of the Templars – not only to take him seriously, but to *adore* him. But, as we will see, the New Testament Gospels are by no means the only information we have about the Baptist, and even in the familiar books of Matthew, Mark, Luke and John there are enough clues to raise a great many suspicions that all is not what it seems between the Baptist and Jesus, that John may not have been merely the over-admiring acolyte of the Messiah.

First, it is strange that although John was infamously beheaded on the request of dancing-girl Salome by Herod, after acknowledging and baptizing Jesus, he is never referred to as the first Christian martyr. Indeed, in an inexplicable way, he barely seems Christian at all. Of all the saints he seems to stand alone, enigmatically isolated in a category by himself. We are not told that he had any dealings with Jesus before the baptism, nor any at all with most of the disciples – including the Magdalene – although it would have been very strange if he were unaware of them. For John not only baptized thousands, but he has always been closely linked with Mary in the heretics' minds. Why? What is the Baptist's secret?

### In search of the real Baptist

The New Testament tells how John was the very late child of Elizabeth and the priest Zechariah: indeed, both parents were well into old age when Elizabeth miraculously conceived. The angel Gabriel told Zechariah that the coming child had a single purpose, and that was to 'make ready a people prepared for the Lord'.[28] Elizabeth, who was a kinswoman of Mary the Virgin, visited her and was moved to declare: 'Blessed are you among women, and blessed is the child that you will bear!'[29] Clearly inspired by this show of respect from the older woman, Mary then speaks the song known as 'The Magnificat', which begins, 'My soul glorifies the Lord and my spirit rejoices in God my Saviour' which is so familiar to Christian women the world over.

After his birth – and another paean of praise, this time from his father – John is born, circumcized and 'went to live in the desert until he appeared publicly to Israel'.[30] It seems no one was interested in what John got up to before appearing in order to baptize Jesus – perhaps, it might be thought, he simply lived the unremarkable but difficult life of a hermit away from the crowds and therefore there was really nothing to say. In fact, yet again in this gradual unravelling of the Christian story, nothing could be further from the truth.

In fact, John the Baptist had a flourishing sect – more properly an international organization – that was already well established by the time Jesus began his mission:[31] indeed, it seems that the new Messiah began his spiritual life as one of John's disciples. What happened to John's religion – or his 'Way' as it was known – is a matter for academic conjecture: most scholars think it simply fizzled out, or was absorbed into the new Christian sect. Either way, it is not of much interest to the world of Academe – but perhaps it should be, for in the real history of John's cult lie some of the darkest secrets of Christianity, even perhaps of Christ himself.

The apparent disappearance of John's sect may simply be a footnote in religious history as far as most academics are concerned, but of course we know that certain cabals within the Templars – and others – preserved the Baptist's cult. Yet even the very idea that John *had* a cult will be surprising to most Christians, to whom he is merely a necessary adjunct to the story of Jesus.

## The Church of John in the East

We have seen how Leonardo championed his cause – to the great detriment of the Holy Family as depicted in his artworks – and how the Knights Templar revered the Baptist, perhaps to the point of worshipping replicas of his severed head, or even the head itself. And the group behind the Priory of Sion seems also to have distinctly Johannite undertones. The Templars were said to have learned their reverence for the Baptist from a mysterious group called 'the Church of John in the East' while on their travels as crusaders and seekers for arcane artefacts and lost knowledge. And although most scholars seem not to know where to look for this group of peculiar heretics, their identity is uncovered soon enough with a little delving.

Known to Victorian explorers as 'St John's Christians' – although this is way off the mark – the strange hybrid tribe known as the Mandaeans lived for many years in what is now Iran and the southern marshlands of Iraq, although the depredations of Saddam Hussein after the Gulf War prompted a mass exodus of the survivors – an estimated 15,000 – to more welcoming lands scattered across the globe.[32] Indeed, some survived in Iraq, where reporters in the aftermath of the 2003 conflict were fascinated to record the presence of an Arab tribe that reveres John the Baptist. Is it significant that their centre is the town of Nasiriya – surely too similar to the term 'Nasorean' to be coincidental?

Although their origins are unclear, it seems that they came from the area around Egypt – one of their sacred texts declares that 'the people of Egypt were of our religion'[33] and their holy books contain Egyptian words[34] – roughly 2,000 years ago, moving slowly and almost continually towards modern Iraq, suffering persecution from almost every dominant religion and culture as they went. Somewhere along their route they appear to have encountered representatives of the Knights Templar – perhaps at Harran, impressing them with their own unique take on the relationship between the Baptist and Jesus. (This tribe is called 'Sabians' in the Koran, linking them to Sheba's country of Saba.)

By the time the Mandaeans were first seriously studied – in the 1930s by the British explorer Lady Drower – they had accumulated doctrine and practice from other religions, although their basic tenets still appear to shine through. However, as many of their secrets were withheld even from the sympathetic Lady Drower, it is impossible to know the full extent of their beliefs. According to their holy books – such as the *Hawan Gawaita*, *The Ginza* or *The Book of John* – the Baptist was the greatest in their long line of priestly prophets, and although they revere him with great passion, they do not believe him to be divine. He is their most beloved and honoured Gnostic teacher, going under the Arabic name of Yahya, by which he appears in the Koran, and the Aramaic Yohanna.

In fact, the Mandaeans are the world's only surviving Gnostic religion, their cosmology being recognizably similar to that of the *Pistis Sophia*, and their regard for the 'Light' of gnosis is all-consuming. Indeed, John is known as 'the High King of Light', defender of the ultimate good against the opposite and equal forces of evil, which includes the dark goddess Ruha, whose benign aspect manifests as the Holy Spirit. Many prayers are still said to a goddess Libat, who has been identified with Ishtar, *and therefore with Isis*, and they have both male and female priests. Even this minor piece of information has the power to astonish, for surely the puritanical Jewish wildman at the heart of this sect would have eschewed all signs of goddess-worship? John the Baptist was surely the last person to have been a *pagan* sympathizer! But, once again, our image of Christ's forerunner is derived from the late first-century and early second-century Christian spin doctors, and therefore there is a major reason to be open to a radical re-interpretation.

(Indeed, a similar sect in some ways, the Nosairi of Syria, while seemingly utilizing both Christian and Muslim elements in their beliefs and practices, are basically pagan, congregating in sacred groves in 'high places', just like the worshippers of Asherath in Solomonic times. Their two most important symbols are the Light and a chalice, from which they drink sacramental wine, saying: 'I drink to the Light'. They claim the Holy Grail was a symbol given by Christ to John the Beloved alone of great mystical secrets.[35] As 'Nosairi' is the correct interpretation of the word usually understood to mean 'of Nazareth/Nazarene', it seems that Jesus himself shared some of this sect's beliefs and practices, although he was not their originator.)

There are further surprises: as the Mandaeans believe celibacy to be sinful – to them, the only men who are condemned to be reincarnated are those who refuse to marry – it follows that their prophet John had a wife (Anya, or Anna/Anne) and several children. It must be said that the idea of John the Baptist as a family man is somewhat at odds with the Church's image of the inflexible ascetic, presented as almost a prototype for one of the more crusading monks.

However, the most striking and significant factor about the Mandaeans' beliefs is that they *loathe and despise* Jesus, whom they call 'Yeshu, the lying Messiah' or 'Messiah Paulis' – Paul's Messiah.

They call him the 'perverter of all the cults', 'son of a woman' (that old eastern insult again) and anathematize him as an evil usurper of John's Way of light. In their saga of the baptism of Jesus we read ( in rather quaint language):[36]

Who told Yeshu Messiah, son of Miryam, who told Yeshu, [that he could go] to the shores of the Jordan and [say] unto Yahya [John]: 'Yahya, baptize me with thy baptizing and utter o'er me also thy Name thy wont is to utter. I show myself as thy pupil, I will remember thee then in my writings; [if] I attest not myself as thy pupil, then wipe my name from thy pages.'

Then Yahya answered Yeshu Messiah in Jerusalem: 'Thou hast lied to the Jews and deceived the priests . . . thou hast lied to them . . . and spread abroad disgrace . . .'[37] John tests Jesus with riddles, and although Jesus appears to give wise and pleasing answers, the Baptist continues to have his doubts about him – and the dark goddess Ruha in the form of a dove throws a cross over the River Jordan, changing the water into rainbow colours. She declares: 'The Jordan in which Messiah Paulis was baptized have I made into a trough . . . the staff which Messiah Paulis receives have I made into a dung-stick.'[38] [The text ends, like all Mandaean holy books, with the words: 'AND LIFE IS VICTORIOUS'.]

Clearly, this is a very different version of the baptism of Jesus, which according to the New Testament was prefaced by John's public declaration of spiritual and moral inferiority to Jesus, saying: 'I baptize you with water for repentance. But after me will come one who is more powerful that I, whose sandals I am not fit to carry . . .'[39] In the Bible story, confronted with the promised Saviour, he tries to persuade Jesus not to be baptized, saying: '*I* need to be baptized by *you,* and do you come to *me*?'[40] But faced with stern words about the ritual only being right and proper, John agrees to officiate, at which the 'Spirit of God' descended 'like a dove', 'and a voice from heaven said, "This is my Son, whom I love, with him I am well pleased".'[41]

To the Mandaeans the dove was the manifestation of the dark goddess, her presence a dire warning thrown across the Jordan about the future iniquities of the Lying Messiah, whereas to the

Gospel writers it is a sign of God's presence, as his Shekhina, or Holy Spirit. That this is a unique phenomenon is explained by Desmond Stewart:

> Although Yahweh supposedly sent ravens to feed one prophet, he did not customarily manifest himself in descending birds. Doves, in any case, were sacred to the pagan goddess of love, whether known as Aphrodite or Astarte [or, indeed, Isis]. Yahweh had preferred to appear in more violent symbols: the burning bush, the plagues . . . the flame-pillar . . .[42]

He adds:

> Mystical apparitions are in any case probably too swift for ornithological exactitude . . . For what Jesus thought he saw, Egypt provides better guidance than a bird-book . . . When Re [the sun god] held his beloved, the pharaoh, to his bosom, he did so in the guise of Horus, whose commonest symbol was the hawk . . .[43]

Yet here it is no martial hawk that descends on the Chosen One, but a *dove*, although not quite the vapid symbol it might appear, for as Barbara G. Walker writes, it was:

> Aphrodite's totem, the bird of sexual passion, symbolically equivalent to the yoni [vulva].[44] In India, too, the dove was *paravata,* the symbol of lust.[45] Joined to her consort, the phallic serpent, the Dove-goddess stood for sexual union and 'Life'.
> The phrase attributed to Jesus, 'Be ye therefore wise as serpents and harmless as doves' (Matthew 10:16), was no random metaphor but a traditional invocation of the Syrian God and Goddess.[46]

Clearly, there were elements in the baptism of Jesus that came from pagan – even sexual – mysteries, although the Jewish Gospel writers either misunderstood or deliberately set out to misrepresent them.

But what of the baptismal rite itself? It has been suggested that John (and possibly Jesus) was a member of the Essene community at Qu'mran (where the Dead Sea Scrolls were found), a mystery school of puritanical Gnostic Jews whose practices included immersion as a symbolic cleansing ceremony. Was John's baptism simply the Essene rite made public? Although there are some similarities between the Essenes' beliefs and practices and those of the Mandaeans, that may stem from their mutual background in the Egyptian mystery schools, where spiritual and physical discipline were requirements of those who sought the mystical *gnosis* of the god or goddess. Yet the Essenes' regime does not match the lifestyle of either John or Jesus. Both men in their different ways were too fond of women – John of his wife Anya (his love for her being made touchingly clear in the Mandaean texts), and Jesus not only for the special Magdalene, but also the company of many others.[47] And while John famously fasted and lived a teetotal life, Jesus was often accused of being 'a gluttonous man and a winebibber, a friend of tax collectors and sinners'[48] – even if this were an exaggeration, a fondness for raffish company and the odd spot of alcohol still amounted to a lifestyle that would hardly be guaranteed to win him the Essenes' approval. In any case, neither the New Testament nor the writings of their enemies refer to either John or Jesus as Essenes, which is adequate proof that they were not members of the sect.

So if John's rite of baptism was not directly inspired by their ceremonies, where did it come from? Once again, the signs point towards the mystery schools of the land of Egypt. As Desmond Stewart notes: 'The elements in John's rite were as old as near eastern religion. The pharaohs had undergone a rite of baptism which was seen as a rite of royal renewal corresponding to the sun's daily submergence in the sea. The mystery cults of the Roman empire also used immersion . . .'[49,50]

That John's rite was completely unfamiliar to the crowds that flocked to hear him preach in Palestine is demonstrated by the fact that he was not known as '*a* baptist', not one of many, but simply as 'John *the* Baptist'. And we know from Josephus' *Antiquities of the Jews* that whatever John preached caused astonishment and wonder – not just among Jews, but among Gentiles, too. As John's religion reached as far away as Ephesus, it is clear that his Palestinian work was only one leg of a much wider mission, and that he saw his message as being beyond the confines of Judaic law. Indeed, one of the reasons that he fell foul of the authorities in Jerusalem was because he encouraged outdoor worship, thus denying the Temple the revenue from animal sacrifices (prefiguring to some extent the Cathars' refusal to use churches, which they saw as unnecessary and a corrupting influence).

Although it is obvious that John baptized a great many people in several different countries, it is still possible that he was waiting for his epiphany in the form of the greater 'one who is to come', and that this Messiah was indeed Jesus – although even so, he was to change his mind somewhat radically . . .

John's story came to an abrupt end when he was arrested by Herod – according to the New Testament, for criticizing the illegal marriage of Herod Antipas[51] to Herodias – and thrown into the dungeons of the puppet-king's palace. The Bible tells us that the king's step-daughter so pleased him with her dancing that he promised her anything her heart desired, to which – prompted by her mother Herodias – she responded that she wanted the head of John the Baptist. Although Herod was an admirer of the holy man, he reluctantly agreed, and John's head was brought to her on a platter. His grieving disciples removed his body, although whether this includes his head is unclear. The New Testament is silent on the subject of Jesus' own grief.

Although this story has given rise to some extraordinarily fevered paintings, films and plays (including Oscar Wilde's *Salome,* in which he himself played the eponymous dancer),[52] in the Bible accounts it is extremely brief and bald. In fact, only two of the four Gospels even carry it,[53] which is remarkable for such an important event as the death of Jesus' forerunner. And although most people are familiar with the name of the homicidal dancing girl, it comes as a great surprise to discover she is actually anonymous in the biblical accounts: we only know her as 'Salome' from Josephus, whose version of the story is somewhat different.

In his *Antiquities of the Jews* he gives the reason Herod seizes John as a pre-emptive strike against a mass uprising, for not only was the Baptist hugely popular, but he had implicitly sided with Herod's enemy, King Aretas of Nabatea. The problem was not the status of the woman whom Herod had married, as the Gospels state, but the fact that he had divorced King Aretas' daughter in order for that union to be possible, and therefore a state of tension existed between the two countries. If the crowds that followed John were to agree with him about Herod's effective insult to the Areteans, they might revolt against his rule.[54]

Why should Matthew and Luke be at such pains to obscure Salome's name? Why should Mark and John ignore the entire story? If Josephus knew it, surely they did: their source of information on political and royal matters would have been much the same. And finally, why have the Gospels changed the reasons for John's imprisonment, from the threat of his leadership in a mass uprising to the criticism of Herod's marriage? (Although of course the two are not mutually exclusive: it is quite likely that John rebuked the king for his cavalier attitude to marriage. We know from the Mandaean texts that he was a very uxorious man.)

John was seen by the multitudes as the reincarnation of the Old Testament prophet Elias, adding authority to his rumoured status as the 'forerunner' of the coming Christ. It must be said that so far there is nothing in the story of the Baptist to suggest any reason for the enduring hatred of the Mandaeans for Jesus, nor that of the cross-trampling Templars, but now the emphasis shifts, grows darker and more sinister, and certain previously unthinkable ideas begin to bubble away under the surface.

## The rivals

The New Testament leaves no doubt that John was Jesus' moral and spiritual inferior, a situation with which he seems to be content, as the prophesied forerunner. As we have seen, he kneels before Jesus, declaring that it should be Jesus who baptizes him and not the other way round. Although the Gospel of John has no mention of the Baptist's arrest and the bizarre circumstances surrounding his execution, he does include John's unequivocal statement: 'I am not the Christ',[55] but then he also goes on to deny that he is Elias/Elijah, despite the fact that Jesus claims he is. There is something suspicious about John's willingness to grovel before Jesus, which has not escaped modern theologians. Hugh Schonfield notes the 'bitter rivalry' between the followers of the two leaders, writing: 'We are made aware from Christian sources that there was a considerable

Jewish sect in rivalry with the followers of Jesus, who held that John the Baptist was the true Messiah . . .'[56]

It is inevitable that faced with such new and radical considerations a whole raft of disturbing questions arise. What if what we have in the biblical Gospels is no more than propaganda on behalf of the Jesus sect – which, according to an accident of history, happened to become the victor? As we know, history is always written by the faction that triumphs. Perhaps John never knelt to Jesus, never grovelled, declared he was unworthy, or denied that he was the Christ. Perhaps he only became this craven figure in the spiteful minds of the New Testament public relations officers, keen to present their own version of the rivals' relationship to an unknowing posterity.

If not just their respective groups of disciples, but also the two leaders themselves were in fact bitter rivals, then the preliminary baptism scene would be analogous to the apparently veracious description, 2,000 years later, of how the far-left miners' leader Arthur Scargill knelt to Tory Prime Minister Margaret Thatcher![57] If the only accounts of the 1980s that were available to future generations consisted of fanatical Tory Party fantasies, how would the people of 4000 CE know any different?

An objection to the rivalry hypothesis might be that Jesus pays John an enormous compliment, which is hardly the behaviour of an ambitious competitor, when he says: 'I tell you the truth: Among those born of women there has not risen anyone greater than John the Baptist',[58] which certainly appears to be hugely flattering, although it is immediately followed by the puzzling coda: 'yet he who is least in the kingdom of heaven is greater than he'.[59] Modern westerners naturally interpret 'among them that are born of women there has not rise anyone greater . . .' as 'there is no one alive who is greater', but the Mandaeans – and any other son or daughter of the Middle East – would be quick to point out that 'born of women' is a *terrible insult*, meaning 'bastard' – a fatherless child – or perhaps, by extension, 'son of a bitch'. In their book *The Treasure of Montségur,* Walter Birks and R.A. Gilbert go even further, believing that this phrase meant that Jesus thought John was a *demon*.[60] Indeed, the Mandaeans call Jesus 'son of a woman' and they are not known for their unbridled love and respect for him. In the light of this interpretation, Jesus' next pronouncement about John finally makes sense: 'He that is least in the Kingdom of heaven is greater than he' – in other words, John the Baptist is a complete so-and-so, and even the least significant of Jesus' own followers is more important than him.

Rather ingenuously, the Gospels include an episode that reveals something strange about the Baptist's alleged certainty that Jesus was the prophesied Christ. When Jesus began his mission by teaching and preaching in the towns of Galilee, John – who by that time was languishing in prison – seems suddenly to have been assailed by doubts. Matthew says: 'When John heard in prison what Christ was doing, he sent his disciples to ask him, "Are you the one who was to come, or should we expect someone else?"'[61] As he had allegedly fallen at Jesus' feet in a rather sickeningly obsequious manner and announced him to be the chosen one – and presumably witnessed the voice of God and the descending dove – this is passing strange. However, if there was never any such pro-Jesus scene (although it is likely that he was baptized by John, for thousands were), John's question does not seem out of place. But why should he respond so dubiously to reports of Jesus preaching and doing good? Perhaps he heard more alarming versions of the early mission. It is interesting that Jesus' answer to John's question includes the 'born of women' insult and the extraordinarily defensive statement: 'For John came neither eating nor drinking, and they say "He has a demon". The Son of Man [Jesus] came eating and drinking, and they say, "Here is a glutton and a drunkard, a friend of tax collectors and 'sinners'." But wisdom is proved right by her actions.'[62] (Note that 'wisdom' is clearly the feminine Sophia, and may even imply a connection with the Magdalene.)

(The subject of food and drink seems to obsess Jesus, for we are told that when people asked him why the Baptist's disciples fasted, whereas this was not a custom among his own followers he replies grandly: 'How can the guests of the bridegroom fast while he is with them? . . . But the time will come when the bridegroom will be taken from them, and on that day they will fast.'[63] Apart from its cult-leader arrogance, this passage is interesting because Jesus refers to himself as the 'Bridegroom' – an association with Solomon in the *Song of Songs* – and because such a pronouncement would effectively permit him not to have to fast himself. A man who loved his food would hardly encourage others to do without, especially if he was expected to set them an example.)

Yet none of this tussle between rival holy men explains the seething and enduring hatred of the Mandaeans for Jesus and the apparently similar emotions of the Johannite Templars, some of whom spat at and trampled upon the cross and worshipped a bearded, severed head. What else do they know – or think they know – about the relationship between the two men?

The Mandaeans refer to Jesus – 'son of a woman' – as the 'perverter of all the cults' and as John's usurper, and it is interesting to note that in Luke the 'whole assembly' of the priests accused Jesus before Pilate of 'subverting our people'[64] ('perverting our people' in some versions), which hardly seems to accord with Jesus' image as a gentle peacemaker. It may be that they were acting on wicked rumour and that Jesus was innocent of all charges, but the Baptist had heard something while in prison that alarmed him so much he changed his mind, either about Jesus' Messiahship or at least about his integrity.

Whatever it was that John knew or thought he knew about Jesus, his doubts were his last public announcements, for it was immediately after this that he was killed. And then Jesus took over most of his following. On the surface, this may seem perfectly acceptable, for John's disciples would be grief stricken and in need of strong leadership, a visible and potent rallying point – just as the crowds mourning Princess Diana demanded that the Queen return to London to be their figurehead in the time of national grief. Even if John and Jesus had had their personal difficulties, surely it makes sense that the charismatic young leader should step into the Baptist's shoes at such an hour?

Perhaps. Yet we know from other sources that Jesus was not John's intended successor – indeed, from all the evidence, it seems he would have been the last person the Baptist would have appointed even to lead the Judaean end of his mission. And the identity of John's true heir is surprising to the point of being shocking, given our image of the Baptist as a sort of Billy Graham character, a fire-and-brimstone preacher with archetypally rigid morals. It was Simon Magus, the Church's 'First Heretic', so anathematized because he allegedly tried to buy the Holy Spirit from Simon Peter that he gave his name to the sin of *simony,* or the purchase of ecclesiastical favours. And Simon, we recall, travelled around the Middle East with a black woman called Helen, spectacularly dancing while bedecked with chains – his partner in sacred sex rituals. How could Simon Magus of all people possibly be John the Baptist's named successor when Jesus himself was not?

In the third-century *Clementine Recognitions* there is the following interesting passage:

> It was at Alexandria that Simon [Magus] perfected his studies in magic, being an adherent of John [the Baptist][65] through whom he came to deal with religious doctrines . . .
> Of all John's disciples, *Simon was his favourite* [my emphasis], but on the death of his master, he was absent in Alexandria . . .[66]

Although John's second choice, one Dositheus, did eventually take over the organization, for an unspecified amount of time – at the critical moment just after the Baptist's death – the Judaean mission looked as if it fell into the hands of Jesus. Was Simon's absence in Alexandria at exactly this time merely a coincidence – or an intrinsic part of someone else's plan?

It is tempting to see the violent silencing of the Baptist as an essential precursor to the beginning of Jesus' own mission – indeed, Australian theologian Barbara Thiering has suggested that John's death had some connection with Jesus' disciples.[67] And although the argument for the unthinkable – the possibility of the Jesus movement's responsibility for the death of the Baptist – is presented in detail elsewhere,[68] it is necessary to consider it briefly now as the background to the story of the historical Jesus and the real motivation of Mary Magdalene.

The Gospels present a strange and unconvincing explanation for his execution: the dancing girl story is extremely weak – what Roman puppet king would have dared allow a top political prisoner to be killed on a silly girl's whim? Was John's death more suspicious than that? Was the accepted version of events a hastily cobbled-together story to explain the awkward fact that John had been beheaded while under Herod's 'protective' custody? The fact that the Gospel writers clearly *believe* there is something contro-versial about the Baptist's death is enough to ask the usual question in cases of murder: who stood to gain the most from it?

It might seem to be an impossible task from the distant perspec-tive of the twenty-first century to re-open the case of the Baptist's murder, but curiously it is possible, even now, to suggest a possible agent for his sudden death. Why else would the Gospel writers – when they include the episode at all – omit the name of Herod's dancing step-daughter, even though the chronicler Josephus knew her to be Salome? Yet she does appear in the list of female disciples who attend the crucifixion, and is featured very prominently in the Nag Hammadi text *The Gospel of Thomas*,[69] where she even familiarly lies on a couch with Jesus. And, as we have seen, she appears in the interesting little passage that was removed from Mark's gospel, which we know of from the letter of Clement of Alexandria: 'And the sister of the youth whom Jesus loved and his mother and Salome were there . . .' Was the passage edited out not only to remove any association between Jesus and Mary of Bethany, but also because Salome was specifically mentioned? Admittedly, it was a common enough name, but this is the second time we have noted its conspicuous absence, as if the Gospel writers were acting like guilty men denying all knowledge of a key witness. If this Salome was the same as the sadistic dancer at Herod's court – or even if there was a danger she would be confused with her – then there was potential for Jesus' name to be dragged into the murder of John the Baptist, whether or not that was justified. And in any case, he had another contact within Herod's palace – his disciple Joanna, wife of the king's steward Chuza.[70]

On the other hand, if Herod had imagined that John's death would have benefited him in some way, then he was soon relieved of that misapprehension, for when he lost a battle shortly afterwards, the people let it be known that he was reaping his reward for killing the holy man. Jesus, however, was to receive a bizarre and back-handed compliment as he proceeded with his wonder-working. In the first flowering of his mission, after the death of the Baptist, he must have felt enormous resentment as he went about the countryside working miracles, for the people, although impressed, ascribed his powers to the notion that Jesus had somehow absorbed the Baptist's spirit. They declared that 'he does great things' *because* he 'is' John, which while evidence of magical thinking, also implies that John was known to work wonders, whereas Jesus previously was not.

The belief in a magically composite being, a Jesus possessed by – or possessing – the spirit of the Baptist may lie behind much of the heretics' otherwise incomprehensible secrets, and explain the true role of Mary Magdalene in her long years in exile after Christ's crucifixion.

But although the churches acknowledge the existence of miracles, it is beyond the pale to suggest that they were evidence of the paranormal, or of magical ritual – in other words, the hated *occult*. Jesus' special effects were evidence of the divine in him, whereas the very similar performances of others, such as Simon Magus, the result of diabolism. It is interesting to note the words of the Platonist Celsus on this subject: 'And since [Jesus] foresaw that others too, having learned the same arts, would do the same, boasting that they did so by the power of God, he orders that such men shall be expelled.'[71]

## The bizarre legacy of the Baptist

There is evidence that, in his own day, not only did Jesus' own followers believe him to be a gifted occultist, but that his abilities were ascribed to the post-mortem influence of John the Baptist: 'Some were saying: "John the Baptist has been raised from the dead, and *that is why* [my emphasis] miraculous powers are at work in him."'[72] Even Herod agreed, declaring guiltily (and no doubt fearfully): 'John, the man I beheaded, has been raised from the dead!'[73] Apart from other considerations, the Gospel writers clearly thought that including these episodes would enhance Jesus' status, for although the Baptist was known to be a wonder-worker, Jesus now improved on him.

To those people it made perfect sense that when the famous and well-loved holy man was abruptly removed from the scene and the new leader demonstrated a gift for miracles, then Jesus must have access to John's earth-bound spirit. As Professor Morton Smith writes: 'Jesus was called "John" because it was believed that he "had", that is, possessed, and was possessed by, the spirit of the

211

Baptist.'[74] Smith presents three possibilities – as far as the first-century Judaeans were concerned – for the source of Jesus' power: the Baptist's spirit; Beelzebub, an independent supernatural entity; or his genuinely divine nature.[75] Mark tells how the teachers of the law from Jerusalem denounced him as: '... possessed by Beelzebub!'[76] Even the reported paranormal events at Jesus' baptism – the voice of God and the dove – were seen as evidence of him 'having a spirit'. By ancient standards, therefore, the concept of 'having' the dead Baptist was not an improbable explanation for his ability to work miracles, but it was soon suppressed.

In the light of this notion, it is interesting to revisit Jesus' words on the cross – *Eloi, Eloi, lama sabachthani!* – usually interpreted as: 'My God, my God, why have you forsaken me?'[77] However, the bystanders are reported to have said, 'Listen, he's calling Elijah/Elias'[78] (the Old Testament prophet believed by many, including Jesus, to be reincarnated as John the Baptist) which is universally dismissed as meaningless or evidence of foolishness – or simply deafness. This is a very modern attitude, however, for it overlooks Jesus' magical imperative, for which, as we have seen, the evidence is very strong. Perhaps those people did not mishear or misinterpret Jesus' words after all: perhaps the cry referred to the disappearance of the Baptist's spirit from the Messiah's psyche: '*John! John! Why have you abandoned me now?*' As he hung from the cross, was Jesus appalled to discover that his servitor had left him to succumb to the hideous ordeal alone? Maybe the critically injured Messiah had believed that 'having' John would have made him invincible, or at least impervious to pain, just as the disciples asked him for the 'words of power' that would enable them to suffer torture with equanimity, as reported in the *Pistis Sophia*.

However, Jesus was not the only religious leader of his day to be accused of such necromantic activities. As we have seen, John himself was clearly thought to have indulged in similar magical practices, as Jesus said: 'For John came neither eating nor drinking and they say "He has a demon ..."'[79]

Carl Kraeling, author of *John the Baptist* (1951) explains that this meant the Baptist had power over a demon, not that he was possessed by one. He writes: 'John's detractors used the occasion of his death to develop the suggestion that his disembodied spirit was serving Jesus as the instrument for the performance of works of black magic, itself no small concession to John's power.'[80] And, of course, the 'John's detractors' were the Jesus movement.

Magicians believed that possessing paranormal – or even demonic – servitors would not only bring them worldly success, but that such Faustian power games also held out the promise that 'you will be worshipped as a god . . .',[81] which has clear implications for the Jesus story. And the Magical Papyrus of Paris contains the secrets of a spell for gaining power over the spirit of a dead man:

> You will have in him a slave sufficient for whatever (tasks) you may conceive, O blessed initiate of holy magic, and this most powerful assistant, who alone is lord of the Air, will accomplish (them) for you, and the (other) gods will agree to everything, for without this god nothing is (done).[82]

However, perhaps the most significant aspects of this macabre practice were that the demonic contract was only good if the dead man whose soul was to be exploited in this way had been *murdered* and the magus *owned a part of his body* . . . John had met a violent and horrible death, and who knows what fate his severed head had suffered? Had Jesus' contacts at Herod's palace – Salome or Joanna for example – smuggled the Baptist's head out to be used in what was essentially a black magic rite of enslavement?

## CHAPTER ELEVEN

# *Head of the Heretics*

French legends speak of how Mary Magdalene and her party in the leaky boat took the Holy Grail to France, and controversy has raged about whether this was the cup that caught Jesus' blood as he hung on the cross, or the chalice he used for the ritual of the Last Supper; the 'royal blood' as embodied in the pregnant Magdalene or in her child, or something else connected with the story of the black priestess and her would-be divine lover.

However, all these possibilities share the same disadvantage: they emphasize the Magdalene's role as inferior to Jesus, for example in stressing that the 'sacred bloodline' is that of Christ's. But what if this completely misses the point? What if the Magdalene was important in her own right, and not simply as Jesus' chief Apostle? She had authority, with which she anointed him, and put backbone into the flagging, depressed male disciples after the crucifixion so that they were inspired to go out, preach and baptize. The irony is that through her infectious enthusiasm and natural qualities of leadership she sealed the death warrant of her own goddess-based religion. If she had left Simon Peter dejected and demoralized, her future 'church' would no doubt have flourished unhindered by a brutal uncomprehending patriarchy.

There are so many assumptions about Christianity, even the 'alternative' versions. The Holy Grail is always seen as a great mystical artefact associated with *Jesus*. But what if the 'Holy Grail' – the mysterious object said by medieval romance writers to have been taken to France by the Magdalene – had no direct connection with him at all? After all, judging by the earliest of the medieval grail stories, which were inspired or even commissioned by the Knights Templar – with their 'baptized men' and strange rituals of beating a cross in a forest, not to mention bearded severed heads on platters – the concept of the Holy Grail was not Christian, but *Johannite*. In the light of the magical thinking of Jesus' day, and the stories about his dabbling in necromancy, what if the grail *were John the Baptist's head*?

Certainly, the worship of a grisly skull had been an integral part of the Templar initiations, although there is some evidence that it was reserved for the secret inner circle only. During the trial of the Order in 1307 Brother Jean Taillefer of Genay told how he was:

> received into the order . . . [where] at his initiation 'an idol representing a human face' was placed on the altar before him. Hughes de Bure [another Templar] described how the 'head' was taken out of a cupboard . . . in the chapel and that it seemed to him to be of gold or silver, and to represent the head of a man with a long beard. Brother Pierre d'Arbley suspected that the 'idol' had two faces, and his kinsman Guillaume d'Arblay made the point that the 'idol' itself, as distinct from copies, was not exhibited at general chapters, implying that it was only shown to senior members of the order on special occasions.[1]

The exclusivity of the head itself was emphasized by the Templars' tormentor, the French King Philip the Fair, who wrote to his seneschals describing the idol as: 'A man's head with a large beard, which head they kiss and worship at all their provincial chapters, but this not all the brothers know, save only the Grand Master and the old ones.'

These busts were supposedly replicas of John's head, which presumably languished in a secret Templar vault, the exclusive focus for the rituals of the highest grade of initiates. It was widely believed that the Order brought the head back from the sack of Constantinople during the Fourth Crusade in 1203–4, where Robert de Clari described the plethora of relics in the chapel of the Boucoleon Palace, among which was John's head.

That it was not merely intended to gather dust or excite muted respect from pilgrims is, once again, hinted by the knights who either told the Inquisition willingly or through torture about their practices. (Although of course enemies are notoriously liable to exaggerate the confessions of their victims, especially if produced through the thumb-screw and rack, not even the Inquisition was wrong all the time, and in any case the story can be pieced together from other sources.) Like Jesus and others of his day, and in keeping with the prevailing esoteric mind-set of their own, the Templars used the head for magical rituals, which they accomplished (or believed they did) through the raising of an *egregore*, a magical entity created by the power of the magicians' mind which then acts as servitor. As P.R.Koenig writes:

> The representation of the egregore as bust recalls the ancient literary tradition of animated statues or [the story of] Salome, who wanted the head of John the Baptist, probably to master his visionary powers . . . The classic prototype of such an egregore is Baphomet, the alleged egregore of the Templars, who was (as the Roman Emperor of the Gods) likewise worshipped in the form of a bust . . .[2]
>
> Supposedly a medium or statue could then serve as a tenant for the egregore, nourished by the sexual life-powers of the members.

Perhaps the Templars did not have the Baptist's skull after all, but were trying to summon his spirit through the magical activation of other severed heads or plaster or stone replicas.

## Secrets of the Franks Casket
As we have seen, the original grail stories contain ample clues about the true nature of the relic: those who seek it are described as 'baptized men' rather than 'Christians', they encounter a cross in the forest and beat it with sticks, and – most obviously – it is represented as a bearded head on a platter. But there is something else, which arose from an example of that encouraging phenomenon that occasionally attends the despairing researcher – the unannounced arrival of exciting new information. On a short break at Glastonbury in 2002, I was

introduced to Yuri Leitch, an esoteric researcher and gifted artist, who shared with me his discoveries about the Grail stories.

Inspired by the writings of the nineteenth-century polymath, the Reverend Sabine Baring-Gould[3] on the legends of the Sangréal, Yuri noted that he defends the stories of Wolfram von Eschenbach and Chrétien de Troyes against the charge of fabrication by citing an apparently earlier source, the eighth-century *Red Book of Hergest* (the *Llyfr Coch Hergest*), a volume of traditional Welsh legends. This source, however, may initially prove disappointing, for the twelfth century romances of Wolfram and Chrétien may actually pre-date it. However, Yuri has independently made a discovery that seems to back up Baring-Gould's theory: for in the British Museum there is an eighth-century artefact known as the 'Franks Casket' (named after Sir Augustus Franks, who presented it to the museum): a small whale-bone box covered in Anglo-Saxon runescripts and intricately carved scenes of biblical and Saxon/Nordic themes. The runes spell out inscriptions in Old Northumbrian Anglo-Saxon and Latin, but on one side of the casket there is a vowel-less encoded script that has so far eluded the best efforts of several scholars. Yuri writes:

> The back of the casket depicts the sacking of the Temple by the Roman Empire, and in the corner of the temple is a small character, showing the Romans a cup-like object. The runic inscription reads, 'Here fight Titus and the Jews. Here the inhabitants flee from Jerusalem'. A separate word says, 'Judgement', and another says, 'Hostage . . .'[4]

The front of the casket includes complicated references to whales (the box is made of whalebone), together with depictions of the adoration of the magi, and a 'scene from Norse tradition depicting the famous Elven-Smith, Wayland, working at his smithy . . .' As Yuri points out, '. . . this box is well thought out. Nothing on it has been carved due to artistic whim and fancy.' The mythical smith was the maker of sacred relics and magical artefacts, which is particularly significant here because at his feet lies the body of a decapitated man. Yuri describes the scene:

> In one hand Wayland holds in a large pair of Blacksmith's tongs the

decapitated man's head, and, most interestingly of all, in Wayland's other hand, he holds an identical cup-like object to the one held by the small figure in the Temple of Jerusalem . . . Furthermore, scholars have suggested that Wayland is actually making a ritual drinking vessel from the skull of the decapitated man . . .[5]

Yuri sums up this highly thought-provoking discovery:

> on the front of the Franks Casket we have the nativity of Jesus, and the 'Angel' Wayland, making a magical drinking vessel from a human skull; and on the back of the casket we have a figure being set free from the Temple of Jerusalem, holding the same magical vessel.
>
> In *Perceval* by Chrétien de Troyes, the Grail is promoted to be the cup into which Joseph of Arimathea collected the blood of Christ. In *Peredur* and the *Red Book of Hengest*, the Grail is not a cup but actually a decapitated head upon a platter; and if Sabine Baring-Gould is correct, the *Peredur* story is from the same era as the Franks Casket . . . The Knights Templar are said to have been the guardians of the Grail. They are also accused of worshipping a 'head'. Maybe both assumptions are true. Maybe the grail is both cup and head; a ritual drinking vessel made from a human skull, and made by Angelic/Elven forces?[6]

And of course the 'Angelic/Elven forces' could well be the spirit of John himself that Jesus' magic conjured up – at least in the popular belief.[7] It might be objected that the Franks Casket is basically Christian, with its depiction of the holy nativity scene, but even here there is a possible Johannite link for it is now recognized by some scholars that there was a body of 'John' literature – songs, hymns and perhaps even gospels – but it was either destroyed by Jesus' followers *or used by them as the basis at least certain major passages in the New Testament*.

Some of it was completely absorbed, only the name of the main character being changed: thus the nativity of *John* became that of Jesus, and *his* royal pedigree was appropriated by the pretender-Christ, while Herod commanded that the innocents be massacred in an attempt to root out and destroy *John*. Even the words of his mother

Elizabeth on discovering she was pregnant at an advanced age – 'My soul magnifies the Lord and my spirit rejoices in God my Saviour' – became Mary's much-loved 'Magnificat', spoken to reinforce the wonder, and fiction, of the Immaculate Conception. It is thought that the original 'John literature' became most of what are called the 'revelation discourses' in the Gospel of John (the name is thought to be a coincidence, although it may indicate that this John was a disciple of the Baptist). As the German theologian Rudolf Bultmann writes, these 'discourses' were:

> believed to have been originally documents of the followers of John the Baptist who had exalted John and originally given John the role of Redeemer sent from the world of Light. Therefore a considerable part of the Gospel of John was not originally Christian . . . but resulted from the transformation of a Baptist tradition.[8]

The realization that the *John* Gospels leaked into what became the New Testament may go some way towards explaining why it often seems as though there are two Messiahs in the scriptures: one, the hard cult leader with his exhortations to division and hatred and spiteful cursings of pigs and fig trees, and the other who urges forgiveness, neighbourly love and self-sacrifice. Perhaps the authors of the Gospels, writing towards the end of the first century, realized that they had little that was appealing on record about the real Jesus, so they simply lifted some episodes from the John literature with which to impress their readers. (Presumably before burning or hiding their source books.) A Johannite Templar and a Mandaean would have no difficulty in discerning to which 'Christ' should be attributed which sayings.

Yet even if we have all been revering the wrong Christ for centuries, none of this explains why Mary Magdalene – equally beloved of the same heretics who adore the Baptist – should have been on intimate terms with his usurper (or worse). Once again, however, there are many assumptions involved, for it is easy to be beguiled by the Gnostics as well as the mainstream believers. Even though she is portrayed with an apparent authority as the Apostle of the Apostles and acts as Jesus' unstoppable catechist, it must be remembered that these other gospels were written without direct knowledge of the real woman, the writers being unaware of the drama that had been played out between the rival factions of Jesus and John. (After all, the Jesus sect won and made sure that all hints of John's 'reign' were destroyed or subverted into the New Testament version of events.) To the Gnostics as to the orthodox Christians, Jesus was the true Christ and therefore Mary was his devoted servant, even if she was also his lover and/or sexual initiatrix. This, too, may well be a serious misreading of the true circumstances.

The assumptions are that she arrived in Gaul and preached Jesus' gospel, but, as we have seen, it is strange that she remained unmolested after preaching on the steps of the Temple of Diana at Marseilles. Was she in fact spreading *her own gospel*, in which Jesus may have received a relatively minor mention? Was this 'priestess' from a distant country bringing new life to an already well-established, goddess-worshipping tradition?

In *The Holy Blood and the Holy Grail*, Baigent, Leigh and Lincoln suggest that the 'sangréal' should be the 'sang real', or royal blood, the line of sacred kings who could trace their ancestry back to Mary Magdalene and Jesus Christ. But the alleged protectors of that line, the Priory of Sion, are *Johannites* and would never uphold any connection with Jesus. If there is any reverence given to any putative bloodline (and for both Jewish and Egyptian cultures the 'power' came through the female line) it is surely because of *her* involvement, not his. She is the representative of Isis, the goddess of love and magic, who empowers the sacred god-king. Why should she of all women be craven to the man she anoints and spread *his* gospel rather than their shared belief in the goddess?

Of course Isis was only one half of the eternal divine equation, for any powerful goddess of the ancient world there had to be the balance of the equal and opposite male energy in the form of the god. It is assumed even among revisionists and neo-pagans that the Magdalene's 'god' was Jesus, but what if she had seen through him and his showmanship and black magic? In Leonardo's *The Last Supper* she is leaning as far away from Jesus as she can, hinting at some deep rift between them, while St Peter cuts across her neck with his hand, and another raises the 'John gesture' into Jesus' face with unmistakable impertinence, perhaps even quiet anger, as if saying: 'Remember what you did to John the Baptist . . .'

Perhaps, in the end, it was not Jesus who was the Magdalene's consort, but *John*. There are distinct hints of the Isis myth in this: for at Abydos in ancient Egypt there was said to lie the head of the god Osiris, which communicated mystically with his devotees . . . What if even the alternative writers have been linking the Magdalene with *the wrong Christ*?

If the Magdalene and her retinue were consciously – or even unconsciously – enacting the myth of Isis and Osiris there are certain striking similarities between their deeds and those of the prime players in the old story. Osiris, the brother/husband of Isis, is murdered by the wicked Set, and torn to pieces, his head fetching up at Abydos. After magically reassembling his body, and giving birth to the god Horus, Isis then shocks those around her by having an affair with Set – although her motives may well have been to establish ultimate power over her husband's killer. Is this why the Magdalene took up with Jesus, whose followers may have had John executed? Assuming he did not actually die on the cross, is this why she abandoned him to his fate when he recovered from his crucifixion wounds, and fled to France? Was Mary Magdalene not a *Jesus* Christian at all, but the leader of the *John* Christians?

And, just as we know that the 'John literature' was absorbed into the New Testament as the story of Jesus, perhaps so, too, the Magdalene's love for 'Christ' – that useful cover term, as the Templars discovered – has come to be linked with the wrong man . . .

There are no hard-and-fast certainties, but many suggestive questions, which suddenly have free rein once the fetters of the Christian myth fall away. Of course Mary may have been simply Jesus' sexual and mystical initiatrix and never had any personal relationship with him at all beyond the anointing rite – the Gnostics and heretics may have heard a garbled story of the nature of their intimacy. Then again, she may indeed have loved him, almost as much as he was besotted with her, and even had his child or children, but something he did or said caused her to doubt him – and leave. It seems likely that this was his involvement, direct or indirect, with the death of the Baptist under suspicious circumstances.

Although the Bible never so much as hints that the Baptist and the black priestess even met, there is the sense that the Gospel writers were trying to prevent their readers from linking the two, perhaps through their connection with Bethany, scene of the anointing and Lazarus' resurrection ritual. Certainly, as we have seen, there is a mood of evasion about Bethany – calling it 'a certain village', for example – and it may well be because the Bethany family was in some way closely connected with the Baptist, perhaps even relatives. (If he were a close relation, he, too, may have been black . . .) Bethany may have been the centre of essentially *Mandaean* rites, which, if known, could raise suspicions about Jesus as John's usurper. And in this context it is interesting that, as Barbara G. Walker writes: 'In many early societies the old king was killed by the new king, usually called a "son" though he was no blood relative.'[9]

Was John killed to make way for the new chosen king? This implies a possible radical reinterpretation of the many passages in the New Testament when Jesus says 'I and the Father are One' or, more pointedly:

> No one comes to the Father except by me. If you really knew me, you would know my Father as well. From now on, you do know him and have seen him.
> . . . Don't you believe that I am in the Father and that the Father is in me? The words I say to you are not just my own. Rather, it is the Father, living in me, who is doing his work. Believe me when I say that I am in the Father and the Father is in me; or at least believe on the evidence of the miracles themselves . . .[10]

We know that the people – and even Herod – thought that Jesus could work miracles *because* he 'had' the spirit of John the Baptist, and here Jesus boasts that he and the Father 'are one', offering the miracles as proof of this. Was Jesus referring to his magical relationship with the spirit of the Baptist? It is interesting that he says *'from now on* . . . you do know him' as if there had been a specific ritual that marked the beginning of the 'Father's' passing into his own body and soul. (It is also interesting that Jesus uses the term *Abba* for 'Father' which implies a particularly close and familiar relationship – the equivalent of our modern 'Daddy'.)

Was the death of the Baptist in Herod's jail a *ritual murder* – intended to end the 'reign' of one 'king' and mark the beginning of the reign of the next? Let us not forget the enchanted head, which was believed to contain his enslaved soul, bestower of enormous power – perhaps even enabling its possessor to 'be worshipped as a god'? To modern eyes this may seem fantastic, but not to the people of that time and place – nor, much later, to the Templars. To them it made perfect sense, although its necromantic overtones filled many of them with horror.

Indeed, Yuri Leitch suggests a possible scenario whereby John's Head – believed to bestow magical powers – may have become the legendary Grail, or Graal. He writes intriguingly:

Suppose that Herod feared the popularity of John the Baptist so much that he had him killed [which, judging from Josephus, appears to have been the case]. Suppose Herod had kept the head of John the Baptist to 'control' the spirit of John, thereby disabling the confidence to revolt of the Johannite sympathizers.

Suppose that John the Baptist was long dead and beheaded before Salome (a Jesus sympathizer) requested his head on a platter . . . [which became] a massively prized [possession] of Herod's. He promised Salome anything, 'up to half his kingdom' and was yet reluctant to give her John's head.

Suppose that Salome then gives the 'head on a platter' to Jesus [who] gains popularity and Herod fears that Jesus is John reincarnated. (Maybe 'reincarnation' is the wrong translation of the original Hebrew; maybe Herod feared that Jesus was in possession of John's spirit, by possession of the head.)

The oldest Grail romance is the *High History of the Holy Grail,* written in Glastonbury about 1200 AD, based upon a much older, now lost, Latin history of the Grail. (The Franks Casket went to Glastonbury, where it was owned by Abbot Henry de Blois, 'the man who knew all the stories of the Holy Grail more than anyone else', and had an extensive library from which was written the *Antiquities of Glastonbury*, the very first book to recount the Holy Grail story of Joseph of Arimathea.)

In the 'High History' the Graal is specifically a 'most holy vessel' (*not* a cup, but a deep platter, which, according to the 'High History', had been used by Jesus and his disciples during the Last Supper.) *Could it have been John's head [ . . . ]*?[My emphasis.]

A Graal [certainly in France] is a communal eating bowl, in which one dips pieces of bread into the gravy while eating the meat. Jesus said: 'This is *my* body . . . this is *my* blood'![11]

Certainly the biblical stress on the peculiar fact that Herod's step-daughter requested John's head on a *platter* may be a clue as to what it was used for in the extraordinarily intense magical milieu in which John, Jesus and the Magdalene lived in that time and place. To modern thinking such a scenario is quite revolting, and inevitably Christians will react to such a suggestion with both outrage and nausea, but it should be remembered that even the Romans felt the same way about the perceived cannibalism and vampirism of eating the body and drinking the blood of Jesus. (Catholics still believe that the sanctified wafers are *literally* the body of Christ and the wine his blood through the miracle – and, it must be said, high magic – of the process of transubstantiation.) Indeed, when the Spanish imposed Christianity on the Aztecs, the conquered people had no difficulty in accepting the principle of the Mass because they had long drunk blood in their pagan rites.

If Jesus had somehow appropriated John's head from Herod's palace – or even, as Leitch suggests, his personal possession – he would hardly have been content to put it in the equivalent of a glass case to be occasionally dusted and admired. Those were *magical* days and those biblical characters thought in magical terms – especially if, as the *Talmud* indicates, Jesus himself was trained in Egyptian magic. The head would be used in whatever way was deemed to bestow greater power and glory on its owner. And traditionally, the Grail was kept and protected by *women* . . .

However John died, it seems that the heretics believed that the Magdalene ended up being the custodian of the head, or guardian of the Grail as the Templars would see it. But supposing she carried it to France, that was not the end of the story . . .

### The continuing quest

There is an old Templar saying: 'He who owns the head of John the Baptist rules the world', and clearly there are many esoteric groups who believe in its mystical and supernatural powers enough to prize the grisly relic highly. But what happened to it?

The Inquisition was in no doubt as to who had that much-sought after relic: they made it very clear that they believed it had fallen into the hands of the *Cathars*,[12] who guarded it jealously, even though in general they regarded the Baptist as a *demon*. This belief may have come from that abusive passage in the New Testament where Jesus describes John as 'born of women', adding that he is beneath even the most insignificant member of the cult. Or it may be a garbled version of the concept that John was Jesus' 'demon' – his servile spirit, enslaved through the black arts – which remained in this world, somehow magically locked into his skull. Even with a fearsome reputation – and presumably an unpleasant appearance – the relic would have been preserved and protected, for it belonged to the Son, and was of itself believed to be immensely powerful.

Was John's head spirited away from the Cathars' last stand at Montségur in 1244, perhaps with their own version of the Gospels? It seems that it continued to be associated with Mary Magdalene, long after that time, for there she is in Saunière's altar piece kneeling before a skull and an open book, which – in this case – may refer to the Cathar treasures of the Baptist's head and lost gospel.

There is an unusual phenomenon in the Languedoc – and other areas of southern France, besides the west of England – whereby churches dedicated to the Baptist tend to be close to those dedicated to the Magdalene, as if they were spiritually inseparable. Rennes-le-Château's two original churches – in that tiny village – were originally dedicated to the Baptist and the Magdalene, although one, somewhat ironically, was later rededicated to St Peter. It is the Magdalene church that was famously redecorated by the renegade priest Saunière, incorporating peculiar imagery that included a kneeling Magdalene with the book and skull. Indeed, in some places, her traditional jar of spikenard is replaced by a skull, which is interpreted as a reference to her attending Jesus at Golgotha – the 'Place of the Skull' – or as a *memento mori*, a reminder of the end to which we must all come. But what if Saunière's version was intended to speak to 'those with eyes to see' of the rival Holy Grail, the head of John the Baptist? Taken together with the emphasis of the Templarist group behind the Priory of Sion on being 'the swordbearers of the Church of John' – whose Grand Masters, like the kings of Ethiopia, were always called Jean/John/Giovanni – it is suggestive of a tantalizing Johannite connection. Perhaps the monarchist Masons that Saunière worked for were essentially Johannite and Magdalenian; certainly, there were rumours that the priest's ultimate ambition was to start a new religion, with its headquarters in the village, and his building plans included a large open-air baptismal pool. And, as we have seen, there are persistent rumours of Saunière having buried a mysterious chest in the foundations of his Villa Bethany – could it house the head of John? His housekeeper, Marie Denarnaud, wrote to another cleric about 'this thing of M. Jean' which she wished he would remove as she clearly found it repugnant and disturbing. Of course it may have been nothing more than something such as a filthy old beret left in church by a Mr John, but conspiracy theorists will seize on the other more exciting possibility.

(However, one must be wary of even hinting that John's head may be hidden somewhere in the neighbourhood of Rennes-le-Château, for many a promising career has come to grief in the light of similar suggestions. If the heretics' Holy Grail were ever to be found there, it would be an exquisite irony – and signal for the consumption of authorial headgear.)

France is the repository of intriguing connections with both the Baptist and the Magdalene, traditionally the representatives of repentance and penitence respectively, or male and female priestly power. In Provence, for example, close to villages in the area called Sainte-Madaleine, Sainte Marie and Sainte Jean respectively – and near the promontory of St Jean Cap-Ferrat (St John the Iron Head) – stands the chapel of Saint Sebastien, perched high on a rock above the sole road. Inside there is a picture of St Grat, a former bishop of the locality, holding the head of John the Baptist, and just five kilometres away inside the Templar church of Sainte-Croix, are frescos depicting Salome presenting the head of the Baptist to Herodias and Herod. The usual portrayal of John shows him baptizing Christ, but in originally Johannite areas his death is a major feature. And of course in the church at Rennes-le-Château the tableau shows him towering over the kneeling Jesus, whose posture mirrors exactly that of the crouching demon by the door. The Mandaeans would no doubt approve.

In recent years it has been suggested by Keith Laidler in his book *The Head of God* (1999)[13] that *Jesus'* skull is concealed beneath Rosslyn Chapel near Edinburgh – the extraordinary fourteenth-century building, the meaning of whose carvings are still the subject of hot debate[14] – arguing that the Templars discovered it on their travels and brought it back to their traditional Scottish centre. But as the spokesman for the modern Scottish Templars, John Ritchie, told the Edinburgh *Evening News*, 'In all the legends there is indeed worship of a skull, and that would very probably be *John the Baptist's*.'[15] In any case, despite various theories that there are relics or lost gospels under Rosslyn Chapel, there is every reason to believe that there is nothing to be found there at all. As a semi-mythic dumping ground for putative documents, sacred artefacts or heads, it is rapidly becoming Britain's answer to Rennes-le-Château.

Certainly, there are many legends about the strange fate of the Baptist's pitiful remains. There are at present at least two major candidates for the allegedly genuine article, at Amiens cathedral in northern France and in the Ummayad Mosque at Damascus – built over the fourth-century church of John the Baptist – where it lies hidden in a shrine behind a metal grille. One legend has it that Herod sent the head to Damascus so that the Romans could verify his death, while another says that when the Arabs took over the church in the seventh century John's blood bubbled up, and when the church was demolished, his head was found underneath, complete with skin and hair. That it is still deemed to possess magical powers is evidenced by the fact that it is the site of the Mandaeans' annual pilgrimage, where they press their foreheads against the metal grille and reportedly experience prophetic visions.[16]

Yet relics have a way of playing fast and loose with the hopes and faith of their believers: who is to say that the shrivelled skull in the Damascus Mosque is really that of John the Baptist – or, indeed, any of the other claimants?

Theories may be exciting, disturbing, and ironic, but there is little real evidence to suggest what really happened to John's skull. Perhaps it has simply rotted in the ground. Perhaps some group of modern Templar knights have it in their crypt, producing it for meetings and secret orgies of mystical rapture. Or perhaps an individual collector of antiquities has it – all unknowingly – stacked along with his or her other treasures: there it gathers dust, and – if there is any truth in the old ideas of magical rituals – the enslaved soul of John the Baptist, who may be the true Christ, groans quietly in the gloom.

Perhaps we shall never find John's head, if indeed it has somehow survived the sound and fury of two millennia. But if it did survive until at least the late fifteenth century, there may be a clue as to its whereabouts, which brings this investigation round in a neat circle. A nineteenth-century Rosicrucian poster from Paris depicts Leonardo da Vinci as 'Guardian of the Grail': we now know of his unambiguous Johannite devotion, so there can be little debate over what might be, to him at least, the Holy Grail. If he somehow came into possession of the Baptist's head – and as he clearly had Templar sympathies even 200 years after their suppression, he could well have known very high-ranking groups indeed – where could he have hidden it? It may not be too mischievous to suggest that his one remaining work of sculpture – of John the Baptist, which now stands over a porch of the Baptistry at Florence – may contain some clue, even part of the elusive relic itself.

This was a joint work, Leonardo's colleague being Giovan Francesco Rustici a notorious alchemist and necromancer, with whom he spent a considerable time shut away: Giorgio Vasari, the sixteenth-century art historian, says in his *Lives of the Artists* that while Leonardo and Rustici worked on this figure no one was allowed anywhere near them. Perhaps they were simply taking their time to perfect the job, or maybe there was even a sexual sub-text in their seclusion. But the Renaissance artists were also magicians who believed it was possible to imbue works of art with real life, even a form of consciousness, through what others would think of as the black arts – creating an egregore – just as Jesus was said to have used John's spirit to give himself greater powers. Did Leonardo and his friend take the opportunity to imbue their 'John the Baptist' with slightly more than a temporary breath of life? If the sculpture does contain something of the Johannite Holy Grail then life has not been too kind to it, for although the sculpture has been preserved, it now serves as target practice for flocks of pigeons.

Leonardo was buried in the church of St Florentin in Amboise, but when the church was destroyed by Napoleon's men it was said his skull was used as a football – if, indeed, it was *his* skull . . .

In the legends, the Grail was always attended by *women*, and we know of one woman who was an inseparable part of John's story, as she was of Jesus'. Her relics, too, may really exist somewhere, be they the object of fanatical devotion or forgotten in a remote cave or grave. If they were ever found, it would be interesting to have them tested for DNA, for then her racial background could be ascertained. The thought occurs, however, that no matter how authentic her bones may be, once they would be revealed to be those of a black woman the Church would deny they were hers.

As we end this examination of the hidden story of the Magdalene – and because it is impossible to understand her in isolation – also those of Jesus and John the Baptist, it is time to consider what suggestions we have uncovered after 2000 years of remorseless obfuscation, cover-up and conspiracy by those who have always hated her and all she stood for.

Mary 'called Magdalene' was not a prostitute as the Church taught until recently, neither – it seems – was she from Galilee, although she may have been ethnically a Jewish woman. Piecing together her true background from often fragmentary evidence, hints and clues – and even significant omissions – she emerges as one of the most significant of all religious and historical figures.

Known to the heretics as Jesus' 'Apostle of the Apostles', and as his *koinonos,* or sexual companion, clearly she was on intimate terms with the man who is still widely believed to have been a celibate, indeed eternally virgin, God incarnate. Yet there are strong suggestions, centred on the mysterious anointing, that she was not his legal wife, but rather his lover or even sexual initiatrix into the ancient pagan rite of the *hieros gamos,* or sacred marriage. With such authority to bestow divine kingship, it may be inferred that she was spiritually *superior* to Jesus, at least at the time of the anointing ceremony (which the male disciples only understood in terms of the waste of such costly ointment, completely missing the point of the age-old sacred ritual).

Certainly, the Magdalene of the Gnostic Gospels was central to the first days of Christianity, both as a preacher in her own right and as the woman with whom Jesus appears to have been besotted – a situation that did not meet with the approval of the insular and patriarchal Judaean men of his movement, especially Simon Peter who is believed to have hated her ('and all the race of women') so much that he threatened her life. This personal tension prefigured the later situation between his Roman Catholic Church and her secret underground women's movement, which found its apotheosis in southern France. (Where clues abound about the nature of her legacy: the Rennes-le-Chateau mystery includes the enigma of a real historical individual called Marie de Negre d'Hautpoul, or Mary the Black/of Darkness, the High Prostitute, or sexual initiatrix.) St Peter's Church was male-dominated, misogynist, exoteric – for the masses – and based on such inflexible dogma that to disobey or disbelieve was to invite a horrific death; her movement was essentially feminine and esoteric, apparently incorporating ancient goddess worship and initiatory rites of a sexual nature, and was much more intuitive and fluid.

The term 'Magdalene', while carrying the figurative meaning of 'elevated' or 'magnificent' may also refer to her place of origin – not a town on the shores of Lake Galilee as is usually claimed, for there was no Magdala there in her day – but perhaps the Egyptian Magdolum or even the Ethiopian Magdala. Certainly, there are strong suggestions that although she was connected with the mysterious family at Bethany during the Judaean mission, she had spent much of her life elsewhere: her behaviour – and indeed that of Jesus – was very much that of a foreigner, someone who either was not aware of the prevailing cultural requirements or even the Jewish Law, or was not inclined to take it seriously. According to the non-canonical gospels, she was well-known for behaving like a rich, independent and very un-Judaean woman: assertive, outspoken and feisty, completely lacking in the coy timidity expected of women in that time and place.

If of Ethiopian or even Egyptian origin she may well have been black, her colour inspiring the cult of the Black Virgin, which has always been associated both with her and with ancient pagan goddesses, including the equally black Isis, who is repeatedly linked with her among the heretics. There is another traditional connection between the Magdalene and blackness, for even the Church sees her as a Sheba figure – and that mysterious Queen is claimed by several black African countries as their own, especially Ethiopia. Besides, there are clues about blackness in the Grail legends, and in the comparison between the Magdalene and Simon Magus' Helen, who is unequivocally described as being black-skinned.

The Magdalene may well have been from Ethiopian-Jewish roots *and* a goddess worshipper, for King Solomon, said to have converted Sheba to Judaism, actually revered a version of Isis. Mary seems to have been a priestess of an Isian cult, a sexual initiatrix who took her religion to France, where it was immediately recognized and accepted by the priestesses of Diana. It seems that she preached her own version of the old religion.

The strongest candidate for that religion in the modern world is Mandaeanism, of which John the Baptist is deemed the greatest prophet and which, as we have seen, still harbours a profound dislike for Jesus as his usurper. Its complex – and, by the twenty-first century, apparently somewhat confused – theology includes the worship of the one true God, but also, along ancient Egyptian lines, reverence for several lesser gods and goddesses. Indeed, the Mandaean texts include references to Egyptian deities such as Ptah, so their roots may well have been heavily influenced by Egypt – and even later developments such as the riverine mystery religion of Serapis – while at the same time encompassing many of the older Judaic elements.

The Mandaeans originally boasted female high priests, but it was deemed politic to quietly drop this tradition when they settled among the Arabs because of the more misogynist attitude of Islam to women in public or religious office.[17]

*Was Mary Magdalene a Mandaean high priestess?* Was Bethany essentially the Judaean headquarters of John the Baptist's and the Magdalene's Mandaean mission? The Mandaeans consider Jesus himself as an ambitious member of the cult who usurped the prophet's following with lies and deceit, but *not* otherwise a major figure in their religion. His relatively minor status – and the possibility that the Magdalene was actually his spiritual *superior* sheds some light on the otherwise mysterious problems of their relationship. Perhaps he was not quite the hen-pecked man he appeared to be, after all, at least from reading between the lines of the Gnostic books, but was instead merely acknowledging her elevated status – which the non-Mandaean Judaean men found incomprehensible. Was early Gnostic Christianity therefore essentially the result of the only known major Mandaean mission? Certainly, John the Baptist was an uncompromising proselytizer – and he was their greatest prophet. Was Mary also a Mandaean missionary?

The Mandaeans are the world's only surviving Gnostics, having triumphed over every conceivable kind of persecution – if only just.

Yet today's followers are the first to admit that they have lost touch with much of their roots: a great many of their holy books remain untranslated and unknown to the modern generation, and the secrets of the old high initiates – especially in the tradition of female priests – may well have been lost for ever. What were their most jealously-guarded esoteric rites?

We know that the Magdalene and her brother John were involved in something that disturbed the uncomprehending writers of the canon-ical Gospels, something that involved Bethany, a place that seems to have made Matthew, Mark, Luke and John very uncomfortable. But why? Was it because of sexual rites that appear to have taken place there? We are told that John/Lazarus spent the night alone with Jesus clad only in a sheet, a fact that the early Church Fathers tried very hard to suppress. Perhaps the cult practised both heterosexual and homo-sexual initiations, while being otherwise celibate. One is reminded that the old temple of Solomon included not only goddess worship – and therefore sexually active priestesses – but also the services of sacred male prostitutes: were John/Lazarus and his sister Mary keeping that ancient tradition alive?

Certainly, there are strong hints of a sexual thread running through the early Jesus mysteries, for it is now acknowledged that he began as one of the Baptist's disciples, and we know that John's favourite was actually Simon Magus, who practised a sort of tantrism or sex magic with his consort Helen. Sexual mysteries, perhaps based on the well-established Isian tradition, seem to underpin both John and Jesus' esoteric teachings, a fact that has been ferociously covered up by the Church – and largely, but not entirely, the Gnostic groups, few of whom understood the basic principle of sexual alchemy, or the process of achieving supreme enlightenment through controlled orgasm.

Although there is nothing in the Bible to suggest that the Magdalene and the Baptist even met: both are marginalized in the same way, their celebrity used and abused in order to present a sani-tized version of the Jesus story as written by his followers. We know now that he and the Baptist were in fact bitter rivals, and there is even the possibility that Jesus' disciples had a hand in John's death – perhaps a magical ritual murder designed to imprison his spirit in his severed head and control it as a magical servitor. (Certainly the

Johannite Knights Templar are believed to have worshipped a bearded, severed head and trampled and spat upon a cross in their secret rituals.) Perhaps, too – as the original Grail stories strongly suggest – his head was used as a ritual cup or platter by the Jesus group, but whether this was with the connivance and approval of the Magdalene or viewed by her with absolute horror must remain a matter for conjecture.

Certainly legend has her taking the Holy Grail to France after the crucifixion, either effectively as a widow, running away from the naked hatred of Simon Peter, or – more shockingly – because she and the still-living Jesus had suffered a terminal rift, perhaps because of his hand in John's death. This would help explain the curious composition of the Johannite Leonardo's *The Last Supper,* in which John/Mary is depicted leaning as far away from Jesus as possible. The Magdalene's adopted homeland of France became the focus for many later Johannite groups, such as the mysterious Priory of Sion, the alleged 'Swordbearers of the Church of John', whose very name – 'Sion' – is Celtic for 'John'. Was Mary primarily a *Johannite* and *not* a Jesus Christian at all? Is this why the same heretical groups who revere John also venerate her, while being at best lukewarm towards Jesus and the Virgin Mary? Did she carry off the *Johannite* Grail – John's head – to prevent it falling into the hands of the Church, and to keep his earthbound spirit safe from its depredations?

The Languedoc still buzzes with rumours of tombs of 'Christ', graves of the Magdalene and the resting place of the Holy Grail. But while it would certainly be intriguing to discover her bones and the real head of John the Baptist – and whatever secret went to the grave with them, perhaps a lost gospel or two – death, skeletons and skulls are not the point of the missions of John, Jesus and Mary, for in their own ways they were not about death but life, believing it was possible to become divine. That this knowledge has been denied us for so long is a crime, and the self-hatred and brutality engendered by the organization that speaks for them can only result in yet more Magdalen laundries, more spiritual isolation and imbalance, yet more pain and despair. Who will now speak for the Magdalene? Who will have the love and courage to honour the black goddess of a very different Christianity, and in the stillness of their heart, listen to her ancient secrets?

# Afterword

*'Good is that which promotes life, evil is that which destroys it.'*
Albert Schweitzer (1875–1965)

One hears a great deal about 'Christian values' in the English-speaking world – indeed, that phrase is probably current wherever the churches have planted their flag. These values of honesty, decency, compassion, forgiveness and the desire for a happy family life are supposedly unique to those who profess the religion, but of course this is manifestly untrue. What about Jewish, Muslim, Hindu, pagan and even atheists' standards of integrity and ethical behaviour? Clearly, Christianity has no more a monopoly of the everyday virtues than it has of historical truth and spiritual gnosis. (Indeed, given the Church's history of violence, corruption and deceit – only some of which has been discussed in these pages – it might even be said that good Catholics exist not because of their religion but despite it.)

Once, before our tiny world was invaded by the uncomfortable truths of multi-culturalism, it was easy to equate the very word 'Christian' with inherent goodness: there was a time not so long ago in insular England when to declare that one was not a Christian would have been a very shocking thing indeed. Yet as we have seen, there is little about Christianity that actually encourages human goodness – Jesus himself said he came not to bring peace, but division, and urged his followers to abandon their families in order to be his disciples in ways worryingly reminiscent of modern cult leaders such as David Koresh. There has always been a harsh, unyielding background to the fabrication of 'Gentle Jesus, meek and mild', although few knew of it and those that did ensured that it did not become common knowledge.

In several senses, organized religions do humanity no favours: they do make wise and sensible rules, of course – few can argue with 'Thou shalt not kill', except in wartime, when the line between a God-given command and an urgent necessity suddenly becomes blurred – but they sometimes make more questionable and often ludicrous commandments. After the famous ten commandments (Exodus 20:1–17) comes the small print, which is justly less well known – including the instruction of how to deal with a Hebrew slave who refuses to be made a freeman after he has served his statutory six years with his master because he does not wish to abandon his wife and family, who are also part of the household. God told Moses how to deal with such a miscreant: he must have his ear pierced with an awl, then he will be the master's servant for life (Exodus 21:5), for which he was no doubt expected to be grateful. (Why not simply tell the slave he can stay?) Taken together with the complex dietary rules that not only forbid the eating of pork, but also a huge variety of creatures many of which no one in their right minds would want to consume, sometimes one almost suspects Yahweh of testing our sense of discernment – not to mention our sense of the absurd.

It could be said that the moment God's word is written down, it is subject to an incessant process of contamination by scribes, editors and the ruling priest caste, who shamelessly adapt it to suit their own ends. On the other hand, God has apparently given his word in so many forms over the centuries and to so many people that it is impossible to discern what was divinely inspired and what was not. If, indeed, any of it was.

It is fashionable to be pessimistic about humankind – look at the assorted messes we've got ourselves into, and the undoubted evil that pervades the whole earth: war, poverty, child abuse, slavery, drugs, corruption of various sorts, racism and sexism, bigotry, hypocrisy – the list is depressingly long. Finding it impossible to comprehend that a good God would be concerned with such a hell, the Gnostics developed the idea that there were two Gods – the evil one who ruled the Earth, and the good God who lived in Heaven. Undoubtedly almost every individual who has ever lived has had some experience of this life as living hell, but without necessarily adding to it him- or herself.

Most men and women are not all bad (although a very few undoubtedly are, and perhaps the sooner this non-politically correct fact is faced the better): people from all walks of life, all religions and no religion at all have shown a magnificent capacity for compassion and selfless courage. Faced with the evidence, it is hard not to concede that so-called 'Christian values' are in fact simply part of being human and have little connection with the worship of Jesus Christ. There is no need to believe in a miraculous Virgin Birth and a physical resurrection or the word of a long-dead desert prophet to feel and care for others.

Of course there is no denying that to ignore all the evidence about the Jesus of history and focus one's heart and soul on the Christ of faith can create a comfort-blanket *par excellence*. And who is to say that worshipping even what appears to be the total fabrication of a consistently gentle and compassionate Jesus, and taking him as a role model is always, ultimately, a pointless exercise? Many former hardened criminals have been converted by the immediacy of their belief in 'this myth of Christ', and of course that is no bad thing. But the radiant goodness they ascribe to the revelation of Jesus was arguably always inside them anyway, just waiting for the right trigger to make it manifest – and perhaps there are other ways of bringing it to the surface.

Faith is always an intensely personal matter – or at least it should be. Yet it can so easily make fools of us all: Christian cult-busters delight in excoriating groups whose leaders' prophecies fail lamentably, without a flicker of irony. But in his own day Jesus' Second Coming was expected at any moment – and he failed to show up. Many fundamentalist groups in the United States believed he would return in glory at the millennium, when all the true believers would be carried off in the 'rapture' in bodily form, to heaven, leaving the rest of us with our jaws on the ground, waiting to be claimed by the Devil. It is easy to mock, but Christianity is essentially a religion that still awaits the coming of the Lord, just as the Jews hope for the legendary Messiah. Faith all too often does make fools of us, in its many shapes and guises, be it the championing of alleged miraculous relics like the Shroud of Turin or the newer movements that have mushroomed in recent years into a massive sub-culture.

The great white, middle-class Anglo-Saxon Empire of the New Age, with its intricate re-workings of the Christian story – centred on the 'Master Jesus', who may or may not come from Venus – the Grail legends and the role of the Magdalene, is desperately trying to be Gnostic, but like the originals, has a serious problem with the awkward objectivity of history. To many New Agers the Grail stories are literally true – despite the facts that they are just as much works of fiction as any modern blockbuster, there is more than one of them, and even these are contradictory. Ironically any gem of truth hidden in the storytelling is usually overlooked because there is no historical framework in which to set the tales. As we have seen with the Gospels, context is almost everything, but there is a lamentable lack of serious research among the New Age: instead there is a tendency to sit at the feet of a variety of self-appointed gurus, much as the early Christians – both mainstream and Gnostic – sought a leader who could make sense of an essentially senseless myth. One may applaud their relentless questing, but all too often it recalls the classic line from that brilliant cinematic satire *Monty Python's Life of Brian*: 'You're the Messiah. I should know – I've followed a few.' One reads much of the New Age's literature with rising hysteria and quiet despair: one Glastonbury workshop of recent years in all seriousness offered to teach its goddess-worshipping attendees how to 'knit your own womb'.

In any case, although the goddesses had their own priestesses and mystery schools, the whole point of the Feminine Principle was that it was a constant balance and check to the opposite and equal Male Principle, the god who loved and respected the goddess' magic. Many of the new wave of goddess devotees are in danger of setting the pagan movement back centuries with their uterine exclusivity and neo-Gnostic silliness. Undiluted oestrogen can be a killer.

No doubt there will be those who mutter about sooty pots and kettles in the context of an author who apparently pitches her tent on the side of John the Baptist and the ancient Egyptian religion, but who also takes such an uncompromising stance in the subject of a great religion that millions hold dear. However, I should point out that I am hardly a committed Mandaean – no daily baptisms in the Thames for me – nor do I accept without serious questioning the often curious ancient Egyptian thinking. While I may find certain passages in the *Book of the Dead* fascinating because they are strikingly similar to the words of Jesus, and happily admit I find some of the Egyptians' more profound ideas exciting, hopefully even in my post-mortem state I will never find myself uttering lines like 'O Nosey who came forth from Heliopolis, I have not been rapacious'.[1] One has to draw the line somewhere.

Those qualifications notwithstanding, it does seem that many – if not most – people have an inherent need to worship, to express an upwelling of transcendent emotion and in doing so, to become personally transformed. Perhaps, as certain scientists are now suggesting, there is a 'God spot' in the brain, or perhaps as many mystics have claimed over the millennia, we are not simply bodies of dense matter, but also intrinsically refined spirit, which constantly strives to connect with its own world.

As I discovered for myself (see the Introduction), there are few more transformational events than the surprising and life-changing process of conversion: unfortunately, despite the sense of exclusivity that is the hallmark of conversion – and which reinforces the idea that one is joining the one true faith – precisely the same feelings pertain when becoming a Christian, Buddhist, Muslim, and probably even a Voodoo priestess. It is as if the sudden certainty and almost atavistic sense of belonging to a great spiritual tribe flicks on a switch that illuminates the entire world. Suddenly the Magdalene's titles of 'Lucifera' or 'Illuminatrix' take on a new and personal meaning. Losing that permanent secure glow is often terrible, but it certainly makes one grow up.

Reality can be almost unbearable: coming down to earth after the other-worldly joys of total belief in the characters from the fairy-tale propaganda brings with it a bone-wrenching thud. I can recall many occasions when something I read may have shown me the door to freedom, but it also made my heart thump and the blood rush in my ears. I have left libraries many times trembling and upset, for even decades after I had officially abandoned Christianity something in me still quivered in agony when exposed to the bleak imperatives of research.

To a Christian there can be few bleaker: the historical character of Mary the Mother was certainly not a virgin and, as we have seen, may even have been an adulteress; Jesus was probably a charlatan trained in the Egyptian conjurors' art who coveted the Baptist's popularity and may have taken drastic steps to usurp it; even the relative 'goodies' such as the Baptist and the Magdalene are by no means perfect. He was a prophet whose almost criminal naïveté ended in his own death and the scattering and persecution of his followers, while she could easily be seen as a strident harpy who lived out her own lust for glory.

The problem is that Jesus, John, Mary and all the other great religious names that are still revered from long ago are seen as it were in the glow of the haloes imposed on them over the centuries by generations of Christian worshippers. The average Christian sees Jesus as a fragrant and athletic hero who preached sentiments that would not be out of place at a liberal-minded middle-class dinner party. The average New Ager sees Mary Magdalene as a luminously white woman of movie star looks who spoke of her affection for 'the Master Jesus' as one might speak of a crush on a pop idol, embodying the tentative feminism of their own movement, not the vibrant outspokenness of the out-of-place priestess at one extreme, or the hugely influential power-behind the throne at the other. Yet of course the awkward fact is that not only would both of them be malodorous and – by modern standards – old before their time, not to mention notably non-Aryan in appearance (more probably in the case of the Magdalene) but they would embarrass and offend most modern Westerners by their sheer fanaticism. There is no possibility of dressing this up in acceptable modern fashions: such landmark preachers were fiery and uncompromising in their absolute belief in good and evil and the reality of heaven and hell, be they fuelled by a belief in ancient Solomonic goddesses, a new version of the Isis and Osiris story or even a heretical form of Judaism. They were very much the products of their time, place and to some extent cultural expectations – especially where Jesus' assumed Messianic role was concerned – and to understand them at all, they should be seen in their historical context. If the safe Sunday School story is rejected in favour of openness to a slice of real first-century life, it must be said that few of us would want much to do with it.

As we have seen, even many of the 'forbidden' or Gnostic gospels are as likely to contain flights of fancy, besides long and complex fanatical rants, as the biblical books. (Although they are remarkably consistent in providing real insights into the character and true status of the Magdalene.) Life at the time of Jesus, John and Mary was not subtle or sophisticated, and the original Christian compassion sat easily alongside a belief that sinners would suffer hellfire for all eternity. Some of the heretics, especially the Cathars who are so beloved of the New Age, behaved like the sort of extreme cult that is so despised by those same people today – starving themselves to death, taking poison and maltreating their physical bodies to the greater glory of their God. And of course the mysterious Knights Templar, who excite so many who read of them now, and who suffered so atrociously at the hands of the French king and the pope, were also happy to annihilate the 'heathen' with particular gusto and remarkable ferocity. Their times are not our times, their mentality almost incomprehensible to us, and in any objective investigation that touch on those eras one has to be very careful not to impose our own world-views on them, for the result can only be a travesty of what they were really about.

Yet the fact remains that however unacceptable a fanatical Magdalene may be to us today, what she stood for makes her perhaps *the most important woman in history*. Probably a black goddess-worshipping priestess, certainly of uncompromising assertiveness, a lover of Jesus and his spiritual equal, if not his superior, the very fact that the Church so zealously redrew and reinvented her has enormous implications for any serious evaluation of the progress of the world. It seems that it was because of the patriarchy's fear and hatred of the real Mary Magdalene that the gospels of the New Testament – in which she barely appears – were chosen out of so many others that lauded her to the skies, providing the male-dominated thinking for the whole of European history of the last two millennia, which then went on to infect many empires and colonies across the world. The ghost of the real Magdalene haunted the Church, even as it complied in the subjugation of other races and the spread of mass horror in the form of slavery. She pervaded the disenfranchisement of the Victorian women until even the richest were little more than their menfolk's chattels and was constantly at the back of the Church Fathers who ranted against the ordination of women priests, and the higher education of girls. And of course Mary Magdalene cried out for justice for the terrorised 'Maggies' and their outcast children, and for all those who still suffer abuse at the hands of nuns and priests, besides those who prey on the vulnerable in all religions and walks of life. Make no mistake, fear and hatred of that one woman, and a terror that the truth about her would come out, actually created much of the world's misery and changed the course of history.

The Church may be in its death throes, awash with seemingly endless scandals, but it is still possible to extract something helpful, even spiritual, from the crumbling edifice of the West's dominant religion, which may speak to our bruised souls and help them heal. Jesus/John said: 'The kingdom of God is within you' and 'By their fruits you will know them'. Perhaps it is unfortunate that few took the abjuration about the quality of the fruit seriously, allowing corrupt organizations to rise in power and take over mankind's hearts and minds. It may take centuries to know 'them' by their deeds, but it is still good advice, and the lesson of the Magdalen laundries is never to take anything on trust, and be unceasingly vigilant for abuses of the innocent.

'The kingdom of God is within you' also strikes home. We have sought divine archetypes on whom to project our own power, and perhaps this was a necessary stage in the spiritual evolution of our species. Where the ancient Egyptian teachings and the other pagan mysteries were superior to the three great patriarchal religions was that they encouraged ordinary men to believe they could be an Osiris or a Tammuz, and womenfolk to feel the power of the great goddesses within themselves, reaching to each other to know its full force.

The Isis/Osiris mysteries held out the potential for every individual to know, and be, God in one or another of his/her manifestations. Yet no one is suggesting that this was the one and only, ultimate answer. Make no mistake, no objective researcher could deny that the baser forms of Gnosticism and pagan practice were just as given to error as the most mindless and bigoted Christian way of life, but on the whole their adherents did have a precious personal knowledge that God was not shut away in his remote heaven: s/he – the indescribable divine, potentizing light – was inside each one of us.

Ironically, Jesus/John also said 'the truth shall set you free', and there is no doubt that it does: the problem is that there is a ragged gaping hole deep inside where the comfortable, if largely fictitious, religion once reigned supreme. What to put in its place?

Those of us who had been passionate believers know the pain of disillusionment, which is why so many take up another religion, or join another sect. Such natural acolytes become serial believers, in an almost endless cycle of falling in love with one creed or another, only to divorce it sooner or later on the grounds of mental cruelty. The desire to believe and to belong is often greater than the regard for objectivity. But in looking for another teacher, a Master to reveal the great secrets to us, they are constantly passing the buck – and completely missing the point. Free of priests, gurus and dogma, the progress of our spirit is – perhaps terrifyingly – nothing more or less than our own responsibility.

After years of making God in our own image, perhaps it is appropriate to allow him/her to return the favour, but this time from the inside out.

# Notes and References

## Introduction

1. Luke 10: 38–42.
2. *The Gospel of Mary Magdalene*, translated from the Coptic with commentary by Jean-Yves Leloup, Rochester, Vermont, 2002, translated into English by Joseph Rowe.

## Prologue  *Dirty Linen*

1. Starring Anne Marie Duff, shown on 26 March 2002, BBC1.
2. 27 January 1999.
3. Ibid.
4. Ibid.
5. For example, the actress Maggie Smith's mother worked in a Glaswegian laundry in 1912 where, according to Mrs Smith's son Ian: 'the hard and degrading work instilled in her a life-long horror of such soul-destroying employment'. See *Maggie Smith: A Bright Particular Star* by Michael Coveney, London, 1992, p. 33.
6. James Walvin, *Black Ivory: Slavery in the British Empire*, Oxford, 1992, p. 56.
7. *The Standard Times*, 1998.
8. Ean Begg, *The Cult of the Black Virgin*, London, 1996, p. 129. He credits Jean Markale with the discovery of the fact that women once celebrated Mass in Ireland.
9. I am indebted to Robert Brydon for his anecdote about visiting this

institution as a young man, and the memory he carries to this day of its repressive and hopeless atmosphere.

**Chapter 1**  *The Outsiders*

1. See, for example, *The Templar Revelation*, Lynn Picknett and Clive Prince, London, 1997, p. 21.

2. Walter Pater, *The Selected Writings of Walter Pater*, Columbia University Press, 1982, p. 46.

3. In the National Geographic's 2002 video 'Leonardo: The Man Behind The Shroud?', produced by Stefilm, directed by Susan Gray. Clive Prince and myself were also featured.

4. It was a lizard painted silver, with wings stuck on. Pope-frightening was one of Leonardo's hobbies.

5. See *Turin Shroud: In Whose Image?* Lynn Picknett and Clive Prince, London, 1994. However, for those inclined to dismiss the Leonardo theory out of hand on the grounds that the carbon dating put the likeliest years for the faking of the Shroud – 1290–1390 – before the birth of the artist (1452), first: the carbon dating did allow an upper date of 1500, and second: does one seriously suppose that a genius and perfectionist like da Vinci would use new cloth for something that was supposed to be 1500 years old?

6. This fact has not been lost on other authorities, such as Serge Bramley who admitted as much in the video 'Leonardo: The Man Behind The Shroud?' (see (3) above).

7. See *The Templar Revelation*, Chapter One.

8. Such as Maria Consolata Corti, the Italian author who also argues that Leonardo created the Turin Shroud. However, she believes he did so out of *Christian piety*, although this neither matches his known cynicism about religion nor the mind-set of a late medieval Christian, who would never have dared put his own face in the place of Jesus', especially covering it with *fake* redemptive blood.

9. As described in *Turin Shroud: In Whose Image?* Leonardo basically created the so-called miraculous Shroud image by using a basic photographic technique: chemically-treated cloth, a pin-hole camera and large doses of light. If this sounds implausible, it is known that Leonardo was obsessed with optics and the basis of what we now call photography – and that he built his own camera obscura. It is remark-

ably easy to produce a 'Shroud' image in this way, although time consuming. The instructions are given in our book: try it!

10. At the *Fortean Times* UnConvention in spring 1999. We are indebted to Bob Rickard for the many opportunities he has given us to present talks to his conferences.

11. Although the delegates of the UnConvention may seem to outsiders to be the usual mix of anoraks and eccentric enthusiasts for the unexplained, in reality they are usually tough-minded sceptics for some reason.

**Chapter 2**  *The Magdalen Alternative*

1. Given on pp. 110–12 of Wolff (ed.), *Documents de l'histoire de Languedoc*, which also give three other contemporary accounts of the atrocity. The extracts reproduced here were translated by Clive Prince.

2. Walter Birks and R. A. Gilbert, *The Treasure of Montségur*, London, 1990, p. 78.

3. Ibid., p. 79.

4. Ibid., p. 81.

5. Although he refused to eat meat, declaring that he would not permit his body to become the 'charnel house' for dead creatures, his accounts list payments for fish. It should be pointed out that vegetarianism was seen to be nothing less then heresy – it was called 'the devil's banquet' – because God had given mankind domination over the creatures of the earth, and therefore it was sacrilege to avoid eating them. Getting away with vegetarianism was only one of many instances of Leonardo apparently leading a charmed life.

6. Despite the denial of the churches and continuing theological arguments, there seems little doubt that Jesus and his followers did believe in reincarnation. For example, Jesus himself spoke of the prophet Elias coming again as John the Baptist. (Mark 16:15–34 and Matthew 28:46–47)

7. Written in the Langue d'Oc, and published by Clédar in 1887, it can now be found in the Lyon Library. (Translated into French by E. Nelli in his *Ecritures Cathares*.)

8. Stoyanov draws our attention to the fact that the 'Rainerius' tract has been printed in Dondaine, *Un traité néo-manichéen*, pp. 64–78.

9. Stoyanov, p. 164.

10. Ibid., p. 139.

11. H. T. F. Rhodes, 'Black Mass', *Man, Myth and Magic*, no. 10 (1971), pp. 274–8.
12. See, for example, Ean Begg's *The Cult of the Black Virgin*, p. 107.
13. Stoyanov, p. 223.
14. All Bible quotations are taken from the New International Version, 1973.
15. See Carla Ricci, *Mary Magdalene and Many Others*, Tunbridge Wells, 1994, p. 42, note 52.
16. Ibid., p. 50.
17. H. von Campenhausen, *Ecclesiastical Authority and Spiritual Power*, London, 1969; first published in German as *Kirchliches Amt und geistliche Vollmart*, Tübingen, 1953.
18. See Mark 16:9; John 20:11–17.
19. Elaine Pagels, *The Gnostic Gospels*, p. 39.
20. Ibid., p. 39.
21. Mark 15:40.
22. See, for example, the note on p. 721 of the New International Version of the Bible.
23. Mark 16:9.
24. Luke 8:1–3.

**Chapter 3** *Sacred Sex and Divine Love*

1. Quoted in Henry Corbin's *La topographie spirituelle de l'Islam iranien*, La Différence, 1990.
2. Susan Haskins, *Mary Magdalene: Myth and Metaphor*, p. 93.
3. Picknett and Prince, *The Templar Revelation*, p. 251.
4. *The Gospel of Mary Magdalene*, pp. xvi–xvii.
5. See, for example, Barbara G. Walker, *The Woman's Encyclopedia of Myths and Secrets,* San Francisco, 1983, p. 886.
6. Luke 7:39.
7. Luke 7:44–47.
8. The importance of the shadowy Bethany family is closely argued in Hugh J. Schonfield's *The Passover Plot*, London, 1965.
9. *The Templar Revelation*, p. 241.
10. Pagels, p. 81.
11. Morton Smith, *The Secret Gospel,* London, 1973, p. 17.
12. Picknett and Prince, p. 242.
13. See Desmond Stewart's *The Foreigner,* London, 1981, p. 108.

14. John 1:28.
15. See Hugh Schonfield, *The Passover Plot*, p. 156.
16. Timothy Freke and Peter Gandy, *The Jesus Mysteries*, London, 1999, p. 95.
17. Stewart, p. 62.
18. Mark 14:4.
19. Jean-Yves Leloup, p. xxi.
20. Kiddushim 1:7.
21. Walker, p. 501. She refers to J. J. Bachofen's *Myth, Religion and Mother Right*, Princeton, N.J., Princeton University Press, 1967.
22. See *The Scottish Coronation Journey of King Charles I*, by Robert and Lindsay Brydon, Privately printed, Edinburgh.
23. Walker, p. 584.
24. Leloup, pp. xx–xxi.
25. See the last chapter of Picknett and Prince's *The Stargate Conspiracy*, and Jeremy Narby's seminal work, *The Cosmic Serpent: DNA and the Origins of Knowledge*, London, 1998.
26. *The Stargate Conspiracy*, p. 350: 'The role of Isis [in the ancient Egyptian shamanic process] is particularly interesting because it portrays the feminine principle as being essential to the shamanic journey. In fact, the whole concept of female initiates has been sadly neglected, but perhaps for unexpected reasons. At a London conference in October 1996 . . . Jeremy Narby was questioned on why all the shamans he had mentioned in his talk were men. He replied that specially selected women often sit with [them] as, fuelled with [a] drug, they embark on their out-of-the-body adventures. The women actually accompany them and share in their experience, and afterwards, when they have returned to normal consciousness, help them remember what took place in those other realms. But the important point is that the women do all this *without taking ayahuasca* [a psychoactive drug]. Clearly, the female companions of the shamans have no need of chemical aids for their spiritual flights.'
27. Edersheim, vol. i. p. 571.
28. *A Dictionary of the Bible: Dealing with its language, literature, and contents including the Biblical theology,* edited by James Hastings, M.A., D.D., Edinburgh, 1900, p. 284.
29. Hugh Schonfield, *The Pentecost Revolution*, London, 1974, p. 278.
30. See Hugh Schonfield's, *The Passover Plot*, p. 209.

31. Burton L. Mack, *The Last Gospel: The Book of Q and Christian Origins*, Dorset, 1994, p. 51.
32. I am indebted to Keith Prince for providing this information.
33. See G. R. S. Mead (ed), *Simon Magus: An Essay*, 1892, pp. 28ff. He is quoting from the third-century *Clementine Recognitions*.
34. Acts 10:9ff.
35. The British won: there is now a move to have the gold and sacred objects they looted returned to Ethiopia.
36. See Baigent, Leigh and Lincoln's *The Messianic Legacy*, London, 1986.
37. Starbird, p. 50.
38. Walker, p. 570.
39. The Gnostic *Gospel of Thomas,* for example – see next chapter.
40. For example, Morton Smith, *Jesus the Magician*, London, 1978, p. 25.
41. Matthew 11:19.

**Chapter 4**   *Apostle of the Apostles*
 1. Elaine Pagels, *The Gnostic Gospels*, 1979, p. 14.
 2. *The Gospel of Mary Magdalene,* translated by Jean-Yves Leloup, Introduction by David Tresemer Ph.D. and Laura-Lee Cannon, Rochester, Vermont, 2002, p. xi.
 3. Hippolytus' *Refutations of All Heresies* VIII 12, translated by Kraemer, *Maenads,* 255. For the surviving oracles spoken by these women prophets see Ronald Heime, *The Montanist Oracles and Testimonia*, North American Patristic Society, Patristic Monograph Series no. 14, 2–9 Macon, GA, Mercer University Press, 1989. Of course the remnants of the female prophecies were kept by the misogynist Church Fathers, who may well have been somewhat selective in their choice of material and radical in their editing.
 4. *The Gospel of Mary Magdalene,* translated by Jean-Yves Leloup, 1997, p. xi. Their own reference reads: 'James Carroll, *Constantine's Sword*, New York, Houghton Mifflin, 2001.'
 5. Ibid., pp. 14–15.
 6. *Gospel of the Egyptians: 40:12–13,* in the Nag Hammadi Library (NHL) 195.
 7. Pagels, p. 15.
 8. Ibid., p. 19.

9. Elaine Pagels indicates that some words in this passage are missing and have been supplied by scholars. I have reproduced the extract without indicating these words for the sake of clarity and readability.

10. Irenaeus, AH *Praefatio*, quoted on p. 17 of Pagels.

11. Ibid., AH 3.11.9.

12. Pagels, p. 17.

13. Karen Jo Torjesen, *When Women Were Priests*, San Francisco, 1993, pp. 158–159.

14. Tertullian, *De Praescriptione Haereticorum*, 41.5.

15. Pagels, pp. 72–73.

16. Ibid., p. 73.

17. *Trimorphic Protennoia*, 42.4–26, in NHL 465–6/45.2–10, in NHL 467.

18. See for example, the *Daily Mail*, 'Vicars Told To Treat God "as a woman"' by Chris Brooke, 3 April 2002.

19. This is usually given as 'Thunder, Perfect Mind', but I take the point of Timothy Freke and Peter Gandy, who, in note 1 to Chapter Five of their book, *Jesus and the Goddess*, state: '*The Thunder, Perfect Mind*, NHC, 6.2.13 and 16, in Robinson, J.M. [*The Nag Hammadi Library*], 1978, 297, 299. The introduction to this text in the NHC makes clear that the two parts of the title are unrelated. We have consequently omitted *Thunder*, as it appears nowhere in the text.'

20. *Thunder, Perfect Mind* 13.16–16.25, in NHL 461–2.

21. Armstrong, p. 38.

22. I Corinthians 15:3–8.

23. See the Introduction of the *Pistis Sophia*, translated by G.R.S. Mead, Kila, MT., USA, 1921.

24. Ibid., First Book, 36.

25. Ibid., Second Book, 72:3.

26. *The Gospel of Mary Magdalene*, p. 18.

27. Ibid., p. 9.

28. Ibid., p. 7.

29. Ibid., First Book.

30. Ibid., p. 231.

31. *Gospel of Thomas*, 51:23–6; in NHL 130.

32. Pagels, p. 86.

33. They are now in the Royal Collection at Windsor.

**Chapter 5** *The French Connection*
1. *Pistis Sophia,* Second Book, 72:161.
2. I am indebted to Mike Wallington for suggesting this theory.
3. De Voragine, *The Golden Legend,* vol. 1, pp. 374ff.
4. Such as *The Templar Continuum* by Alan Butler and Stephen Dafoe, Ontario, 1999.
5. For details see Picknett and Prince.
6. Baigent, Leigh and Lincoln, *The Holy Blood and the Holy Grail,* London, 1982, p. 83, citing Michelet, *Procès des Templiers,* Paris, 1851.
7. John 1:29.
8. See *The Hiram Key* by Christopher Knight and Robert Lomas, London, 1996.
9. See *The Sign and the Seal* by Graham Hancock, London, 1992.
10. Raymond Lull, Catalan occultist and mystic, 1232–c.1316.
11. From Lull's *Liber de acquisitone terrae sanctae* (March 1309), quoted in Hillgarth, *Lull and Lullism in Fourteenth-century France,* p. 104. I am indebted to Keith Prince for the translation.
12. Susan Haskins, *Mary Magdalen,* London, 1993, p. 22.
13. Such as the new Liverpool Cathedral, built in the 1960s.
14. See Lee Irwin, 'The Divine Sophia: Isis, Achamoth and Ialdaboath', in David Fideler (ed.), *Alexandria 3,* Grand Rapids, 1995.
15. Hancock, p. 306.
16. Such as Notre Dame de Souterrain (Our Lady of the Underworld) at Chartres.
17. Barbara G. Walker, *The Woman's Encyclopedia of Myths and Secrets,* San Francisco, 1993, p. 866–7.
18. See, for example, the reception ceremony described in Appendix B of Malcolm Barber, *The New Knighthood: A History of the Order of the Temple,* Cambridge, 1994.
19. And even a form of credit card: having deposited their money at one preceptory, and received a receipt, they could then spend their money at any other Templar property.
20. Including, of course, *Monty Python's Search for the Holy Grail.*
21. Ean and Deike Begg, *In Search of the Holy Grail and the Precious Blood,* London, 1995, p. 79.
22. Malcolm Godwin, *The Holy Grail: Its Origins, Secrets and Meaning Revealed,* London, 1994, p. 47

23. See *The Templar Revelation,* which devotes two chapters to the subject, and the Selected Bibliography.

24. Perhaps this has something to do with the fact that although the village boasts a bar, a hotel (Saunière's Bethany House) and an occult bookshop, there is no grocery store. For a village perched on the very top of an almost vertical hill, this is more than a passing inconvenience. For all his great plans for the village, Saunière seems to have overlooked the basic necessities.

25. Notably Richard Andrews and Paul Schellenberger, *The Tomb of God,* London, 1996. For a refutation of their theory, see Appendix II of *The Templar Revelation.*

26. The Grand Master of the Priory of Sion at the time Baigent, Leigh and Lincoln were writing their book, Pierre Plantard de Saint Clair, said that the Order of the Temple (of which the Priory was allegedly the secular arm) was: 'the swordbearers of the Church of John and the standard-bearers of the premier dynasty, the arms that obeyed the spirit of Sion'. 'Sion' is usually taken to refer to the biblical land, is also *Welsh for 'John'* – and the Priory has an inexplicable interest in the Celtic language.

27. I am very grateful to Clive Prince for sharing his groundbreaking research with me.

28. St Sulpice also has darkly heretical connections. For example, it is the setting for J. K. Huysmans' satanic novel *Là bas (Down There),* which contains a description of a Black Mass. The church also served as headquarters for the mysterious seventeenth-century secret society called the Compagnie du Saint-Sacrement, which is said to have been a front for the Priory of Sion (which in turn is a front for various Templarist Masonic organizations).

29. Ean Begg, *The Cult of the Black Virgin,* London, 1985; revised 1986, pp. 193–4.

**Chapter 6** *'Black, but Comely . . .'*

1. Begg, pp. 8–9.
2. Ibid., p. 8.
3. Barbara G. Walker, *The Encyclopedia of Women's Secrets and Mysteries,* San Francisco, 1983, p. 670.
4. Ibid., p. 671.

5. E. Cobham Brewer, *Dictionary of Phrase and Fable,* New York, 1894.

6. Martin Bernal, *Black Athena*, London, 1987, p. 116.

7. Ibid., pp. 116–117.

8. Although at the time of writing Mary the Mother is still only the 'Blessed Virgin Mary', there are moves afoot – largely the initiative of Pope John Paul II himself – to acknowledge her as joint ruler of Heaven with her son.

9. Morton Smith, *Jesus the Magician,* New York, 1978, p. 25. He notes that Jesus snubs his mother on two occasions: Mark 3:31ff and Mark 6:1ff – and she is not even mentioned in the 'Q' source material for the gospels.

10. Matthew 12:46–50.

11. Mark 6:3; Matthew 13:55–6.

12. Picknett and Prince, p. 78.

13. Begg, p. 72.

14. Ibid., p. 125.

15. Susan Haskins, *Mary Magdalen*, London, 1993, p. 63.

16. *Song of Songs* 3:1–4.

17. See for example,
www.colorq.org/Bible/Tanakh/SongofSolomon.htm

18. Numbers 12:1.

19. Graham Hancock. *The Sign of the Seal*, London, 1992, pp. 269–75.

20. Pliny, *Hist. Nat., VI*, 35.

21. Acts 8:26–27 and Jerome 53:2–5.

22. For example, at the time of writing in mid-2002 the British Museum is currently showing an exhibition about the excavations in the Lebanon that are believed to reveal the ruins of her ancient palace.

23. 1 Kings 10ff.

24. http//www.swagga.com/queen.htm

25. Matthew 12:42.

26. The fourteenth-century *Kebra Negast (Glory of Kings)* was translated from a Coptic original found before 325 CE among the treasures of St Sophia in Constantinople.

27. Robert Silverberg, *The Realm of Prester John*, Ohio, 1972, pp. 177–8.

28. BBC Online Network, 31 May 1999 See http://news.bbc.co.uk/hi/english/world/africa/newsid_353000/353462.stm

29. Ibid.
30. Ibid.
31. Jacqueline Pirenne, 'Des Grecs à l'aurore de la culture monumentale "Sabéenne"' in R. Fahd (ed.), *L'arabe preislamique et son environment historique et cultural*. (Actes de colloque de Strasbourg, 24–27 June 1987), published by Université des sciences humaines de Strasbourg, 1989. Quoted in Hancock, p. 460.
32. Hancock, p. 75, quoting Wolfram von Eschenbach, *Parzival*, (trans. A. T. Hatto), London, 1980.
33. Ibid., p. 75.
34. Ibid., p. 75.
35. Ibid., p. 78–9.
36. Ibid., p. 47.
37. Luke 8:3.
38. Matthew 12:42.
39. John Romer, *Testament: The Bible and History*, London, 1988.
40. Hugh Schonfield, *The Essene Odyssey*, Shaftesbury, 1984, p. 165.
41. Karl Luckert, *Egyptian Light and Hebrew Fire*, New York, 1991.
42. The Acts of Peter, quoted in Owen St Victor, *Epiphany*, Leuvens, 1991, p. 37.
43. Ibid.
44. Barbara G. Walker, *The Encyclopedia of Women's Myths and Secrets*, San Francisco, 1983, pp. 602–3.
45. Magdala was used as the base of operations for the Emperor Tewodros II in the middle of the nineteenth century, during his attacks on the neighbouring countryside, but in 1867 he made the grave error of imprisoning several British diplomats. This was his undoing: the following year a military expedition led by Sir Robert Napier seized Magdala and rescued them. The Ethiopian king committed suicide, while Sir John became Baron Napier of Magdala for his heroism. Unfortunately, the British made off with a huge haul of gold and sacred relics, which is the subject of an ongoing and highly controversial attempt by the Ethiopian government to take back these looted treasures, their version of the Elgin Marbles.

**Chapter 7**  *The Rise and Fall of God's Wife*

1. Kings 10:1.
2. Kings 10:3.

3. King Solomon, *Kebra Negast*.
4. Queen of Sheba, *Kebra Negast*.
5. Raphael Patai, *The Hebrew Goddess*, Detroit, 1990, p. 25.
6. Ibid., p. 25.
7. Ibid., pp. 28–29.
8. Exodus 19:15.
9. Karen Armstrong, *The End of Silence*, London, 1993, p. 38. Her comments were inspired by the writings of Jewish feminist writer Judith Plaskow. See her *Standing Again At Sinai*, San Francisco, 1990.
10. Armstrong, p. 38.
11. Patai, p. 34.
12. William F. Allbright, *From the Stone Age to Christianity*, Baltimore, 1940, p. 78.
13. Patai, p. 38.
14. Genesis 30:10–13.
15. 1 Kings 11:4.
16. 1 Kings 11:6.
17. Patai, pp. 44–45.
18. William G. Denver, 'Asherah, Consort of Yahweh? New Evidence from Kuntillar "Arjund"', *Bulletin of the American School of Oriental Research (BASOR)*, vol. 255, 1984, pp. 21–27.
19. André Lemaire, 'Who or What Was Yahweh's Asherah?' *Biblical Archaeology Review*. vol. 10 no. 6, Nov/Dec 1984, p. 42.
20. Armstrong, p. 24, referencing 1 Kings 12:28; 1 Kings 21:3 and 2 Kings 21:3.
21. 1 Kings 15:12–13; Chronicles 14:2–4; 15:8,16.
22. Julian Morganstern, 'Amos Studies III', *Hebrew Union College Annual*, vol. 15, 1940, p. 121, note 98.
23. Patai, p. 50.
24. 1 Kings 15:11–14.
25. Patai, p. 221.
26. A. T. Mann and Jane Lyle, *Sacred Sexuality*, Shaftesbury, 1995, p. 137.
27. Jean Robin, *Le royaume du graal,* Paris, 1992, p. 266.
28. Picknett and Prince, p. 86.
29. Patai, p. 96.
30. Proverbs 8:22–31.
31. Patai, p. 98.

32. Ibid.
33. See the *Pistis Sophia,* for example.
34. Nelson Glueck, *Deities and Dolphins, The Story of the Nabataeans,* New York, 1965, p. 166.

**Chapter 8** *Resurrecting Egypt*
1. See, for example, Aishylius' play *The Suppliants,* which was apparently intended to be a trilogy. One of the lost pieces was called *The Egyptians,* and in any case the extant play concerns the settlement of Argos with fugitives from 'Aigyptos'.
2. For example, Professor Karl Luckert, *Egyptian Light and Hebrew Fire,* New York, 1991.
3. Whose name is the truncated form of 'Thothmoses', Thoth being the Egyptian god of wisdom.
4. R. O. Faulkner, *The Ancient Egyptian Book of the Dead,* New York, 1972, revised edition London, 1985.
5. The pyramids at Giza lie about twelve miles to the south-west of Heliopolis.
6. Adbel-Aziz Salah, *Excavations at Heliopolis, Ancient Egyptian Ounu,* 2 vols., Cairo, 1981–3, p. 23.
7. Jamieson B. Hurry, *Imhotep, the Vizier and Physician of King Zoser and afterwards the Egyptian God of Medicine,* revised ed., Oxford, 1928, p. 11.
8. Picknett and Prince, *The Stargate Conspiracy,* London, 1999, p. 3.
9. Ibid., p. 4.
10. Mark Lehner, *The Complete Pyramids,* London, 1997, p. 142.
11. The standard translation is that of R.O. Faulkner: *The Ancient Egyptian Pyramid Texts,* revised ed., Oxford, 1969. However, many passages remain obscure.
12. Picknett and Prince, p. 9.
13. See *New Scientist,* 12 September 1998.
14. Picknett and Prince, p. 11. I am indebted to Filip Coppens for his original insight.
15. Martin Bernal, *Black Athena vol. I,* London, 1987, p. 2.
16. Ibid., p. 15.
17. André Vandenbroek, *Al-Kemi: Hermetic, Occult, Political and Private Aspects of R. A. Schwaller de Lubicz,* Hudson, 1987, p. 203.
18. R. A. Schwaller de Lubicz, *Sacred Science,* p. 100.

19. Ian Shaw and Paul Nicholson, *British Museum Dictionary of Ancient Egypt*, London, 1995, p. 239.
20. C. de Brosses, *Du culte des dieux fétiches ou parallèle de l'ancienne religion de l'Egypte avec la religion actuelle de Nigritie*, Paris, 1760. See also F. E. Manuel, *The Eighteenth Century Confronts the Gods*, Cambridge, Mass., 1959, pp. 184–209.
21. Bernal, note 81 to p. 244.
22. J. A. de Gobineau, *Oeuvres*, Paris, 1983, vol. I, p. 221.
23. Bernal, p. 241.
24. Gobineau wrote: 'I need not add that the word honour, like the concept of civilization which contains it, are equally unknown to the Yellows and the Blacks.' *Oeuvres*, vol. I, p. 342.
25. Bernal, p. 241.
26. Ibid.
27. http://news.bbc.co.uk/hi/english/world/africa/newsid_353000/353462.stm
28. Macrobius, *Saturnalia*, 1.20.13.
29. Apuleius, *The Golden Ass*, translated by Robert Graves, London, 1950.
30. Spell 78.
31. Spell 80.
32. Ibid.
33. R. Melkelbach, 'Isis', *Man, Myth & Magic*, no. 51, p. 1461.
34. Hosea 11:1.
35. Matthew 2:13–15.
36. Karl W. Luckert, *Egyptian Light and Hebrew Fire*, New York, 1991, p. 319.

**Chapter 9**  *The Jesus Myth Exposed*

1. Desmond Stewart, *The Foreigner*, London, 1981, p. 14.
2. The Nero deification myth also had the magi returning by a different route for diplomatic reasons. I am indebted to Keith Prince for pointing this out.
3. Authors of *The Jesus Mysteries*, London, 1999 and *Jesus and the Goddess*, London, 2001.
4. Hector Hawton, Introduction to Robertson, *Pagan Christs*, New York, 1993, originally published 1903, p. 8.
5. Ibid., p. 68.

6. Ibid., pp. 52–3.
7. Raphael Patai, *The Hebrew Goddess*, p. 51.
8. Freke and Gandy, p. 6.
9. For example, Hugh Schonfield, whose *The Passover Plot*, London, 1965, argues that Jesus was primarily a political figure working for Palestine's independence from Rome, who consciously shaped his own career to fit that of the expected Messiah.
10. Isaiah 7:14.
11. Stewart, p. 15.
12. See, for example, Mark 6:3: 'Isn't this the carpenter? Isn't this Mary's son and the brother of James, Joseph, Judas and Simon? And aren't his sisters here with us?'
13. In Josephus' *Antiquities of the Jews,* (XX.200) we read about: 'the brother of Jesus, the so-called Christ, James was his name' as one of the people executed by the High Priest in 62 CE.
14. John 8:41.
15. Mark 6:3.
16. The Platonist Celsus, *Against Celsus*.
17. Sanhedrin 67a.
18. Ibid., p. 17.
19. Stewart, p. 33.
20. Talmud Shabbat 104b, Sanhedrin 67a. 'Did not Ben Stada bring witchcraft from Egypt . . . ?' Ben Stada is Ben Pandira, one of the Talmud's names for Jesus.
21. John 12:23.
22. Barbara G. Walker, *The Woman's Encyclopedia of Myths and Secrets*, San Francisco, 1993, p. 750.
23. John 14:2.
24. Wallis Budge (trans.), *The Book of the Dead*, p. 440.
25. 'Mansion' was also Egyptian slang for 'prostitute', although the religious meaning is more likely to be relevant here.
26. Wallis Budge, *Egyptian Magic*, p. 116
27. Ibid., p. 27.
28. Luke 8:21.
29. Mark 14:26.
30. Matthew 5:3.
31. Mark 9:42.
32. Mark 9:37.

33. John 10:9.
34. Matthew 26:64.
35. John 5:21.
36. John 5:23.
37. Although Jesus is believed to have been a carpenter, the word is *naggar*, which can also mean 'learned man'. Of course he could have been both carpenter and a learned man, *and* a swine-herd in his young days in Egypt.
38. Flavius Josephus, *The Jewish War*, p. 139.
39. Acts of the Apostles, 21:38.
40. Ibid., 21:39.
41. *Against Celsus*, 1:6.
42. Stewart, p. 123.
43. See Matthew 9:14–16.
44. Professor Etherbert Strauffer, *Jesus and His Story*, New York, 1959, p. 201.
45. Quoted in Smith, p. 60.
46. Tertullian, *De Spectaculis*, p. 30.
47. Celsus, *Against Celsus*, 1:28, 38.
48. Luke 15:11–13.

**Chapter 10**   *Jesus and the Death of the Baptist*

1. Morton Smith, *Jesus the Magician*, New York, 1978, p. 49.
2. Tacitus, shortly after 115 CE.
3. Smith, p. 51.
4. See Mark 6:32ff, 8:1ff.
5. Mark 4:39.
6. Mark 11:12ff.
7. See Smith, p. 119.
8. John 20:22.
9. Matthew 10:35ff.
10. *Pistis Sophia,* 4th Book, 132:349.
11. Smith, p. 109.
12. Mark 5:13.
13. Smith, p. 110.
14. Matthew 21:18.
15. Matthew 21:19–22.
16. J. R. Ackerley to Francis King, 11 October 1964.

17. Smith, p.1.
18. Ibid, p. 49.
19. Desmond Stewart, *The Foreigner,* p. 118.
20. John 12:10.
21. For example, Matthew 26:14–16.
22. Stewart, p. 133
23. *The Golden Ass,* trans. by Robert Graves.
24. And this militates against the idea that Jesus' shroud, miraculously imprinted with his image, was spirited away by his disciples to resurface centuries later as the Shroud of Turin – not to mention the concept that the Holy Grail is a cup that caught his blood as he hung on the cross. The people of that time and place would have *abhorred* such an action, no matter how much they loved the man.
25. For example, in Wales: see Graham Phillips' *The Marian Conspiracy,* London, 2001. This book so incensed the Vatican that the author was excommunicated – even though he had never been a member of the Church!
26. Hugh Schonfield, *The Passover Plot,* p. 177.
27. Is 'Sion' in this context Welsh for 'John'?
28. Luke 1:17.
29. Luke 1:42.
30. Luke 1:80.
31. Acts of the Apostles, 19:1–7. Perhaps it is no more than the unvarnished truth that these Johannites then went on to become *Jesus* Christians, but under the circumstances it does read remarkably like one-upmanship.
32. Mandaeans are now found in Australia, the United States (in particular Florida), Holland – and, unromantically, Catford in South London! Because of their emphasis on ritual bathing in running water, they prefer to live near rivers or canals.
33. E. S. Drower, *The Mandaeans of Iraq and Iran: Their Cults, Customs, Magic, Legends and Folklore,* Oxford, 1937, p. 264. Lady Drower was the first European to make a major study of the Mandaeans.
34. Such as the name 'Ptah-hil'. Ptah was the ancient Egyptian god of abundance.
35. Birks and Gilbert, pp. 151ff.
36. This translation is taken from the book *Gnostic John the Baptizer:*

*Selections from the Mandaean John-Book*, by G. R. S. Mead, pp. 48–52.

37. Ibid, p. 48–52.
38. Ibid, p. 48–52.
39. For example, Matthew 3:11.
40. Matthew 3:13.
41. Matthew 3:16–17.
42. Stewart, p. 60.
43. Ibid, p. 61.
44. Robert Graves, *The White Goddess,* New York, 1958, p. 123.
45. L. Austine Waddell, *Tibetan Buddhism,* New York, 1972, p. 108.
46. Franz Cumont, *Oriental Religions in Roman Paganism,* New York, 1956, p. 118.
47. This is made very clear in the Gnostic texts, where he is described as spending much time with the likes of Joanna, Martha and Salome. Indeed, Jesus' fondness for the company of women was one of the charges levelled against him by his enemies.
48. Luke 7:34.
49. Stewart, p. 58.
50. In Egypt, the most popular celebration took place on 25 December, the birthday of Isis' son Horus, followed twelve days later (our 'Twelfth Night' and the Orthodox Church's Christmas) with that of her other son, Aion. The festivities and religious observances included baptisms – preceded by confessions of sins and public repentance – in holy pools in temples beside the Nile. In *Man, Myth & Magic,* S. G. F. Brandon notes the 'evident influence of the festival of Isis on popular Christian customs . . .' More specifically, R. Merkelbach states that '[the Isian religion] was popular because it appealed to the desire for personal salvation . . . Sins were forgiven through immersion in water . . .' Isis, like the much later Jesus Christ, was known as the 'Saviour', through whom salvation was possible, and whose love would ensure both resurrection of the body and eternal life for the spirit. The companion mystery school of the goddess' consort Osiris, also practised baptism – immersion to symbolize the purification of the soul and renewal of the psyche. As S. G. F. Brandon notes: 'This two-fold process for the achievement of a blessed immortality is not found again until the emergence of Christianity.'

51. He had married Herodias, the former wife of his half-brother Philip: since she had divorced Philip first, the union was against Jewish law.
52. The furore and scandal was such that the play closed after just one performance.
53. Matthew 14:1ff and Luke 3:19ff.
54. The Gospel writers make another mistake: Herodias' ex-husband was not Philip, but another Herod. He was Salome's father.
55. John 1:20.
56. Hugh J. Schonfield, *The Essene Odyssey*, Shaftesbury, 1984, p. 40.
57. The often violent miners' strike of the 1980s marked a particularly bad patch in the course of relations between left and right wings.
58. Matthew 11:11.
59. Ibid.
60. Walter Birks and R. A. Gilbert, *The Treasure of Montségur*, London, 1987, p. 82.
61. Matthew 11:1ff.
62. Matthew 11:18–19.
63. Mark 2:18–20.
64. Luke 23:2.
65. The term used is 'Hermobaptist', which means 'day-baptist', although little is known about the meaning of the word.
66. G. R. S. Mead (ed.), *Simon Magus: An Essay*, London, 1892, pp. 28ff.
67. Barbara Thiering, *Jesus the Man*, pp. 84–5 and 390–1.
68. See Picknett and Prince, *The Templar Revelation: Secret Guardians of the True Identity of Christ*.
69. *Gospel of Thomas* 61. See *The Gnostic Scriptures*, translated by Bentley Layton, London, 1987.
70. Luke 8:3.
71. *Against Celsus*, 1.6
72. Mark 5:14.
73. Mark 5:36.
74. Morton Smith, *Jesus the Magician*, p. 34.
75. Ibid., p. 81.
76. Mark 3:22.
77. Mark 15:34.
78. Mark 15:35.
79. Matthew 11:18.

80. Carl H. Kraeling, *John the Baptist*, London, 1951, p. 160.
81. Smith, p. 97.
82. PGVM IV: 1930–2005.

**Chapter 11**   *Head of the Heretics*

1. Quoted in Noel Currer-Briggs, *The Shroud and the Grail*, London, 1987.
2. P. R. Koenig, *Too Hot to Handle*, New York, 1990.
3. Writer of the famous hymn, *Onward, Christian Soldiers*, besides over 150 books on a huge variety of subjects.
4. E-mail to the author, May 2002.
5. Ibid.
6. Ibid.
7. The reality of magical entities lies beyond the scope of this book: what matters here is what people *believed*.
8. Edwin Yamauchi, *Pre-Christian Gnosticism*, London, 1973, p. 25.
9. Walker, *The Woman's Encyclopedia of Myths and Secrets*, p. 502.
10. John 14:6–11.
11. E-mail to the author, 15 December 2002. Understandably Yuri adds: 'Scary stuff, eh?'
12. Walter Birks and R. A. Gilbert, *The Treasure of Montségur*.
13. Keith Laidler, *The Head of God*, London, 1998.
14. See Picknett and Prince, *The Templar Revelation*, pp. 127–30.
15. John Ritchie, quoted in the Edinburgh *Evening News*, 22 August 1998.
16. I am indebted to Rick Gibson for this information. He discovered this by talking to Mandaeans at Damascus in the early 1990s.
17. I am indebted to Steve Wilson for his ground-breaking – and ongoing – researching into the Mandaeans, which, at the time of writing, seems to provide long-awaited clues for the solution to some of the most enduring problems surrounding Jesus, John the Baptist – and of course, Mary Magdalene.

**Afterword**

1. See *The Ancient Egyptian Book of the Dead*, trans. R. O. Faulkner, London 1985, Spell 125 (p. 31), 'The Declaration of Innocence Before the Gods of the Tribunal', to be spoken by the dead in the Hall of Judgement.

# *Acknowledgements*

There are many people who have made positive contributions to this book, either directly by supplying information and aiding my research in a variety of ways, or indirectly by ensuring that I had the time, resources - not to mention home comforts - with which to be able to focus on the long hard task of researching and writing about the Magdalene. Among the many, certain friends and colleagues deserve special mention:

Clive Prince, my constant and unshakeable rock and closest colleague, whose very practical help and moral support is, as always, unsurpassed. He managed to make me laugh whenever I felt depressed and discouraged, and his enthusiasm for, and unique understanding of, this material has opened many doors. His unselfishness and generosity quite simply ensured that this book was written.

Stephen Prior, whose uniquely generous hospitality has provided a refuge in times of discouragement and the perfect venue for celebrations, and for whose practical assistance – and Goonish sense of humour – I will always be very grateful.

Francesca Norton, for those many long conversations, delicious food and very jolly weekends in the country.

Craig Oakley, whose company is a joy and who can always be relied upon to understand – a Magdalene man to his fingertips.

Robert Brydon, for sharing the astonishing breadth of his knowledge on a vast range of subjects, and for being so supportive.

And to Lyndsay Brydon, thanks for always making me feel special – and for the unlimited red wine and bacon sandwiches in their Edinburgh home.

Debbie Benstead and Yvan Cartwright for great affection, intuitions, surreal fun and serious frolicking in the shadow of the Forest of Gloom.

Keith Prince, for his unique insights into the ancient world, and understanding of the real Leonardo da Vinci.

Sheila and Eric Taylor, for wonderful breaks in my home city of York, for their well-appreciated hospitality, kindness – and lots of laughs.

David Bell, one of my oldest friends, who is always interested and always there for me.

Nigel Foster, whose humour, wisdom and kindness mean a lot.

Ashley Brown, for his friendship, continued support and generosity.

Yuri Leitch, who although a new friend nevertheless, generously shared with me his breakthrough discovery about the Franks casket and many other insights.

Steve Wilson, for his extremely important and ground-breaking research into the Mandaeans, which he has generously shared with fellow researchers.

Paul Weston, for the things of the spirit.

Graham Phillips, for some riotous evenings, and for his understanding about the difficult world of the lone writer.

Mike Wallington, for his support and insight about the Magdalene in France.

Robin Crookshank-Hilton, for her generosity and fun, especially on the memorable, bitterly cold day of the esoteric London tour.

Christy Fearn, for zealously championing the Magdalene.

All my fellow researchers of the 'No Name' group, whose company, conversation and emails mean so much.

Andrew Roberts, whose book-lined study is an oasis of calm and erudition.

Susanna Sinclair, a firebrand among Magdalene women and a most original and gifted photographer.

Professor Lola Young, for her kind help in making this book known to the black community.

Harold Wilson, whose enthusiasm and refusal to give up in the face of prejudice and arrogance is an inspiration.

Geo Thom, a very irreverent theologian, for the joys of that Blackpool conference and many other evenings, some in the British Museum.

Emma Virtue, who inspired much about this book.

For their friendship, help and inspiration in all manner of ways: Vida Adamoli; Georgina Bruni; Michael Carmichael; Andrew Collins; Moira Hardcastle; Louise Hodge; Michéle Kaczinsky; Durdana Khan; Ian Lawton; Sarah Litvinoff; Jane Lyle; Mary Nielson; Chris Ogilvie-Herald; the O'Callaghan family of the O'Conor Don pub/restaurant; Nick Pope; Bob Rickard and Caroline Wise.

Thanks are also due to Krystyna Green, Gary Chapman, Gina Rozner and Sarah Smith at Constable, for their exceptional enthusiasm, easy gift for friendship and for the remarkably trouble-free gestation of this book – and to Adrian Andrews for his understanding of the time-honoured angst of authors.

And to Cormac Kinsella, thanks for a marvellous Irish tour.

Finally, I would like to thank Anabel Lopez and the staff of the St John's Wood Library; the staff of the Westminster Reference Library and the British Library, for their tireless running about to find obscure reference material.

# The Mandaeans and the Sabians

The obscure past of the Mandaeans – the strange Middle-Eastern tribe who uphold John the Baptist as their greatest prophet and loathe Jesus – may yet yield up certain thought-provoking links with many underlying themes of this story, as Clive Prince has suggested to me. They are mentioned in the Koran as the 'Sabians', perhaps suggesting that during their travels they stayed for some time in the Queen of Sheba's Arabian territory of Saba. Yet there is another interpretation of their Islamic name, which also provides new insights into certain aspects of this investigation. According to British author Tobias Churton, in his book *The Golden Builders* (2002), 'Sabian' derives from the Semitic word meaning 'washers' (this interpretation and the 'Sheba' one being mutually exclusive).

There were Mandaean communities in Harran (forty miles south of Edessa) and Baghdad in the 2nd century, but they were apparently the subject of persecution in the mid-3rd century and driven out. After this the pagan scholars who were forced out of Alexandria by the Christians settled in Harran, bringing with them the Hermetic (secret occult) philosophy and other learning from the classical world.

By the time of the Arab conquests of the 9th century nobody could remember what a Sabian was. The accepted story (originating with Arab writers about 70 years after the event) is that when the Caliph al-Mamum passed through Harran in 830 CE, he demanded to know what religion the inhabitants professed, threatening that if they were not of those named in the Koran they would all be slaughtered. These pagans hurriedly decided that they were Sabians, naming their prophet as Hermes Trismegistus ('Thrice Blessed Hermes' – or the Egyptian god of secret knowledge and wisdom, Thoth, after whom the Hermeticists were named), and their holy book as the Hermetica, the Hermeticists' legendary secret writings.

According to Tobias Churton – following conventional wisdom – the term 'Sabians of Harran' refers to two distinct groups: before 830 CE 'Sabian' indicated a Mandaean. But after that, and up to c.1000, it referred to the learned pagans of Harran, and subsequently to pagans in general. But because Arab chroniclers were unaware of the distinction, it is nigh-impossible now to be certain what they mean by 'Sabian'.

But, as Clive Prince suggests, what if the accepted idea is wrong and the two groups of Harranian Sabians were in fact one and the same – that is, Mandaeans? If so, there are some exciting suggestions for the Johannite connection.

The post-830 Sabians of Harran, who established an important centre of learning in Baghdad (also an earlier Mandaean base) were the most learned people at that time in either Europe or the Middle East. What we regard today as medieval (Muslim) Arab science is really *Sabian* science, which included astronomical, alchemical, medical and architectural knowledge that filtered into Europe via the Arabs (and partly through the Templars). Churton believes that the Sabians had a direct effect on the rise of gothic architecture in medieval Europe, through Arab architects brought to Europe by noblemen.

Excitingly, Churton argues that the Sabians strongly influenced Wolfram von Eschenbach's *Parzifal*, suggesting that his account of the origins of the Grail stone is modelled on that of the *Hermetic baptismal bowl*, described in Book IV of the *Corpus Hermeticum*, the sacred writings of the Hermeticists.

Through the associations with the Sabian/Mandaeans' extreme veneration of John the Baptist, and the idea of the Grail as a baptismal bowl, we are faced with an alternative *Johannite* origin for the Holy Grail, perhaps a rival theory to the concept of the drinking vessel made from John's head, or even simply another version of it and one with its roots in the sacred, occult knowledge of secret initiations. Of course this concept is a world away from the common idea that Christianity was always intended to be based on exoteric worship, for the masses. In fact, all the indications are that it was always a religion of mysteries and secrets, initiations – and initiatrixes.

# Select Bibliography

There are hundreds of books on the subjects covered in this book; in my view these are the best currently available. Others are given in the notes and references.

Armstrong, Karen, *The End of Silence: Women and the Priesthood,* Fourth Estate, London, 1993.

Ashe, Geoffrey, *The Virgin,* Arkana, London, 1976.

Baigent, Michael, Richard Leigh and Henry Lincoln, *The Holy Blood and the Holy Grail,* Jonathan Cape, London, 1982; revised edition; Arrow, London, 1996.

Begg, Ean, *The Cult of the Black Virgin,* Arkana, London, (revised) 1996.

Begg, Ean, and Dieke, *In Search of the Holy Grail and the Precious Blood,* Thorsons, London, 1966.

Bernal, Martin, *Black Athena Volume I,* Vintage, 1991

Birks, Walter and R.A. Gilbert, *The Treasure of Montségur,* The Aquarian Press, London, 1990.

Budge, Sir E.A. Wallis, (trans.) *The Book of the Dead,* British Museum, London, 1899.

*Egyptian Magic,* Dover Publications, New York, 1971.

Burkett, Elinor and Frank Bruni, *A Gospel of Shame: Children, Sexual Abuse and the Catholic Church,* Penguin USA, New York, 1993.

Butler, Alan and Stephen Dafoe, *The Templar Continuum,* Templar Books, Belville, Canada, 1999.

Cawthorne, Nigel, *Sex Lives of the Popes,* Prion, London, 1996.

Churton, Tobias, *The Golden Builders: Alchemists, Rosicrucians and the First Free Masons,* Signal Publishing, Lichfield, 2002.

Crossan, John Dominic, *Who Killed Jesus?* HarperCollins, New York, 1995.

De Voragine, Jacobus, *The Golden Legend: Readings on the Saints,* trans. William Grayer Ryan, 2 volumes, Princeton University Press, 1993.

Doresse, Jean, *The Secret Books of the Egyptian Gnostics,* Hollis & Carter, London, 1960, first published as *Les livres secrets des Gnostiques d'Egypte,* Librarie Plon, Paris, 1963.

Drower. E.S, *The Mandaeans of Iraq and Iran: Their Cults, Customs, Magic, Legends and Folklore,* Clarendon Press, Oxford, 1937.

Drury, Nevill, *The History of Magic In The Modern Age,* Constable, London, 2000.

Dumas, Monique and Jacques François Réglat, *Le monastère dynamité: Histoire du Carol, près Baulou – La vie du révérend père de Coma (The Dynamited Monastery: History of Le Carol, near Baulou – The Life of the Reverend Father de Coma),* Édition La Truelle, Moulis, 1995.)

Eisler, Robert, *The Messiah Jesus and John the Baptist,* Methuen & Co., London, 1931.

Faulkner, R.O., *The Ancient Egyptian Book of the Dead,* British Museum Press, London, 1972.

Freke, Timothy and Peter Gandy, *The Jesus Mysteries,* Thorsons, London, 1999.

*Jesus and the Goddess,* Thorsons, London, 2002.

Godwin, Malcolm, *The Holy Grail: Its Origins, Secrets and Meaning Revealed,* Bloomsbury, London, 1994.

Hancock, Graham, *The Sign and the Seal,* William Heinemann, London, 1992.

Haskins, Susan, *Mary Magdalen,* HarperCollins, London, 1993.

*Mary Magdalen: Myth and Metaphor,* Magdalen Enterprises, 1994.

Heyob, Sharon Kelly, *The Cult of Isis among Women in the Graeco-Roman World,* E.J. Brill, Leiden, 1975.

Jansen, Katherine Ludwig, *The Making of the Magdalen: Preaching and Popular Devotion in the Later Middle Ages,* Princeton University, USA, 2001.

Jenkins, Philip, *Pedophile Priests: Anatomy of a Contemporary Crisis,* Oxford University Press Inc., USA, 1996.

Josephus, Flavius, *The Complete Works,* trans. William Whiston, Thomas Nelson Publishers, New York, 1999.

*The Jewish War,* trans. G.A. Williamson, Penguin, London, 1970.

Kraeling, Karl H., *John the Baptist,* Charles Scribner's Sons, London, 1951.

Laidler, Keith, *The Head of God,* Headline, London, 2000.

Layton, Bentley, *The Gnostic Scriptures,* SCM Press, London, 1987.

Leitch, Yuri and Oddvar Olsen (eds), *The Temple,* (periodical booklet), Glastonbury. For details email: templeavalon@yahoo.co.uk

Leloup, Jean-Yves, *The Gospel of Mary Magdalene,* (trans. Joseph Rowe), Inner Traditions, Rochester, Vermont, USA, 2002.

Lyle, Jane and A.T. Mann, *Sacred Sexuality,* Element Books, Shaftesbury, 1996.

# SELECT BIBLIOGRAPHY

Luckert, Karl W., *Egyptian Light and Hebrew Fire*, State University of New York Press, 1991.

Mead, G.R.S., *Pistis Sophia*, Kessinger Publishing Company, Kila, MT, USA, 1921.

*The Gnostic John the Baptizer: Selections from the Mandaean John Book*, John M. Watkins, London, 1924.

'Simon Magus', An Essay, London, 1892.

Newman, Barbara, *From Virile Woman to Woman Christ*, University of Pennsylvania Press, Philadelphia, 1995.

Osman, Ahmed, *Out of Egypt: The Roots of Christianity Revealed*, Century, London, 1998.

Pagels, Elaine, *The Gnostic Gospels*, Penguin Books, London, 1982.

Patai, Raphael, *The Hebrew Goddess*, (3rd ed.). Wayne State University Press, Detroit, 1990.

Phipps, William E., *The Sexuality of Jesus*, Harper & Row, New York, 1973.

*Was Jesus Married?* Harper & Row, New York, 1970.

Picknett, Lynn, and Clive Prince, *Turin Shroud: In Whose Image?* Bloomsbury, London, 1994.

*The Templar Revelation: Secret Guardians of the True Identity of Christ*, Bantam Press, London, 1997.

*The Stargate Conspiracy*, Little, Brown, London, 1999.

Pope, Marvin H., *Song of Songs: A New Translation with Introduction and Commentary*. Doubleday, New York, 1983.

Qualls-Corbett, Nancy, *The Sacred Prostitute, Eternal Aspect of the Feminine*, Inner City Books, Toronto, 1988.

Redgrove, Peter, *The Black Goddess and the Sixth Sense*, Bloomsbury, London, 1987.

Ricci, Carla, *Mary Magdalene and Many Others*, Burns & Oates, Tunbridge Wells, 1994.

Robinson, James M., (ed.) *The Nag Hammadi Library in English*, HarperSan Francisco, 1978, revised edition, 1988.

Robinson, John A.T., *The Priority of John*, SCM Press, London, 1986.

Romer, John, *Testament: The Bible and History*, Michael O'Mara, London, 1988.

Rudolph, Kurt *Mandaeism*, E.J. Brill, Leiden, 1978.

Saul, John M and Janice A. Glaholm, *Rennes-le-Chateau: A Bibliography*, Mercurius Press, London, 1985.

Schonfield, Hugh J., *The Essene Odyssey*, Element Books, Shaftesbury, 1984.

*The Passover Plot*, Hutchinson, London, 1965.

*The Pentecost Revolution* Hutchinson, London, 1974.

Silverberg, Robert, *The Realm of Prester John*, Ohio University Press, 1972.

Smith, Morton, *Clement of Alexandria and a Secret Gospel of Mark*, Harvard University Press, Cambridge, Mass., 1973.

*Jesus the Magician,* Victor Gollanz, London, 1978.

Starbird, Margaret, *The Woman with the Alabaster Jar,* Bear & Co., Sante Fé, 1993.

Stewart, Desmond, *The Foreigner,* Hamish Hamilton, London, 1994.

Stoyanov, Yuri, *The Hidden Tradition in Europe,* Arkana, London, 1994.

Thiering, Barbara, *Jesus the Man,* Doubleday, London, 1992.

Torjesen, Karen Jo, *When Women Were Priests,* HarperSanFrancisco, 1993.

Vermes, Geza, *Jesus the Jew,* William Collins, London, 1973.

Waite, Arthur Edward, *The Hidden Church of the Holy Graal: Its Legends and Symbolism,* Rebman, London, 1909.

Walker, Benjamin, *Gnosticism: Its History and Influence,* Crucible, 1989.

Walker, Barbara G., *The Women's Encyclopedia of Myths and Secrets,* HarperSan Francisco, 1983.

Walvin, James, *Black Ivory: Slavery in the British Empire,* Blackwell Publishers, 1992.

Webb, Robert L., *John the Baptizer and Prophet,* Sheffield Academic Press, Sheffield, 1991.

Welburn, Andrew, (Introduction and commentary), *Gnosis: The Mysteries and Christianity: An Anthology of Essene, Gnostic and Christian Writings,* Floris Books, Edinburgh, 1994.

Wilson, A.N, *Jesus,* Sinclair-Stevenson, London, 1992.

Witherington, III, Ben, *Women and the Genesis of Christianity,* Cambridge University Press, 1990.

Wolff, Philippe (ed.), *Documents du l'histoire du Languedoc,* Edouard Privat, Toulouse, 1969.

Wolfram von Eschenbach. *Parzival,* (trans. A.T. Hatto), Penguin, London, 1980.

Yamauchi, Edwin, *Pre-Christian Gnosticism,* Tyndale Press, London, 1973.

# Index